T0301282

The Artisan Brand

NEW HORIZONS IN MARKETING SERIES

Books in the New Horizons in Marketing series make a significant contribution to the study of marketing and contexts in which it operates. As this field has expanded dramatically in recent years, the series will provide an invaluable forum for the publication of high-quality works of scholarship and show the diversity of research on marketing.

Global and pluralistic in its approach, this series includes some of the best theoretical and analytical work with contributions to fundamental principles, rigorous evaluations of existing concepts and competing theories, stimulating debate and future visions.

Titles in the series include:

Social Marketing and Advertising in the Age of Social Media
Edited by Lukas Parker and Linda Brennan

Youth Marketing to Digital Natives
Wided Batat

Strategies for the Digital Customer Experience
Connecting Customers with Brands in the Phygital Age
Wided Batat

The Artisan Brand
Edited by Jon Mulholland, Alessandra Ricci and Marta Massi

The Artisan Brand

Entrepreneurship and Marketing in
Contemporary Craft Economies

Edited by

Jon Mulholland

Associate Professor, University of the West of England, UK

Alessandra Ricci

Post Doctoral research fellow, Department of Business, Law, Economics and Consumer Behavior, IULM University, Milan, Italy

Marta Massi

Assistant Professor, Trent University, Canada

NEW HORIZONS IN MARKETING SERIES

Edward Elgar
PUBLISHING

Cheltenham, UK • Northampton, MA, USA

Published by
Edward Elgar Publishing Limited
The Lypiatts
15 Lansdown Road
Cheltenham
Glos GL50 2JA
UK

Edward Elgar Publishing, Inc.
William Pratt House
9 Dewey Court
Northampton
Massachusetts 01060
USA

A catalogue record for this book
is available from the British Library

Library of Congress Control Number: 2022943103

This book is available electronically in the **Elgar**online
Business subject collection
http://dx.doi.org/10.4337/9781839106132

ISBN 978 1 83910 612 5 (cased)
ISBN 978 1 83910 613 2 (eBook)

Printed and bound by CPI Group (UK) Ltd, Croydon, CR0 4YY

Contents

List of figures   vii
List of tables   viii
List of contributors   ix
Foreword by François Colbert   xiii
Acknowledgements   xv

1   Introduction to *The Artisan Brand*   1
     Jon Mulholland, Marta Massi and Alessandra Ricci

PART I   UNDERSTANDING CRAFT AND ARTISANAL
            MARKETS

2   Understanding of the concept of 'craft' from the
     perspective of Italian consumers   14
     Alessandra Ricci and Marta Massi

3   The UK market for craft: a review of Crafts Council evidence   26
     Julia Bennett

4   Social embedding, artisanal markets and cultural fields:
     quality, value and marketing in the cases of new wave
     custom motorcycles and boutique guitar pedals   42
     Jon Mulholland and Peter Webb

PART II   FROM TRADITION TO INNOVATION:
            TRENDS AND ISSUES IN ARTISANAL AND
            CRAFT MAKING

5   Neo-artisanal practice and the nostalgic: traditional
     makers' identities, innovation and sustainability in
     neo-artisanal production   63
     Laura Quinn

6   Innovation in craft: creating new value through art   81
     Giacomo Magnani and Laura Bresolin

7   The innovative logics of digital manufacturing: the case
       study of 3DiTALY   102
       Daniela Corsaro and Mirko Olivieri

PART III   ENTREPRENEURSHIP AND BUSINESS
            MODELS IN CRAFT AND ARTISANAL MARKETS

8   Entrepreneurs in action? Motivations for crafting a career
       in handmade goods   120
       Victoria R. Bell

9   New business models for craft: the case of Artemest   136
       Chiara Piancatelli and Alessandra Ricci

PART IV   MARKETING IN CRAFT AND ARTISANAL MARKETS

10   The new rise of artisanship in Kenya: evidence from
       artisan entrepreneurs   157
       Alisa Sydow and Isabella Maggioni

11   Slow production, less consumption: righteous approaches
       to the paradox of craft businesses   177
       Richard E. Ocejo

12   The resurgence of craft retailing: marketing and branding
       strategies in the food and beverage sector   193
       Alessandro Gerosa

13   Innovating through craft: from happenstance to strategic culture   209
       Ginevra Addis

Afterword by Maurizio Dallocchio   226
Afterword by Franco Cologni   228
Index   230

Figures

2.1   Over the last year, which of these craft products have you purchased?   20

2.2   How do you learn about new artisanal products?   21

2.3   Thinking about your experience of buying craft products, how often do you buy in the scale listed here?   22

2.4   Can you select the terms that link to the craft world?   22

3.1   Time line 1990–2020   30

3.2   Strategies for developing the market for crafts   36

5.1   3D printed vortex whiskey tumbler prototype and glass blowing mould positive   71

5.2   Finished vortex whiskey tumbler   72

5.3   Instagram post discussing an early stage of the process   73

5.4   Emotionally durable design through service teaching and narration   77

9.1   Artemest's market   149

Tables

2.1	Descriptive statistics	19
7.1	3DiTALY details	107
7.2	Key informants' profiles	108
10.1	Data collection	165
10.2	Data structure	166

Contributors

Ginevra Addis is an Adjunct Professor of Contemporary Art Management at USCS-Milan, where she received her M.A. in Economics and Management of Art, Culture and Entertainment, and where she has also worked as an Adjunct Professor and Faculty Member in the Master of Arts Management since 2017. She holds a Ph.D. in Analysis and Management of Cultural Heritage, which she obtained at IMT School for Advanced Studies, Lucca (IT) in December 2019 co-advised by Professor Eva Ehninger at Humboldt, Berlin.

Victoria R. Bell is currently a Principal Lecturer in Criminology and Sociology in the Department of Humanities and Social Sciences at Teesside University. Victoria's research interests are varied and her expertise includes research methodologies, in particular qualitative and visual methods; prison teaching and research; and craft research. Victoria does linocut and other printing in her own time, but has no plans to put her work on the market.

Julia Bennett is the Crafts Council's Head of Research and Policy. She develops policy and advocacy strategies, writes about craft and manages research projects. Recent research commissions include *The Market for Craft*, and *Measuring the Craft Economy*, a set of proposals which resulted in DCMS including craft data in its economic estimates. As an experienced researcher, research manager, policy specialist and strategist, Julia has worked independently with small charities and arts organisations, as well as for national organisations.

Laura Bresolin accomplished an MA degree in Arts Policy and Management in London. For more than 10 years she has been working as a manager in the field of art, design and new technologies. She collaborates with foundations, galleries and prominent international artists, as well as design and engineering corporates.

Daniela Corsaro is Associate Professor of Marketing and Sales at IULM University in Milan. She has been Assistant Professor at the Catholic University of Milan and Rome, where she obtained a PhD in Business Administration and Management. Her main areas of interest include relationship value management, business to business marketing, sales transformation, business negotiations in international contexts as well as marketing and sales automation.

She is director of the Research Center for International Marketing & Sales Communication and of the Executive Master in International Marketing & Sales Communication. From 2018 she is Rector Delegate for the relationship with companies.

Alessandro Gerosa is a Lecturer in Marketing at the Birmingham Business School, University of Birmingham. Alessandro's main research interests cut across the disciplines of sociology, consumption studies and marketing, focusing on authenticity as an aesthetic regime of consumption, neo-craft industries in the context of the creative economy, and digital cultures. His works have been published, among others, in *Consumption, Markets & Culture*, *The International Journal of Cultural Policy* and *Space and Culture*.

Isabella Maggioni is Associate Professor of Marketing at ESCP Business School. Isabella's research interests cover the area of consumer behavior and psychology, with a specific focus on consumer well-being, identity-based consumption, and ethical consumption behavior in retail and tourism research settings. Isabella has published her research in journals such as *Journal of Business Research*, *Journal of Retailing and Consumer Services*, *European Management Journal*, *International Journal of Hospitality Management*, and *International Journal of Tourism Research*.

Giacomo Magnani is adjunct professor of Business Economics at Università Cattolica del Sacro Cuore. He teaches Business Economics and Management and Museums' Management and Accountability. His research focuses on arts organizations' strategy and accountability, services firms' business model and family business.

Marta Massi is Assistant Professor at Trent University. She has been Assistant Professor at the Catholic University of the Sacred Heart and Lecturer at McGill University. Her research focuses on consumer behaviour, digital marketing and branding. She has published in the *International Journal of Market Research*, *Journal of Strategic Marketing* and *Journal of Business & Industrial Marketing*. Recently, she co-edited the book *Digital Transformation in the Cultural and Creative Industries: Production, Consumption and Entrepreneurship in the Digital and Sharing Economy* (Routledge, 2021).

Jon Mulholland is an Associate Professor in Sociology at the University of the West of England, Bristol. Jon's research interests are in the fields of sustainability, environment and craft economies, in addition to migration, diversity and nationalism. Jon leads modules in the sociology of 'race' and ethnicity, sustainable futures and green criminology.

Richard E. Ocejo is Professor of Sociology at John Jay College and the Graduate Center of the City University of New York (CUNY). He is the author of *Masters of Craft: Old Jobs in the New Urban Economy* (Princeton University Press, 2017) and *Upscaling Downtown: From Bowery Saloons to Cocktail Bars in New York City* (Princeton University Press, 2014) and has published in several sociology journals. He is also the editor of *City & Community*.

Mirko Olivieri is a Ph.D. candidate in Communication, Markets and Society at the department of Business, Law, Economics and Consumer Behavior of IULM University. He is also member of ALMED Communication School at Università Cattolica del Sacro Cuore (Milan, Italy), where he received his master's degree in corporate communication and marketing management. His research interests lie in the field of marketing communication, digital channels and corporate reputation management.

Chiara Piancatelli, PhD, is Lecturer of Digital Marketing at SDA Bocconi School of Management, Milan. Since January, 2020 she is Executive Program Director of the courses Digital Communication (Ed. Online & Ed. Blended) and Marketing (Ed. Evening) and Adjunct Professor of Marketing at Bocconi University. Her research activities focus on Digital Marketing, Social Media Marketing, Event Marketing and Big Data & AI Marketing. She is research associate at Deakin University, Australia, where she spent a visiting period during her PhD in Management & Innovation. Chiara earned an MSc in Economics and Management from Bocconi University and a PhD in Management & Innovation from Cattolica del Sacro Cuore University.

Laura Quinn is a glass maker, designer and educator. Quinn graduated from the National Collect of Art and Design, Ireland, with a joint BA (hons) degree in Glass Design, and Art and Design History. She received her MA in 3D Design Crafts from Plymouth College of Art, UK, specialising in glass blowing and digital design for craft. She is currently the Glass Technical Tutor at the University for the Creative Arts, UK, where she continues to develop her artisanal practice.

Alessandra Ricci is a post-doctoral Fellow at IULM University, Milan Italy. She obtained her PhD in Management and Innovation at the Catholic University of the Sacred Heart, Milan. She has been research fellow at Bocconi University, Milan, and Adjunct Professor at the University of Gastronomic Sciences, Pollenzo. Her research focuses on artisanship, luxury, high-end sector and Made-in-Italy from different perspectives such as marketing sustainability and value creation.

Alisa Sydow is an Assistant Professor of Entrepreneurship & Innovation at the ESCP Business School, Turin Campus. Her research focuses on entrepreneurship in developing economies, with a particular interest in the African context. She has published in *Entrepreneurship Theory and Practice*, *Journal of Business Ethics* and *Journal of Business Venturing Insights*.

Peter Webb is a writer, lecturer and musician who specialises in research into popular and contemporary music, subcultures, politics, social theory and his idea of 'milieu cultures'. He is a Senior Lecturer in Sociology at the UWE, Bristol. He previously worked in the music industry 1990–2002 as an artist and tour manager. He is the owner and creative director of PC Press, publishing books on Test Dept, Killing Joke and Massive Attack.

Foreword by François Colbert

What is the difference between the artist and the artisan? Is there a difference? Is the artisan an artist? What is the place of artisans in the cultural industries, and how did this place evolve over time? Why are we asking ourselves these questions?

For thousands of years societies have produced fine sculptures and paintings. Artists had to master their craft if they wanted to please their rich sponsors. They combined fine craftmanship with high artistic skills. But people also needed objects in their day-to-day lives, pottery to store wine or grains, weavers to fabricate clothes, and so on; those were the labour of the artisans. In the last century or so, artists have explored different means of expressing themselves. They no longer need to rely on, or to please, private sponsors. Their art is no longer required to be figurative. Even if they master their craft, exact replicas of what nature offers is no longer necessarily the goal. There is abundant space for abstract ideas.

In the contemporary world, technology has influenced the way we fabricate objects. Designers are often seen as artisans, and 3D machines are used to create and reproduce those objects in a fraction of the time. From artisans creating a unique piece, to artisans reproducing a model, the field has evolved tremendously.

But this evolution is not only technical. It is also related to what consumers perceive, or regard, as craft. Production in the artisanal field ranges from low-end objects fabricated by amateurs, to highly artistic pieces, to industrial fabrication. We may find ourselves using products that are created by industrial designers, but from a mould assembled by artisans. Some people buy objects produced by their neighbours. Others are interested in unique pieces created by artisans who may readily be seen as artists producing highly skilled craftmanship. One can be astonished by the beauty and uniqueness of glass sculptures, with collectors keeping a close eye on such artists' outputs, being prepared to pay a fine price to acquire a unique object from them.

A capacity to distinguish a valuable object from an ordinary product can be a signal sent by connoisseurs to those constructed as lacking the capacity to assess the unique from the ordinary: in other words, the authentic versus the non-authentic. This discussion about authenticity is linked to the distinction effect proposed by Bourdieu (1979). Several authors have built on the concept of high art consumption as a mode of social class distinction (Courchesne et al., 2021). Enlarging the discussion, Peterson and Kerns (1992) have challenged the claim that the consumption of high art continues to function as a way to stand out from the crowd. Rather, the capacity to be eclectic in one's choices (being omnivorous) has been established as the new paradigm. More recently, Hahl et al. (2017) proposed that preference for authentic low-brow art has emerge as a means for elites to confirm their own authenticity. Selecting and buying craft considered as low-brow but authentic can be associated with such omnivorousness.

As a consequence, we are witnessing an emergence of scholarly interest in the artisanal and craft sectors, though with a need to advance our understandings further. This book makes an interesting contribution, because it offers several perspectives on the subject under study: in terms of both pertinent case studies and conceptual dimensions. An additional interest within the book lies in the spectrum of academic perspectives included, such as marketing, sociology and ethnography. This book is useful both as an introduction to the subject, but also as a resource for more established researchers. Both will find plenty of food for thought here.

Professor François Colbert
HEC Montréal

REFERENCES

Bourdieu, P. (1979), *La distinction: critique sociale du jugement*. Paris: Éditions de Minuit.

Courchesne, A., A. d'Astous, F. Colbert (2021), 'Socialization of Cultural Consumers in the Family: A Synthesis of 50 Years of Marketing Research', *International Journal of Arts Management*, 23(3), 10–20.

Hahl, O., E.W. Zuckerman, M. Kim (2017), 'Why Elites Love Authentic Lowbrow Culture: Overcoming High-Status Denigration with Outsider Art', *American Sociological Review*, 82(4), 828–56.

Peterson, R.A. (1992), 'Understanding Audience Segmentation: From Elite and Mass to Omnivore and Univore', *Poetics*, 21(4), 243–58.

Acknowledgements

We would like to thank Ellen Pearce of Edward Elgar Publishing for her support and patience in the production of this book. We would also like to extend our gratitude to the authors who have contributed to this text, without whom of course this book would not have been possible. Jon would like to thank Aga, Iza and Daniel for their enduring support throughout the process of producing this book. He would also like to extend his gratitude to the University of the West of England, whose funding support for the project, *Being Authentic: Exploring Dynamics of Consumption and Production in the Vintage-Retro Market*, played such an important role in making this text possible. Finally, Jon would also like to thank Dr Pete Webb for his collaboration in the above project, and the chapter included here. Alessandra would like to thank her parents, sisters and family for their support. Gratitude also goes to Alisa, Andrea, Cecilia, Le Mure, Marta, Michele, Miriam.

She would also like to thank Professor Maurizio Dallocchio for inspiring and leading her on the path of academic, Professor Daniela Corsaro and Professor Francesco Massara for believing in her work and Professor Nicola Sorrentino for the caring support.

She is sincerely grateful to Bocconi University, the Catholic University of the Sacred Heart of Milan and the IULM Free University of Languages and Communication, three institutions of excellence of Italian education, that have allowed her to carry on her studies and research on craftsmanship. Special thanks to Fondazione Cologni, Franco Cologni and Alberto Cavalli for their kind helpfulness

1. Introduction to *The Artisan Brand*

Jon Mulholland, Marta Massi and Alessandra Ricci

Traditionally used to identify people with manual skills who can produce unique hand-crafted products (Garavaglia & Mussini, 2020), the term 'artisan' has recently become a marketing cue for signaling product quality and authenticity. But can we really talk about 'artisan grilled chicken' and 'artisan pizza' when such products are distributed by McDonald's and Domino's, respectively? Or should these expressions be considered oxymorons or another example of marketing gimmick, specifically craft washing?

While it is well-established that such descriptors do not correspond to reality, because mass-producers simply cannot make 'craft' or 'artisanal' products' (Wilson & Flohr, 2016), it is undeniable that expressions such as 'artisan' and 'craft' can add great value to goods that are marketed as such (Leissle, 2017). Taking the distance from the historical and traditional understanding of artisanship as labour class, the word 'artisan' becomes, therefore, a brand word (Leissle, 2017) that not only identifies goods and services, but can also signal authenticity, one of the cornerstones of contemporary marketing (Brown et al., 2003).

Thanks to the consumer quest for authenticity, craft products are preferred over industrial products, and consumers are increasingly willing to pay more for craft products. The artisan-brand emerges, therefore, as a guarantee of and a cue for authenticity, that provides craft products with legitimacy in the eyes of consumers and creates a strong attachment between consumer and the artisan figure (Dezecot & Fleck-Dousteyssier, 2016).

The artisan brand produces perceptions of authenticity for a number of reasons. First, because it provides products with an 'aura', that is, 'a strange tissue of space and time; the unique apparition of a distance, however near it may be' (Benjamin, 2008, p. 23/orig. 1936). This aura in turn provides craft products with uniqueness, a characteristic lost in the age of mechanical reproduction where infinite copies can be produced from an original prototype (Benjamin, 1936). The aura of a craft product is the *hic et nunc* (here and now) of an object, that is 'its unique existence in a particular place', which is missing 'in even the most perfect reproduction' (Benjamin 2008, p. 21/orig. 1936).

Second, the artisan brand brings a sense of originality, that is, the unmediated relationship to the origin/source of the product, the human factor. The term 'artisan' by definition refers to production activities based on the manufacture of goods and manual labour that do not include the use of machines, or at least only marginally so, and employ a limited number of workers in small-scale production. In the 'artisan economy', the role of individuals is crucial, as the most elevated criterion for a purchase is neither quality nor price, but rather is the outcome of the quality of the relationship between the producer and consumer. Artisanal companies are often family-based, small-scale organizations that sell their products mostly locally (Marques et al., 2019), thus evoking the idea of uniqueness, originality and personality. By reestablishing an unmediated link with the human resource producing the craft object, the artisan brand is perceived as original by consumers. This unmediated relation, conceptualized as a direct link to the origin or provenance of the product, is a critical dimension of the definition of authenticity as demonstrated by the success of other unmediated forms of markets (such as farmers' markets).

Third, the artisan brand establishes a link between the product and art, providing craft objects with a sacred value, as 'the unique value of the authentic work of art always has its basis in ritual' Benjamin (2008, p. 24/orig. 1936). Before the Renaissance, art was always ritualistic or religious in its character, then became increasingly secular. Like an artwork, a craft object is perceived as unique, arguably exclusive and not mass-produced. For a long time, crafts were regarded as a synonym of 'art'. However, 'art' and 'craft' 'cannot be used as unequivocally as we would want to use them if they were scientific or critical concepts' (Becker, 1978, p. 863). Recently, scholars have distinguished between 'crafts' and 'art'. Some authors distinguished between artists, that is, individuals who create unique and symbolic products and craftsmen 'whose skills contribute in a supporting way' (Becker, 1978, p. 863). Being handcrafted, artisanal products are also scarce and rare as opposed to commodified and mass-produced. The scarcity of artisanal products, therefore, favours the perceived authenticity of the artisan brand.

Fourth, the artisan brand is linked to the idea of continuity and stability. By offering quality products over the long term, artisans demonstrate their know-how consistently and continuously, establishing a tradition of reliability over time and building an ongoing relationship with consumers. This also implies an ethical dimension of the craft brand, that is, its sincerity toward consumers in the manufacture of craft products and the morality that craftsmanship represents (Dezecot & Fleck-Dousteyssier, 2016).

Finally, the artisan brand incorporates a social dimension in that it can lead to consumer participation in a 'community of likeminded people' (Dezecot & Fleck-Dousteyssier, 2016), that is, a 'brand community' (Muniz & O'Guinn, 2001; Sams et al., 2022). Individuals seek to satisfy their need for authenticity through self-authenticating acts (Arnould & Price, 2000), that is, joining communities of people who share the same interests and passions to establish a more authentic relationship (Maffesoli, 1996). These groups have been defined as tribes as they bring about 'the re-emergence of quasi-archaic values: a local sense of identification, religiosity, syncretism, group narcissism [...], the common denominator of which is the community dimension', which is an expression of the postmodern reaggregation of the hyper-individualist society (Cova & Cova, 2002, p. 67). By reconnecting individuals to brand communities – defined as 'specialized, non-geographically bound communities, based on a structured set of social relationships among admirers of a brand' (Muniz & O'Guinn 2001, p. 412), and to communities of consumption (Schouten & McAlexander, 1995, p. 50) the artisan brand becomes 'a religious icon, around which an entire ideology of consumption is articulated' (Schouten & McAlexander, 1995, p. 50).

The implications for marketing, of these developments in the field of crafts, are relevant. Companies are increasingly employing marketing strategies to advertise their products by alluding to the charm of the concept of 'crafts', thus providing their industrial products with a value that belongs to the world of true craftsmanship (see brands such as Five Guys, Tostitos, Amica Chips, etc.). For instance, Leissle (2017) stressed how the term 'artisanal' is a floating signifier in how contemporary American chocolate companies market their product and emphasized how the US food industry uses terms like 'artisan' and 'crafted' to brand and add value to industrial products. In a context in which marketing is treating 'crafts' and 'artisanal' as buzzwords, as heuristics to attract consumers, there emerges a need to clearly define what 'crafts' and 'artisanal' mean, and to set the foundations for future developments of the concepts.

This research-based book offers an overview of marketing and branding in the craft sector. Through cases and examples, the authors examine how artisans and craft firms are facing the challenges posed by globalization and digitalization. In particular, this book examines how the contemporary era has brought about developments that have changed the way artisanal products are marketed and consumed. The authors emphasize how craft firms and organizations are not adequately addressing such profound shifts, as issues of authenticity, personalization, legitimacy, sustainability, and co-creation become increasingly influential features of contemporary consumption patterns. The book engages with some of the principal managerial and entrepreneurial implications that such developments have for craft firms, as they enter a more dynamic era of craft production and consumption.

Surprisingly, studies on craft marketing are scant, both in the mainstream and arts marketing literature. Our book addresses this gap by offering a critical contribution to an understanding of key developments and debates in this under-researched field. The text achieves this task both by adopting a multi-disciplinary approach (in particular: marketing, business studies, sociology and art) to craft marketing, and by drawing on the perspectives of market actors (artisans, craft makers, key stakeholders, and consumers). By focusing on craft marketing from a multidisciplinary academic, and practice, perspective, this book takes into account the respective stances of diverse stakeholders. By gathering together some of the leading scholars and specialists in the field, in providing theoretical, conceptual and empirical contributions, this book also serves as a guide to the current 'state of the art', and as a signal to further productive research avenues going forward.

THE COMPOSITION OF THE BOOK

Part I of the book explores the nature and changing forms of artisanal and craft markets, empirically, theoretically and conceptually. In so doing it sets the context for the remainder of the book. In Chapter 2, Understanding the Concept of 'Craft'; From the Perspective of Italian Consumers, Ricci and Massi engage with key debates associated with the conceptualiztion of the artisanal, and of craft. They then go on to draw on primary quantitative survey data to explore consumer behaviour from a marketing perspective. Specifically, the data is used to examine the perceptions and preferences of Italian craft consumers relating to various categories of craft products, in addition to the role played by price in informing their consumption decisions. The survey data illuminate important gender dimensions to the meanings consumers attribute to craft products, with women attributing to them, qualities of art, authenticity, beauty and creativity. In contrast, male consumers display an orientation towards valuations of 'quality' and 'made-to-measure'. The data give substance to the importance of the relationship between the economic and the cultural, where craft and artisanship can be understood as part of a broader cultural economy in which culture and economy become mutually informing. Ricci and Massi, as with Mulholland and Webb, mobilize an embeddedness framework to conceptualize the relationship between the cultural and the economic in this context. In respect of marketing strategies and practices, the data point to the increasing importance of direct and personal relationships between artisans and their consumers in supporting the quality of consumer experience, and facilitating satisfaction.

In Chapter 3, The UK Market for Craft: A Review of Crafts Council Evidence, Julia Bennett provides a critically reflexive account of the UK's *Market for Craft* report (Morris Hargreaves McIntyre, 2020). The chapter considers the report's findings, and analyses the implications for making, consumption and the role of market intermediaries in the UK. The UK market for craft has expanded over recent decades, a fact that can be attributed to a number of wider trends that are likely to accelerate: the rise of e-commerce, the preference for investment purchases over throwaway objects, a rapidly growing interest in sustainability, support for small businesses, and the growth of the experience economy.

UK craft is a growth industry, with a population of buyers and collectors that is diversifying and flourishing. The marketing of artisanship is becoming as important to the survival and growth of the sector as the sale of its products. There is a growing appreciation of the authenticity, originality and unique provenance of craft items, with buyers and potential buyers keen to understand and experience the skill sets such products entail. The craft sector is demonstrating its ability to flex and innovate in response to changing demand, refining its material knowledge and practice as well as its engagement with audiences and purchasers.

Yet makers and craft businesses face considerable turbulence, potential losses and an unpredictable purchasing environment, requiring resilience and determination. They will need to develop focused strategies to encourage, educate and refine consumer knowledge and understanding, if they are to grow occasional buyers into collectors. They will also need a range of additional support in the context of challenges presented by Covid-19 and Brexit.

In Chapter 4, Social Embedding, Artisanal Markets and Cultural Fields, Jon Mulholland and Pete Webb take two case studies of artisanal production (new wave custom motorcycles and boutique guitar pedals) and argue for the value of adopting a social embedding perspective for understanding artisanal markets. Specifically, they claim that within such markets, understood as 'markets of uncertainty', quality and value are effectively mediated through the embedding of these markets in cultural fields (cultural fields as markets), such that producers and consumers are able to inter-subjectively deliberate on the inherently uncertain nature of quality and value within a context of potentially homologous relationships, as such, embedding works to coordinate artisanal markets. The embedding of producers within artisanal markets, and the embedding of such markets within cultural fields, fulfils multiple important functions for producers, intermediaries and consumers.

Drawing on semi-structured interview data with artisanal producers, the chapter illuminates the many ways in which 'cultural fields-as-markets' function to ameliorate 'problems of coordination' (Beckert, 2007), specifically those associated with value uncertainty, cooperation and competition. Producer embedding in artisanal markets frames: the way in which artisans acquire and communicate their 'know-how'; the (often cooperative) relationships artisans have with a broader network of makers, and market arbiters; makers' innovations in respect of their of their current and future products; artisanal navigations of inevitably difficult trade-offs between quality and economic viability in pursuit of reputational status; and the nature, means and traction of artisans' marketing strategies and content. In this way, the chapter illustrates the value of the concept of embedding as a lens through which to understand the mechanisms and dynamics of artisanal markets, and of marketing in this sector.

Part II of the book, From Tradition to Innovation: Trends and Issues in Artisanal and Craft Making, focuses on some of the key innovation-related developments taking place within artisanal and craft markets, and considers what such developments might mean for the identity and dynamics of the sector. In Chapter 5, exploring neo-artisanal identities and practices, Laura Quinn draws on her own practice as a glass blower to sociologically examine the tensions that exist between nostalgic representations of traditional artisanship, and the realities of the industrial techniques associated with some forms of (neo-)artisanship. The chapter directly engages the question of whether the nostalgic view of the artisan as a custodian of heritage and culture obstructs neo-artisans' potential to evolve both the nature, and public understanding, of artisanal making. Specifically, she considers the central issue of whether the neo-artisanal space occupied by contemporary glass blowers might serve as a platform for the reinvention of the romantic veneration of the artisan, or alternatively might serve as a catalyst for a departure into new public conceptions of artisanal making.

Within this context, the chapter also examines the role that narratives of sustainability may play in such deliberations. Craft and artisanship have been attributed qualities of sustainability, such that those who engage in sustainable, or green, consumption may construct craft and artisanal products in contra-distinction to those of industrial mass manufacture. Undoubtedly, producers across all market sectors have increasingly recognized the market value of 'green washing' their products. The chapter argues that neo-artisans should be careful not to be lured into reproducing nostalgic, and therefore limiting, (mis)representations of artisanal practice as sustainable per se. Rather, neo-artisans should, through the medium of their marketing, enable consumers to develop a more sophisticated and holistic understanding of sustainability that makes space for the reality of neo-artisanal practices that necessarily include industrial processes, processes that taken in isolation, may be deemed unsustainable.

In Chapter 6, Innovation in Craft: Creating New Value Through Art, Giacomo Magnani and Laura Bresolin draw on a case study of the Berengo Studio, an artisanal 'artistic glass' producer from Murano Island, Venice. In its practices and products, Murano glass embodies important tangible and intangible elements of the cultural heritage of Venice, and constitutes one of the earliest expressions of the 'Made in Italy' national brand. Many homes in Italy, and abroad, will display examples of Murano glass, used as decorative household *objets d'art*. The relative success of the Berengo Studio stands in some contradistinction to the malaise of the broader glass sector, both in its artisanal and industrial forms, and as such offers important insights into how an artisanal company may innovate to survive, even in a broader context of crisis.

Specifically, the chapter explores the innovative ways in which the Berengo Studio has built an advantageous market position for its artisanal products precisely through its engagement with 'high art'. By rejoining traditional craft skills with the creative work of artists (as was the case in the past), Berengo Studio has successfully transformed the public perception of their artefacts. Now increasingly signified as 'art', as much as 'craft', Berengo Studio's products have realized new aesthetic and market value, through their renewed distinction, at a time when the broader glass sector struggles. Magnani and Bresolin's account evidences the uses that tradition and heritage may have as a platform for effective innovation. The tangible and intangible assets of cultural heritage may be creatively re-enlisted in the name of securing viable futures, in particular where they are conjoined with other innovations in production techniques, and with effective branding and marketing strategies.

In Chapter 7, The Innovative Logics of Digital Manufacturing, Daniela Corsaro and Mirko Olivieri take the case of 3DiTALY to explore the nature and implications of 3D printing technologies for the manufacturing practices and business models of craft-based companies. Drawing on qualitative data, the chapter explores the dynamic interface between the revolutionary technological transformation that is 3D printing, with an equally significant shift within consumer expectations and practices, associated with personalization, creativity and production democratization. 3D printing plays directly into the hands of the craft economy, in the manner in which it renders small-scale, and even bespoke, production, not only economically viable, but also directly suited to prosumption-based relationships with engaged consumers. 3D printing provides a technological platform to challenge the mass production logic of contemporary globalized commodity manufacturing.

In its place, 3D print-based production techniques facilitate an opening-up, or a democratization, of human creativity, both on the production and consumption side, allowing for new choices to be co-constructed beyond the limits of what an overly rigid system of mass production might provide. The adopted case study 3DiTALY reveals the important linkages that exist between 3D digital technologies and a DIY philosophy and practice, where consumers are empowered to develop their own imaginations and capacities through the technology. 3D printing dramatically reduces the cost obstacles to start-up, prototyping, fabricating and manufacturing, minimizing the economies of scale effect, and hence offering unprecedented access for SMEs to enter markets. By embracing these revolutionary digital technologies, the craft sector is able to open up new competitive advantages, being positioned to offer personalized, cost-effective services to meeting the needs of newly creative consumers.

Part III of the book, Entrepreneurship and Business Models in Craft and Artisanal Markets, engages some of the most important developments currently impacting on the nature and forms of entrepreneurialism and business modelling within the sector.

Victoria Bell draws on data from a longitudinal qualitative study of self-identified artists, designer-makers and crafters in Chapter 8, Entrepreneurs in Action? The data were collected in the North of England, and explore the nature, forms and dynamics and entrepreneurialism within the field. She draws on typological frameworks developed by Susan Luckman and Ian Fillis, in addition to Mainiero and Sullivan's Kaleidoscope Career Model, to explore her participants' motivations for embarking on, and continuing in, a 'career' in craft. Bell's data support the claim that whilst motivations are complex, and connected to individual circumstances that change over time, they reflect Angela McRobbie's proposal that social values, as well as other entrepreneurial characteristics, are influential. Bell's participants were entrepreneurial in how they used their time, their materials, and the opportunities that came their way, though variably so. Important themes emerge in Bell's qualitative data, particularly in respect of her participants' relationship to their role and work. These include the value placed on creativity, control, flexibility in working, social values, intangible added value, the development of skills, the emotional/ affective dimensions of the work, and the development of 'publicly performed narratives of self' (Luckman, 2015, p. 118). Bell finds that such publicly performed narratives of self are mediated through a range of marketing and branding activities.

Bell's participants also gave voice to some of the tensions associated with maintaining 'authenticity' in the context of a diversification of products, and the pressures of commercialization, finding their embeddedness of maker-networks invaluable in sustaining their sense of authenticity in their work. Such embeddedness also provided much-needed sociality and fulfilment, and cooperative skill-enhancement. In the context of a need to self-support, and for some, to engage in portfolio working, the Covid-19 pandemic has brought both challenges and opportunities.

In Chapter 9, New Business Models for Craft: The Case of Artemest, Chiara Piancatelli and Alessandra Ricci examine the role played by digital transformations in reconfiguring the artisanal sector, and specifically, the opportunity structures such transformations have made newly available to artisans for profitable innovation and partnership. A fourth industrial revolution, most clearly expressed in the dramatic evolution of multitudinous digital platforms, promises to transform the artisanal sector. Digital technologies may transform the business models of artisanal organizations, offering innovations in digitally facilitated networking, the adoption of service-dominance logic, user-design driven approaches, mass-customization, production technologies, and also business-to-business and business-to-consumer e-commerce. Rather than replacing traditional operating methods, such technologies can be used in conjunction with them, in advancing new synergies of the old and the new. More specifically, digital tools are enabling innovations of co-creation between stakeholders, one important consequence of which is an emerging 'coopetition' between producers, as against competition. These tools are also supporting new enhancements of customer-experience, and enabling novel e-commerce opportunities in the context of the Covid-19 pandemic and beyond. The chapter takes the case study of Artemest, a curated e-commerce company dedicated to Italian luxury craftsmanship, to ground its analysis of the opportunities presented by synergies of traditional crafts with e-commerce. In providing craft businesses with a curated online marketplace in support of both business-to-customer and business-to-business sales opportunities, allied to related services of logistics, content production, analytics, credit collection and customer care, Artemest has been able to revolutionize traditional craft businesses' access to market.

Part IV, Marketing in Craft and Artisanal Markets, examines some key dynamics characterizing the contemporary transformation of marketing within artisanal and craft sectors. In Chapter 10, The New Rise of Artisanship in Kenya: Evidence from Artisan Entrepreneurs, Alisa Sydow and Isabella Maggioni draw on a range of qualitative data to explore the enablers of, and obstacles to, a flourishing of artisanal entrepreneurship in Nairobi. Focusing on the community of artisans associated with the KI Flea Market, the chapter examines the dynamics associated with building a positive brand identity for craft products under the rubric of 'Made in Kenya', as a national umbrella brand. Artisanal entrepreneurs have understood the importance of, but also the challenges associated with, establishing positive brand associations amongst consumers for local products. For such positive associations to be established, indigenous tradition, as one part of a broader heritage value, must be positioned front and centre, and positively signified against the allure of foreign goods readily regarded by consumers as embodying status value and quality.

Consumers must be enabled to recognize the quality of local artisanal products, and be enabled to feel pride in their consumption. Key to the success of the artisanal entrepreneurs has been their work in building effective collaborative networks and substantive producer communities around the KI Flea Market, and in supporting the co-creation of the Made in Kenya brand. In addition, finding ways to enable consumers to recognize the quality of the local artisanal products has been key. Notwithstanding the evident successes of this innovative community of artisanal entrepreneurs, these artisans have needed to work imaginatively and forcefully against a prevailing negative Country

of Origin effect that has constructed local products in negatively stereotypical terms as of poor quality, in part as a legacy of colonial rule. Sydow and
Maggioni conclude that three principal variables have underpinned the success
of the Flea Market's community of artisanal entrepreneurs: the overcoming
of negative Country of Origin effect, the establishment of a strong artisanal
community, and the enhancing of the reputation of local products.

In Chapter 11, Slow Production, Less Consumption: Righteous Approaches
to the Paradox of Craft Businesses, Richard Ocejo explores the paradox
faced by craft-based businesses in simultaneously promoting consumption
and anti-consumption. Drawing on interviews with craft workers and entrepreneurs, in addition to extensive ethnographic fieldwork, he examines the
ways in which craft businesses seek to resolve this dilemma through a distinct
anti-consumption discourse directed at consumers. This discourse combines
both a framing of the nature and forms of 'righteous consumption', and
a practice of educating consumers on the merits of such consumption; all for
the purpose of inviting consumer reflexivity on what makes for 'better' consumption (and in the process reinstating the rarefied position of the crafts in
question). The anti-consumption promoted by craft workers deploys a critique
of mass consumption as a device for the veneration and even fetishization
of more selective and mindful forms of consumption of craft objects. Such
objects are marked by their provenance, and their claims to 'authenticity'. In
the process, craftspeople promote a new elite form of consumption associated
with the elaboration of culturally omnivorous tastes, with the added appeal of
a sustainability narrative. Whilst consuming less to consume 'better' simultaneously works to venerate the quality and sustainability of craft production
and consumption, customer engagement with such narratives cannot be
assumed. Accordingly, craftspeople deploy a form of marketing as education
(service education), providing formal and informal windows of opportunity for
(potential) customers to understand and ultimately value the 'slow production'
process.

In Chapter 12, The Resurgence of Craft Retailing: Marketing and Branding
Strategies in the Food and Beverage Sector, Alessandro Gerosa explains the
loss, and then the resurgence, of the social prestige of shopkeepers, understood not only as retailers but also artisans and cultural intermediaries. The
development of neo-craft industries paved the way to a resurgence of artisanal
retailing. In a post-Fordist economy, craft not only seems suited to satisfying
consumers' demand for authenticity, but also facilitates the business models of
small and independent retailers; giving birth to a new retail paradigm.

The chapter explores the marketing and branding strategies used by retailers
in this new field of neo-craft retailing in the food and beverage sector, and
specifically the use made of the craft products themselves (as authentic and
distinctive), in addition to the atmosphere of place, in positioning themselves

as artisans within a broader marketplace. In such a context, small and independent brick-and-mortar shops are better able to capitalize on these trends, as long as they are successful in branding themselves as authentic and distinctive in the eyes of the customers they target. This in turn requires an effective deployment of the aesthetic and symbolic canons of the neo-craft sector.

At the same time, however, such retailers must balance these strategies with economic viability through the identification of market niches sufficiently original to allow distinctiveness, yet sufficiently popular to attract enough clientele. This in turn depends critically on the setting of market-optimal prices tailored to an essentially middle-class clientele. In the context of Gerosa's research participants, this balance is manifested in the provision of gourmet products clearly distinct from industrial, mass-produced goods, but without the prices associated with 'highbrow' alternatives. Gerosa's data also foreground the importance of craft retailers' locatedness within their respective neighbourhoods, in respect of building an identity, embedded as these retailers can be in the economic, cultural and social landscape associated with that neighbourhood.

In Chapter 13, Innovating Through Craft: From Happenstance to Strategic Culture, Ginevra Addis asks the question, 'how does strategic culture stem from craft?' Deploying the distinction between happenstance and strategic culture, Addis accounts for the complex interplay of Italy's *arte popolare* and the emergent, imported Pop Art, where *arte popolare* had become established as an important early contributor to the 'Made in Italy' brand; representing both community and heritage through its craftsmanship. The arrival of Pop Art in Italy triggered contestation in its relationship with *arte popolare*, with the former constructed as a modernizing and trans-localizing threat to the traditional and emplaced nature of the latter. In some cases, though often without enduring success, an emergent Italian Pop Art sought to produce artefacts conjoining elements from the Italian crafts tradition with Pop Art motifs.

The chapter goes on to explore the emergence, initially haphazardly, and then strategically, of a distinctive Pop Art branding and marketing strategy, that proved effective in both Italy and the USA. Particular attention is given to understanding the defining role played by Andy Warhol's business models and marketing strategies, as these became defining elements of much of the US Pop Art market. The key features of these strategies were their notably 'mass' character, drawing on universal or North American consumerist images that served to displace the vernacular and local elements of, amongst other forms, *arte popolare*. Addis examines the dilemmas and precarities, but also the opportunities, associated with the deployment of such massified marketing strategies (and their constituent iconographies) for Italian Pop Art.

REFERENCES

Arnould, E. J., & Price, L. L. (2000). Authenticating acts and authoritative performances: questing for self and community. In S. Ratneshwar, David Glen Mick, & Cynthia Hyffman (eds), *The Why of Consumption: Contemporary Perspectives on Consumer Motives, Goals and Desires* (140–63). Routledge.

Becker, F. (1978). The quality of unmercy. *The Hudson Review*, 86–106. https://hudsonreview.com/authors/frawley-becker/#.YqG61qjMIuU.

Benjamin, W. (2008) [1936]. The work of art in the age of mechanical reproduction. In H. Arendt (ed.), *Illuminations* (19–55). Fontana Press.

Brown, S., Kozinets, R. V., & Sherry Jr, J. F. (2003). Teaching old brands new tricks: retro branding and the revival of brand meaning. *Journal of Marketing*, *67*(3), 19–33.

Cova, B., & Cova, V. (2002). Tribal marketing: the tribalisation of society and its impact on the conduct of marketing. *European Journal of Marketing*, *36*(5–6), 595–620.

Dezecot, J., & Fleck-Dousteyssier, N. (2016). The concept of artisan-brand: exploration of the characteristics and consumers' motivations. https://halshs.archives-ouvertes.fr/halshs-02952979/document.

Garavaglia, C., & Mussini, M. (2020). What is craft?—An empirical analysis of consumer preferences for craft beer in Italy. *Modern Economy*, *11*(6), 1195–208.

Leissle, K. (2017). Artisan as brand: adding value in a craft chocolate community. *Food, Culture & Society*, *20*(1), 37–57.

Maffesoli, M. (1996). *The Time of the Tribes: The Decline of Individualism in Mass Society*. Sage.

Morris Hargreaves McIntyre (2020). The market for craft. Commissioned by the Crafts Council and Partners. https://www.craftscouncil.org.uk/documents/880/Market_for_craft_full_report_2020.pdf.

Muniz, A. M., & O'Guinn, T. C. (2001). Brand community. *Journal of Consumer Research*, *27*(4): 412–32.

Sams, D. E., Rickard, M. K., & Sadasivan, A. (2022). The perspective of artisan vendors' resilience, dedication to product authenticity, and the role of marketing and community: 21st century. *Arts and the Market*, *12*(1), 70–83.

Schouten, J. W., & McAlexander, J. H. (1995). Subcultures of consumption: an ethnography of the new bikers. *Journal of Consumer Research*, *22*(1), 43–61.

Wilson, A., & Flohr, M. (eds) (2016). *Urban Craftsmen and Traders in the Roman World*. Oxford University Press.

PART I

Understanding craft and artisanal markets

2. Understanding of the concept of 'craft' from the perspective of Italian consumers

Alessandra Ricci and Marta Massi

INTRODUCTION

This chapter aims to understand consumer perceptions of artisanship. In particular, the research investigates Italian consumer perceptions of artisanship and consumer preference for different types of artisanal products. Most of the research conducted to date in the field of artisanship has been qualitative in nature. As Thorlindsson et al. (2018) state, 'interestingly, all the sociological work on craftsmanship is qualitative. We are not aware of any quantitative research on craftsmanship.' Scholars have investigated the relationship between artisanship and design (Lawson 2009; Bean & Rosner 2012; Adamson 2007, 2013), the relation between art and craft (Arendt 2012; Shiner 2010; Adamson 2016), artisanship from an historical and philosophical point of view (Leslie 1998), anthropological and sociological interpretation (Costin 1998; Herzfeld 2015; Becker 1978), and artisanship in relation to its products (Antoldi et al. 2017). This research will aim to fill a research gap by examining Italian consumer preference for and perceptions of artisanal products. In particular, the survey included questions on respondents' willingness to pay more for artisanal products, frequency of purchase of artisanal products, product category purchased, satisfaction related to quality, packaging, price, and degree of customization. In addition, we asked consumers to indicate their degree of agreement on a number of items that described the concept of authenticity in order to identify factors useful to define the artisanship concept. This chapter is structured as follows. First, we review the definition of artisanship from different perspectives, including economic and sociological. Second, we address the concept of artisanship in the marketing context. Finally, we present the results of research aiming to understand how Italian consumers perceive artisanship.

A DEFINITION OF CRAFT

As Leissle (2017) states:

> Told in a story, a maker's intimacy with any aspect of the 'artisan' endeavor is available to sell to consumers—as their own intimacy with chocolate. Storytelling thus anchors 'artisan,' but to a functional process—a way of selling chocolate, a form of marketing—rather than to a labor class, skill set, or material fact of the food. Stories are malleable and particular, making storytelling a flexible anchor. Naming oneself 'artisan' requires less any particular story than enough of a story—enough intimacy—to compel a purchase.

This statement identifies the perspective of consumers of craft products and their perception of the concept, which has not yet been studied in depth. Principally, the term 'artisanal' is often used to identify people with manual skills who can produce high-quality and unique products (Garavaglia & Mussini 2020; Cavalli 2017; Adamson 2013). Rarely has this concept been provided with a well-rounded definition within the literature. Thus, it is intriguing to identify some of the main themes and dimensions and to garner a greater comprehension of why and how varying approaches to and understandings of the concept are relevant to the marketing field. In this scenario, the European area provides a compelling context as the development of artisanship has its root in this setting (Leissle 2017).

Specifically in economic literature, craft has been defined as a specialized form of labour, (1) quality-driven, (2) material specific and (3) motivated by internal and external rewards (Adamson 2007; Banks 2010; Sennett 2008). Recently, Garavaglia and Mussini (2020) defined craft production activities for the manufacture of goods by manual labour, that is, without the use of machines or with the marginal use of machines, and by employing a limited number of workers in small-scale production. Indeed, artisan producers are often family units that sell their products locally (Marques et al. 2019) evoking the idea of uniqueness, originality and personality (Dallocchio et al. 2016; Cavalli 2017; Ratten & Tajeddini 2017). Thus, the choice of raw materials, production techniques and manufacturing procedure characterizes these artisan products. According to many authors, in fact, the work of the artisans is stimulated by goals of personal satisfaction rather than economic growth (Chatterjee et al. 2017), as the focus of the craftsman is on the consumer (Garavaglia & Mussini 2020). According to Jakob (2013), consumers are willing to pay more for craft products than industrial products thanks to the aforementioned characteristics (i.e. uniqueness, customization, etc.), and this was an opportunity to respond to mass production.

The field of crafts has been defined as a meta-sector cutting across different product categories, markets and consumer types. Craft products could be classified based on their degree of innovation (vs. tradition) and their profession-alization degree (i.e. do it yourself vs. upscale products). For instance, both a hand-made vase and a crafted beer can be considered crafts. In this sense, the concept of artisanship is a multidimensional one. The term 'artisanal' has traditionally been used to identify people with manual skills who can produce excellent and unique products, and to identify a specific class of workers. Rarely has this concept been provided with a well-rounded definition within the literature. For many years, the concepts of 'art' and 'crafts' have been regarded as synonyms. However, 'art' and 'craft' 'cannot be used as unequiv-ocally as we would want to use them if they were scientific or critical concepts' (Becker 1978, p. 863). Some authors (see Becker 1978; Levine 1972; White & White 1993) distinguished between artists, that is, individuals who create unique and symbolic products and craftsmen 'whose skills contribute in a sup-porting way' (Becker 1978, p. 863).

The notion of crafts has been evolving over time to include more contem-porary forms of artisanship, such as the work of the digital makers (Anderson 2013). An explanation of the current evolution of the notion was given by Annie Warburton, the creative director of the British Crafts Council, at the Triennale di Milano in 2017. Warburton reconsidered the relationship between crafts and manufacturing, stating that new technologies, processes and mate-rials can all push the crafts world towards new horizons where contamination with other fields (such as art, science, technology) can provide new lifeblood to the sector.

Further, the concept of crafts has been increasingly associated with those of innovation and economic sustainability. According to the main crafts foun-dations, such as the Institut National des Metiers d'Art (France), Fondazione Cologni dei Mestieri d'Arte (Italy), and the Crafts Council (UK), crafts are facing a crucial phase of strategic development, meaning that the intelligence of the *savoir faire* could turn into economically profitable innovations. The KPMG (2016) report, *Innovation through Craft: Opportunities for Growth*, describes how traditional know-how, driven from the bottom up and with an open-ended approach, is combining with new tools and processes to drive innovation via the culture of artisanship. The artisanal craft economy is, there-fore, providing a reconfigured model of production and leading to alternative patterns of consumption. Given the craft economy's character as a space of culturally embedded skilled making, artisanal craft stands to benefit from the emergence of important trends in contemporary consumption practices, where made-to-measure meets an emerging impetus and need for authenticity, sustainability, personalization, individualization, and new expressions of connoisseurship.

Thus, in this study, we take up this new trend towards understanding con-sumers' perceptions and behaviours. The purpose is to extend the understanding of how consumers buy craft products. To achieve this aim, an empirical study with Italian consumers was conducted.

The study proceeds as follows. First a discussion on extant literature on artisanship and its definition(s) therein is made. Second, a detailed description of how the empirical study of Italian consumers was conducted is provided. Third, the main findings are presented. Finally, a discussion on implications and limitations is offered, providing suggestions for further research.

ARTISANSHIP IN THE MARKETING FIELD

A literature review shows that artisanship (or craftsmanship) has been studied from different perspectives. Much on craft can be found, but very little about the relationship between craft and marketing (Leissle 2017; Wherry 2006). However, as craft and marketing represent an ideal topic to extend the body of the knowledge, Dickie and Frank (1996) provide a conceptual framework on the topic of the artisan occupations in the global economy, referring to the term 'craft' as objects generally viewed in a continuum from the functional to the artistic. From a marketing point of view, authors argue that artisans 'provide the means of economic survival for people shifting from a subsistence to a cash economy' (p. 53). More recently, Leissle (2017) stressed how the term 'artisan' is a floating signifier in contemporary US chocolate marketing and food industries that use terms like 'artisan' and 'crafted' to brand their chocolate and to add value to their products. 'Today, "artisans" are again at the frontlines, this time pitted against the advanced capitalist hegemony of industrial giants. In contrast to exploitative production terms of multinationals, "artisans" offer an intimate market of goods that are materially desirable and ethically sound' (Leissle 2017, p. 44). According to the author, in the 'artisan economy' the role of persons is crucial, as the most elevated criterion for a purchase is neither quality nor price, but that it happens between knowable people.

Hence, a large number of existing studies in the broader literature have examined the concept of artisanship. Based on the previous studies, the following dimensions of the artisanship concept were identified. To date, research on consumer perceptions of artisanal products has been largely qualitative. In addition, the research has been limited to specific product categories. For instance, Lahne and Trubek (2014) conducted focus groups with consumers in Vermont about their everyday perceptions of artisan cheese to develop a conceptual framework for sensory perceptions of the product. Based on this research, it was found that consumers combine information about producer practices, social context and the materiality of the product through an active, learned practice of sensory perception.

Groves (2001) conducted five focus groups with consumers who were responsible for half or more of their household's shopping to investigate their perceptions of authenticity related to both artisan and mass-produced branded products. Groves identified five dimensions affecting consumer perceptions of an authentic British food product, including uniqueness to Britain, a cultural or traditional association with Britain, characteristics of the production process, the presence of an authority, and specific extrinsic characteristics of the product.

More recently, Waldman and Kerr (2015) conducted a survey to investigate consumer perceptions of products at farmers markets including experimental auctions and sensory analysis of pasteurized and unpasteurized cheese and questions concerning attitudes about food safety. The results of this research demonstrated that there is neither evidence of positive demand for pasteurization nor of a trade-off between safety and quality. Consumers of artisan cheese make their purchase decisions based on taste instead of their attitudes towards food safety. Further, Gellyngk et al. (2009) investigated consumer quality perception with respect to bread. The authors identified four consumer segments based on attributes such as sensory, health and nutrition. Results showed that more than 80 per cent of the respondents buy their bread at an artisanal bakery, independent of their quality perception of bread.

Identifying all the facets of the concept of 'crafts' is a difficult task as it involves not only a definitional issue but also a multidisciplinary approach to the subject that includes sociology, anthropology, economics and management. Authors such as Sennet (2008), Adamson (2013) and Arendt (2012) defined craftsmen as individuals embodying a specific human condition. However, this is only one aspect of the multidimensional nature of the concept.

This literature review demonstrates how studies that have been conducted on consumer perceptions and preference for artisanal products are mainly qualitative and that it has concentrated largely on certain product categories, mainly food (e.g. cheese and bread). Thus there is a need to extend these findings to other product categories and to investigate consumer perceptions of the notion of artisanship.

RESEARCH METHODS

The questionnaire was delivered online through personal contacts. One thousand invitations to complete the survey were sent out in September 2018, and 412 complete questionnaires were returned. Table 2.1 presents the descriptive statistics of the sample in order to offer a better understanding of respondents' feedback.

We collected data using a random sample of local consumers working in different sectors and living in different regions of Italy. The survey was pretested with a random sample of 50 consumers in order to understand if the questions were clear. By doing so, we had a higher degree of confidence that the insights

Table 2.1   Descriptive statistics

		Total no.	Total %
Gender	Male	159	38.59
	Female	253	61.41
Age	< 18	1	0.24
	18–25	26	6.31
	26–35	133	32.28
	36–45	76	18.45
	46–65	142	34.47
	> 65	34	8.25
Education	High School	131	31.80
	Bachelor Degree	212	51.46
	Master Degree	44	10.68
	PhD Degree	17	4.13
	Other	8	1.94
Profession	Student	32	7.77
	Lecturer	30	7.28
	Entrepreneur	40	9.71
	Manager	25	6.07
	Dealer	15	3.64
	Artisan	8	1.94
	Architect	12	2.91
	Designer	3	0.73
	Journalist	6	1.46
	Freelancer	71	17.23
	Employee	87	21.12
	Public Employee	15	3.64
	Retiree	27	6.55
	Searching for a Job	9	2.18
	Others	32	7.77
Level of Income	< 25,000€	118	28.64
	25,000€–39,000€	93	22.57
	40,000€–54,000€	68	16.50
	55,000€–75,000€	61	14.81
	76,000€–99,000€	16	3.88
	100,000€–145,000€	25	6.07
	> 145,000€	31	7.52

gained around understandings of 'craft' and artisanship from Italian consumers were reliable.

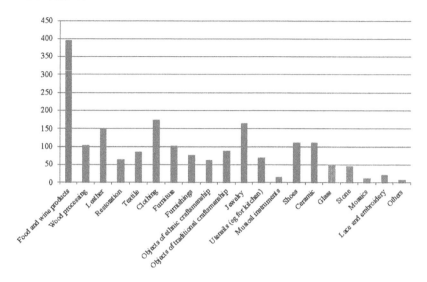

Figure 2.1   Over the last year, which of these craft products have you purchased?

ANALYSIS AND RESULTS

In order to analyse our data, we began by examining the purchasing behaviour of Italian consumers. Almost 400 participants stated that they had purchased food and wine craft products in the last year. This was thus the most prevalent category for craft products, followed by categories such as clothing and jewellery (around 160 participants indicated they had purchased such craft products). Less relevant categories include musical instruments, mosaics, and lace and embroidery (Figure 2.1).

As a next step, we wanted to gain a better understanding of which channels consumers use in order to gather information about new artisanal products. Although we had quite a young group of participants, offline channels dominated their responses (Figure 2.2). Most of the respondents stated that they had gathered information about new artisanal products by word-of-mouth, followed by trade fairs and specific markets dedicated to craft products. Hence, we can deduce that for marketing activities in the sector of artisanship, producers should focus on offline communication and promotion as they seem the strongest channels in order to get new clients.

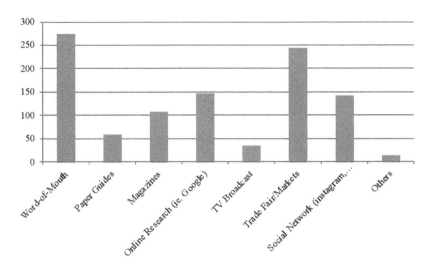

Figure 2.2   How do you learn about new artisanal products?

In line with the strength of offline communication channels, we found that direct contact with artisans is the dominant place where Italian consumers buy craft products. Moreover, shops, labs and trade fairs are popular places for buying artisanal products. This highlights the relevance of direct relations to producers which may also be a criterion for buying craft products. This was also demonstrated by the fact that respondents' least preferred place to purchase craft products is from online shops (Figure 2.3).

Returning to the question of how Italian consumers define and understand the craft world, respondents were asked to indicate terms that they link to the craft world. For this question, we discovered a significant difference between male and female consumers. Thus, we split the results by gender in order to better understand their differences. Terms such as arts, authenticity, beauty, creativity and unity were more strongly connected to the craft world for female consumers than for male consumers, whereas luxury and made-to-measure were terms more strongly linked to the craft world for male participants. Consequently, we assume that words which are generally perceived as more 'feminine' are also perceived more by women to be linked to the concept of the craft world. For instance, the terms 'made-to-measure' and 'luxury' may be considered masculine expressions and thus might be linked to men buying tailored suits. This is why we see a connection among perceptions of the craft world and artisanship and personal identity (Figure 2.4). This also demonstrates that there might be an interrelationship among society and personal behaviour towards the perception and consumption of craft products.

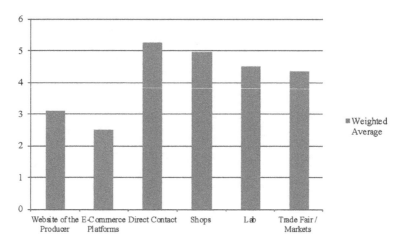

Note: 1 = NEVER; 7 = OFTEN.

Figure 2.3   *Thinking about your experience of buying craft products, how often do you buy in the scale listed here?*

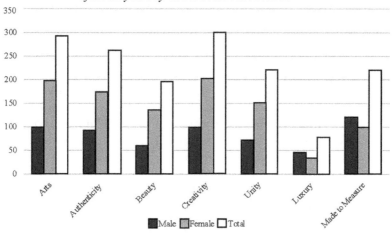

Figure 2.4   *Can you select the terms that link to the craft world?*

DISCUSSION

This study aims to advance understanding of the concept of craft. More specifically, consumer behaviour and perceptions of the craft world in Italy were studied. The results indicate that arts, authenticity, beauty, creativity and unity are terms that are strongly connected to the craft world for female consumers. This insight broadens the perspective of the concept of cultural economy (Villette & Hardill 2010) which has become an increasingly common term both theoretically and empirically in the social sciences (Claval 1995). It presents the ways in which the economic is embedded in the culture and the culture is seen as materialized in the economic (Crang 1997). Based on the findings, basic concepts of cultural economy should be connected in order to gain a better understanding of craft and artisanship. Moreover, the connection between artisanship and marketing was linked in order to gain more insight into how Italian consumers gather information about new artisanal products and where they buy them. Principally, it was identified a tendency towards direct and personal channels between craftsmen and their consumers. It seems to be relevant for craftsmen to build up a direct relationship which supports consumer experience and satisfaction. Thus, it would be interesting to further investigate how marketing activities and distribution channels can be improved for craftsmen in Italy.

Despite the findings of the study, there is a need to outline some of its key limitations. First, the analysis is based on Italian consumers. Due to this fact, and the identified link between personal identity and a cultural and behavioural context, generalizability of the findings might be limited. Further limitations might be induced by the number of participants. In order to strengthen the results, the survey should be extended to more consumers in order to come up with a more representative sample. This improvement would fortify findings and their generalizability. With respect to the link identified to cultural economy, perceptions of the concept of 'craft' are related to the specific culture in which artisanship is embedded.

Studies should be undertaken with respect to other geographical regions in order to confirm or discredit previous findings. Moreover, a geographical extension could lead to new insights as a result of the variety of cultural and historical contexts which could contribute notably to our understanding of the concepts craft and artisanship. In addition, a comparison between different nations could generate further insights of widely accepted elements that are country- or culture-specific.

CONCLUSION

By unpacking the understanding the concept of craft from the perspective of Italian consumers, this study tried to develop theories around the phenomena of artisanship that assist in substantiating emerging research streams. In doing so, this research shifts the conversation of the definition of artisanship and craft made by experts towards understandings of actual consumers. The theory provides a valuable depiction of key insights of understandings of artisanship and consumer behaviours with respect to purchasing artisanal products and gathering information about craftsmen and artisans. Returning to the opening question of how Italian consumers perceive the craft world, significant differences have been identified between male and female consumers. Female consumers connect artisanship to arts, authenticity, beauty, creativity and unity, whereas male consumers relate the terms 'made-to-measure' and 'luxury' with the craft world. In conclusion, this study contributes to the research stream of artisanship by connecting studies to actual consumers. We hope our study stimulates further research addressing those and other connected research questions.

REFERENCES

Adamson, G. (2007). Craft and the romance of the studio. *American Art*, 21(1), 14–18.
Adamson, G. (2013). *The Invention of Craft*. Bloomsbury Academic/V&A Publishing, London.
Adamson, G. (2016). *The Craft Reader*. Bloomsbury Academic, London.
Anderson, C. (2013). *Makers: The New Industrial Revolution*. Random House, London.
Antoldi, F., Capelli, C., & Macconi, I. (2017). Territori che 'suonano'. I fattori critici di successo della produzione italiana di strumenti musicali. *Quaderni di ricerca sull'artigianato*, 3, 323–50.
Arendt, H. (2012). *Vita activa: la condizione umana*. Giunti, Firenze.
Banks, M. (2010). Craft labour and creative industries. *International Journal of Cultural Policy*, 16(3), 305–21.
Bean, J., & Rosner, D. (2012). Old hat: craft versus design? *Interactions*, 19(1), 86–8.
Becker, H. S. (1978). Arts and crafts. *American Journal of Sociology*, 83(4), 862–89.
Cavalli, A., (2017). *The Master's Touch Essential Elements of Artisanal Excellence*. Marsilio Editori, Venezia
Chatterjee, S., Gupta, S. D., & Upadhyay, P. (2017). Empowering women and stimulating development at bottom of pyramid through micro-entrepreneurship. *Management Decision*, 56, 160–74.
Claval, P. (1995). L'analyse des paysages. *Géographie et Cultures*, 13, 55–74.
Costin, C. L. (1998). Introduction: craft and social identity. *Archeological Papers of the American Anthropological Association*, 8(1), 3–16.
Crang, M. (1997). Picturing practices: research through the tourist gaze. *Progress in Human Geography*, 21(3), 359–73.
Dallocchio, M., Ricci, A., & Vizzaccaro, M. (2016). *Costruttori di valore: il ruolo strategico del saper fare italiano*. Marsilio Editore, Venezia.

Dickie, V. A., & Frank, G. (1996). Artisan occupations in the global economy: a conceptual framework. *Journal of Occupational Science*, 3(2), 45–55.

Garavaglia, C., & Mussini, M. (2020). What is craft? An empirical analysis of consumer preferences for craft beer in Italy. *Modern Economy*, 11(6), 1195–208.

Gellynck, X., Kühne, B., Van Bockstaele, F., Van de Walle, D., & Dewettinck, K. (2009). Consumer perception of bread quality. *Appetite*, 53(1), 16–23.

Groves, A. M. (2001). Authentic British food products: a review of consumer perceptions. *International Journal of Consumer Studies*, 25(3), 246–54.

Herzfeld, M. (2015). Heritage and the right to the city: when securing the past creates insecurity in the present. *Heritage & Society*, 8(1), 3–23.

Jakob, D. (2013). Crafting your way out of the recession? New craft entrepreneurs and the global economic downturn. *Cambridge Journal of Regions, Economy and Society*, 6, 127–40.

KPMG (2016). Innovation through craft: opportunities for growth: a report for the Crafts Council. https://www.craftscouncil.org.uk/documents/876/Innovation _through_craft_full_report_2016.pdf.

Lahne, J., & Trubek, A. B. (2014). A little information excites us: consumer sensory experience of Vermont artisan cheese as active practice. *Appetite*, 78, 129–38.

Lawson, C. (2009). 'Made by' vs 'designed by': two approaches in sustainable development collaborations with artisan communities. *Nordes*, 3. https://dl.designresea rchsociety.org/nordes/nordes2009/exploratorypapers/13/.

Leissle, K. (2017). 'Artisan' as brand: adding value in a craft chocolate community. *Food, Culture & Society*, 20(1), 37–57.

Leslie, E. (1998). Walter Benjamin: traces of craft. *Journal of Design History*, 11(1), 5–13.

Levine, E. M. (1972). Chicago's art world: the influence of status interests on its social and distribution systems. *Urban Life and Culture*, 1(3), 293–322.

Marques, C. S., Santos, G., Ratten, V., & Barros, A. B. (2019). Innovation as a booster of rural artisan entrepreneurship: a case study of black pottery. *International Journal of Entrepreneurial Behavior & Research*, 25, 753–72.

Ratten, V., & Tajeddini, K. (2017). Innovativeness in family firms: an internationalization approach. *Review of International Business and Strategy*, 27, 217–30.

Sennett, R. (2008). *The Craftsman*. Yale University Press, New Haven/London.

Shiner, L. (2010). *L'invenzione dell'arte. Una storia culturale*. Piccola Biblioteca Einaud, Torino.

Thorlindsson, T., Halldorsson, V., & Sigfusdottir, I. D. (2018). The sociological theory of craftsmanship: an empirical test in sport and education. *Sociological Research Online*, 23(1), 114–35.

Villette, S. M., & Hardill, I. (2010). Paris and fashion: reflections on the role of the Parisian fashion industry in the cultural economy. *International Journal of Sociology and Social Policy*, 30(9–10), 461–71.

Waldman, K. B., & Kerr, J. M. (2015). Is food and drug administration policy governing artisan cheese consistent with consumers' preferences? *Food Policy*, 55, 71–80.

Wherry, F. F. (2006). The social sources of authenticity in global handicraft markets: evidence from northern Thailand. *Journal of Consumer Culture*, 6(1), 5–32.

White, H. C., & White, C. A. (1993). *Canvases and Careers: Institutional Change in the French Painting World*. University of Chicago Press, Chicago.

3.   The UK market for craft: a review of Crafts Council evidence

Julia Bennett

INTRODUCTION

As a national charity developing and promoting craft in the UK, the Crafts Council builds an evidence base about the sector to inform both policy and practice, seeking to improve the conditions for craft to flourish. Craft skills add economic, cultural and social value in a broad spectrum of creative and non-creative industries that span the creative economy. The Crafts Council champions craft that is analogue and digital, professional and informal, espousing contemporary design and drawing on centuries of heritage skills. We work with businesses and everyday makers,[1] gallerists, retailers and audience participants. In this pivotal role it is vital that we understand the domestic and international market for craft and how to intervene in that market to support its sustainability, relevance and development.

In 2019 the Crafts Council therefore took the decision to collaborate with partners to refresh our understanding of the characteristics of the craft market, having last undertaken such a study in 2010.[2] The market context had changed significantly during this period, with routes to market diversifying through digital sales platforms and collaborations, the UK's international trading context evolving and the popularity of craft, both professionally and in informal participation, showing signs that it was increasing. As partners, we sought to understand the drivers and impacts of those changes and, as a national development agency, the Crafts Council was committed to supporting professional makers and market intermediaries in their ability to respond.

Working with a steering group of partners representing support organisations and market intermediaries across the UK,[3] our aim was to be able to present evidence about the craft market to government, funders and partners, advocating for necessary support mechanisms and interventions, while informing our collective effort to stimulate the market and the professional development of craft businesses. We sought to gather quantitative and qualitative evidence of the volume, value and characteristics of the UK craft market and an analysis of its potential. Following a process of competitive tender, we appointed Morris Hargreaves McIntyre (MHM) to undertake the study. The final report, *The Market for Craft*,[4] was published online in May 2020.[5]

This chapter summarises the approach to the study (including a note on Covid-19) and the size of the market for craft. It goes on to describe how the context has evolved, how consumption patterns and routes to market have changed and diversified and how makers have responded to the market environment. It discusses the implications of the findings, exploring how the craft sector can respond. The evidence informs our understanding of how the contemporary era has brought about changes to the way artisanal products are produced, marketed and consumed. The chapter concludes with the view that the evidence is generating a market that is diversifying and flourishing. However, the sector will need to demonstrate determination and resilience to confront new challenges now integral to the future development of the market.

APPROACH TO THE STUDY

The study used quantitative and qualitative research methods, combining desk research, sample surveys and interviews to build a picture of the market. The approach to each stage of the study was drafted and revised in consultation with the steering group.

Evidence about UK craft consumers and their behaviour patterns was gathered through a nationally representative online population survey sourced from third-party panel providers, for which 5,392 completed the full survey asking about purchasing habits and behaviours. This stage was followed by an online survey of makers (total sample 1,707) which explored market activity and support needs, 28 of whom also returned a further smaller semi-structured qualitative questionnaire. Nine interviews were undertaken with market intermediaries to understand their role in shaping new routes to market for makers. Ten 30-minute in-depth interviews were conducted, using an agreed discussion guide, to test and contextualise the findings from the population and makers' surveys. Interviewees were identified in consultation with steering group partners. They represented organisations which provide craft makers with routes to market (directly to consumers or via commercial opportunities and partnerships) and who may offer services including website development, marketing and branding, professional photography, and training opportunities. Lastly, in order to gauge the potential for UK makers to export craft goods to other countries, a further third-party-sourced representative online population survey was conducted with a sample of 1,716 people in New York City and Los Angeles. In 2016, the USA was the third largest market for UK craft at an individual country level (MHM, 2020, p. 84) and, for makers responding to the survey, the USA was the largest single market where they had sold their work overseas (MHM, 2020, p. 67).[6]

The definition of craft used in 2020 reflects what is now a broader understanding of craft than would have been the case in 2006 (MHM, 2006) and 2010 (MHM, 2010); 'Any object that has been made by hand by a craft maker, including basketry, ceramics, furniture, glass, jewellery, metalwork, paper, textiles, wood. Disciplines can range from furniture to jewellery, encompass stand-alone unique pieces of work and may include the use of more unusual materials.'

This approach was taken in order to reflect in the study the breadth of what is now considered to be craft, whilst taking into account how the historical perspective, context and market conditions have evolved. However, as the market has grown over the intervening periods, it should be noted that some of this growth may be accounted for by a broadening of the popular understanding of what is craft.

A Note on Covid-19

The fieldwork for the study was in its final stages at the time the pandemic was declared. As the research progressed it became clear that the market would be deeply affected by Covid-19 and the report therefore notes early indications of the virus's impact on the craft sector. This chapter seeks to take into account relevant research findings published up until September 2020 and to reflect these in its analysis of the market.

The Crafts Council undertook small-scale surveys of the impact on maker businesses early on in the UK lockdown in April and May 2020 (Crafts Council, 2020) to which 573 people responded. Product orders were down on average by 67 per cent, while 71 per cent of makers had been impacted by the closure of galleries and 64 per cent by the closure of markets and fairs.

The Creative Industries Federation (Oxford Economics, 2020) warned of a 'cultural catastrophe', projecting devastating figures for 2020. Economic modelling predicted that the turnover of the UK's creative industries would contract by £74 billion in 2020. Crafts were at risk of losing £513 million in revenue (53%), with the wider craft economy[7] projected to lose 47 per cent of jobs (58,000) as many craft practitioners experienced the fallout of closed workshops and retail spaces.

Data from the Office for National Statistics published in August 2020 notes that there was a record quarterly decrease in self-employed workers in the first quarter of 2020/21 (ONS, 2020a). Self-employment is the most common mode of employment amongst women makers in the craft sector (Spilsbury, 2018). ONS figures (ONS, 2020b) also reveal that arts, entertainment and recreation was the sector with the highest year on year increase in vacancies in the period up to July 2020. Whilst the overwhelming majority of these jobs will not be in the craft sector, there will be many that are in agencies and intermediary roles that support craft businesses and the market for craft products.

At the time of writing, the future of the economy in general and the crafts business ecology in particular is still very precarious. The impact of the planned withdrawal in October 2020 of Treasury support funds from those eligible to access them (only a proportion of craft business) is also still to be felt.

THE SIZE OF THE UK MARKET FOR CRAFT

MHM found that 73 per cent of the UK adult population (45.6 million) were in the market for buying craft in 2019, with a value of £3 billion.[8] There was an associated four-fold uplift between 2006 and 2020 in the volume of craft objects bought annually from a living maker.[9] However, the rate of growth has not been uniform across disciplines: jewellery witnessed the highest volume of sales in both 2006 and 2020 and the highest volume uplift (+£4.1 million), while glass and metalwork saw the highest rate of growth and wood the biggest increase in price. The average price per object decreased from £157 in 2006 to £124 in 2020, reflecting a broadening of interest in craft and more cautious buyers purchasing at a lower price point, trends which are considered in more detail below.

What's Changing in the Craft Market Context?

A number of different trends have impacted on the craft sector in the 10 years since the earlier analysis, as MHM note in the report.[10] Each is addressed in turn and some of the key milestones over the period 1990 to 2020 are reflected in Figure 3.1.

The wider economy is evolving rapidly as, at the time of writing, the UK continues to face uncertainty: in addition to the impact of Covid-19, there is no confirmed set of future international trade conditions for the UK, with Brexit negotiations still to be finalised by the end of 2020. Amongst more established makers[11] selling at the higher end of the market the proportion trading internationally has grown from 18 per cent who had ever made international sales (specifically to international collections) in 2006, to around half who had sold work internationally in the 12 months prior to the survey (MHM, 2020, p. 67). For sales to the USA (the mostly commonly cited international market by maker respondents to the survey) the potential market (as illustrated in the population surveys in New York City and Los Angeles) is higher than in the UK at 85 per cent of the adult population, yet there is a market penetration rate currently of only 23 per cent for UK craft. It's hard to say how much this market has been directly affected by Brexit uncertainty, but supplier confidence in

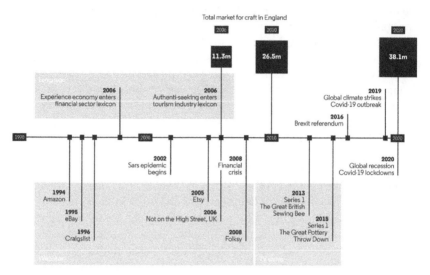

Source: MHM, 2020, p. 44.

Figure 3.1   Time line 1990–2020

international trading is clearly wobbly, with 26 per cent of those responding to MHM's survey of makers indicating that it had already had an adverse effect on their business. Combined with the additional anticipated impact of the Covid-19 pandemic (see above), market conditions are currently very fragile.

The nature of work itself is changing as many more people combine several income-generating activities in portfolio careers.[12] In the creative and craft sectors this has long been a typical mode of working, enabling professionals to maximise their income whilst balancing different responsibilities. 'Creative freelancers are often innovative and entrepreneurial, with many juggling a string of different contracts and work streams in portfolio careers' (Easton & Cauldwell-French, 2017). MHM's survey of makers shows that the most common supplementary roles are teaching craft skills in formal and informal settings, followed by other freelance work connected to craft (MHM, 2020, table 13, p. 66). The more experienced and established a maker is in their career, the more likely they are to be involved in additional work that is related to craft.

The teaching of craft skills is fuelled in part by the increasingly significant role that the experience economy is shown to play in the craft sector:

In the population survey, one in five (21%) of the overall market for craft (buyers and potential buyers) has paid to take part in a craft class, workshop or course, with

5% (2.5m) having done so in the past 12 months with a further 16% (7.1m) having done so at some point in the past. (MHM, 2020, p. 81)

It's interesting to note how this trend is fostering in potential buyers a more profound engagement with the process of making. When the Crafts Council launched the report through a series of well-attended online events, some participants noted that by offering a demonstration of how a piece is created, or a workshop to introduce those new to a craft to the complexity of its skills, the experience would often increase the participants' respect for the skills and time required. As a consequence, there was a stronger appreciation of and understanding of the long-honed technical skills and deep understanding of materials that were reflected in the pricing of objects. This notion of experience will be explored further in the following paragraphs.

In discussing the themes of an experience, Pine and Gilmour (2011, p. 79) argue that 'impressions are the "takeaways" of the experience—what you want customers to have topmost in their minds when they leave the experience', of which authenticity ('original or imitative representations') is one of six 'dimensions of overall impressions'. Peterson (2005, p. 1083) notes that 'this polemic of authenticity is often seen in contemporary mundane product marketing campaigns, as illustrated, for example, in the case of contests over the quality of elite French wines.' He describes how authenticity was created through brand association and emphasis on traditional techniques by French merchants in the development of the international wine market, so enabling them to charge higher prices. The 'traditional' or 'heritage' elements of production are highlighted or, effectively, 'fabricated' in industries, with the knowledge that this has value in attracting tourism. Thus, 'authenticity is a claim that is made by or for someone, thing, or performance and either accepted or rejected by relevant others.' In the case of performing arts, Peterson asserts that 'the constructedness of authenticity is perhaps never so clear as when it is vociferously claimed by the person who is seeking to be identified as authentic' (2005, p. 1086). This translates into a number of identities through which authenticity is constructed, including 'status identity' (for which Peterson quotes Fine's (2004, pp. 65–8) argument that this type of authenticity is dependent on the background of the artist); seeking authentic experiences (in which collectors build authenticity through the story of locating artists and their works); the constructed self; the role of the 'expert' in acting as arbiter of authenticity; and, ultimately, the role of the end consumer in buying into this notion, particularly for contemporary visual and performance artists. Here, the potential for rejection is high if artists are perceived to have copied an earlier accepted authenticity or if the notion of what is perceived to be authentic has shifted over time.

In craft, as in many of the industries cited by Peterson, the notion of authenticity is constructed through a web of relationships between the maker and the consumer/collector across the whole supply chain. The background of the artist or maker is a central part of this construction, including their status amongst their community of peers and their perceived originality, as well as the extent to which the consumer is seeking themselves to identify with a brand, story or tradition. There is a risk, however, that the notion of constructedness also carries with it an implication of falsehood, of artificiality and unworthiness. In the case of craft, the long-honed technical skills and deep understanding of materials referred to above are reflected in the consumer's valuing of the product's authenticity for all the reasons Peterson cites. Furthermore, there is also a recognition of the development of those skills, their refinement and the time it has taken to conceive of, design and realise the product. Authenticity, I would assert, is therefore also an expression of skill, imagination and labour, all worthy of a level of respect which Peterson's characterisation as 'fabricated' may not fully capture.

MHM posit that the desire to experience the activity of making often reflects the growth in the public's own desire for authenticity (MHM, 2020, p. 40). For the consumer or collector highlighted by MHM, it may make sense that at this time of perceived powerlessness in response to growing inequalities and, more recently, a global pandemic, there is a strong desire to connect with more personalised, individual experiences – the 'authentic experiences' to which Peterson refers. Especially during turbulent times, crafting represents stability, a "solace in the tacit" (Stevens, 2011, p. 45). It is a form of resistance to the dominance of capitalism and technology in everyday life and search for authenticity' (Jakob, 2012, p. 128). Campbell echoes this point:

> it is possible to see how the growth of craft consumption in contemporary western societies might represent such a reaction to progressive commodification. For it is possible that, as more and more aspects of modern life become subject to this economic imperative, so more and more individuals might come to experience the need to escape from, or even counteract, this process. (2005, p. 23)

He goes on, 'the arena of craft consumption could become highly valued because it is regarded as an oasis of personal self-expression and authenticity in what is an ever-widening "desert" of commodification and marketization.' The ability of craft to provide a response to this trend is also described thus: 'the distinctive feature of cultural and creative industry work is the tendency to maintain (rather than eliminate) the tension between autonomous impulses of artistic and supplementary craft workers, and the demands of managers for standardised, commercially oriented production' (Banks, 2010).

MHM also point to several related social trends identified in 2010 which continue to impact the craft sector in 2020; for example, an increasing emphasis on ethical consumerism, environmental sustainability and the use of craft as a tool for boosting health and well-being.[13]

The craft market has changed, perhaps most radically, in the channels through which products are taken to market:

> The craft sector has also been strongly impacted by the rise of digital selling platforms in the early to mid 2000s – both craft-specific platforms, such as Folksy (founded in 2008), and platforms with a broader product remit, including Etsy (founded in 2005) and Not on the High Street (founded in 2006). (MHM, 2020, p. 38)

Jakob describes the impact on the crafts sector of the early history of Etsy, a platform which enabled makers to develop their own advertising and promotion and benefit from the new model of 'peer-to-peer' cumulative advertisement to boost consumption (Jakob, 2012, p. 136). MHM argue that this increasing engagement with craft online reflects our wider purchasing habits through the growth of platforms such as Amazon and Ebay:

> This includes the consumer need for immediacy (with next day or quicker delivery), consumer control (informed as to a transaction's progress; the ability to track their item), seamless spending (payments via contactless and wearables) and the concept that 'ease is the new loyalty'. In other words, consumer loyalty is built on the back of intuitive online shopping experiences that prioritise consumer convenience.[14] (MHM, 2020, p. 38)

The proportion of internet users shopping online in 2008 was 49 per cent; in 2018, this had reached 87 per cent.[15] Even though the evidence demonstrates that the majority of consumers still prefer the individual experience of buying (and presumably touching and holding) a piece face-to-face, 33 per cent of buyers are now purchasing online (MHM, 2020, p. 47). The use of websites, newsletters and social media can be seen as increasingly important in conducting potential buyers through their customer journey. The percentage of online purchases is, unsurprisingly, higher in the younger demographic (see the customer segmentation into market buyer group pen portraits, MHM, 2020, p. 13). Sixty-eight per cent of makers now have their own websites, with higher figures for those with more established careers (MHM, 2020, p. 69). Social media is increasingly the route through which to introduce new products, concepts and the personal stories driving makers' creative processes and was already identified by Yair (2012b, p. 12) as having a place in the business and creative development toolkit for almost all makers and craft organisations. Combined with a strategy to increase followers and push traffic to individual websites and newsletter sign-ups, social media is a route to convert interest into sales. It's also a space for experimentation and innovation; artist Matthew

Burrows' #artistsupportpledge[16] on Instagram is an interesting example that emerged during the Covid-19 crisis. Makers sell work using the hashtag and every time an artist reaches £1,000 of sales, they pledge to buy £200 of work from other artist(s). At the time of writing the hashtag had been used over 300,000 times.

The route to market is clearly evolving and adapting as technology and purchasing behaviours are shifting. In a complementary vein, new market models and intermediaries are responding to and shaping the market. MHM (2020) note that

> Whereas a decade ago the approach to selling craft was to elevate it to that of art, to rarefy it and set it apart, now the approach of sales models is based on a confidence in craft's value amongst a new age of craft intermediaries. This approach is far more cognisant of the needs of both buyers and makers.

One intermediary is quoted as saying,

> It was either two extremes, you either had the village craft fairs where work wasn't necessarily understood or celebrated and certainly not their value … and on the other extreme you had quite stark white cubes for galleries. You had to say, 'Applied art galleries,' you weren't allowed to say, 'Craft galleries,' I feel that that definitely changed. (MHM, 2020, p. 77)

MHM describe how such companies and galleries are using market-focused principles from the commercial retail sector, helping makers in their craft businesses to create narratives around their products and creative concept. Understanding the power of brand and the science of merchandising, they may be providing help with presentation and style, photography, creation of collections and even with access to studio space and raw materials. For makers for whom entrepreneurship may not be as high a priority (or such a familiar skill) as spending time developing their practice, these new models are identifying and meeting a need. They are supporting makers and their potential consumers to understand objects, to locate them both physically and aesthetically and to purchase craft items.

Reflecting the growth in interest in craft, entertainment television has celebrated this flourishing of craft activities on screen, reaching audiences of millions with new programming such as *The Great British Sewing Bee* (sewing, BBC2), *The Great Pottery Throw Down* (pottery, series 1, 2 – BBC, series 3 – Channel 4), *Blown Away* (glass, Netflix) and *The Wonderful World of Crafting* (various, Channel 5). The popularity of such programmes and the confidence of programme makers to commission further series demonstrates an increasing interest in and appreciation for making, amongst professional and everyday makers as well as for wider audiences that simply enjoy watching the process.

HOW CAN THE CRAFT SECTOR RESPOND?

The Market for Craft is persuasive in demonstrating how the market is changing, highlighting some of the trends and factors that are active in bringing about this evolution and growth. The segmentation of the market into nine buyer profiles[17] offers an insight into the new, younger demographic who are also buying craft. They may identify as collectors, yet are cautious in their spending habits, often buying at lower price points than buyers identified in earlier research. They are also more ethnically diverse, less dominated by graduates and with lower specialist knowledge.

This rich insight into the behaviours, motivations, buying habits and purchasing channels has the potential to strengthen the knowledge and tools at the disposal of maker businesses as they seek to differentiate their customer base and navigate the market. The report advises that makers, working with their supply chains and support structures, 'focus efforts on the middle market of new consumer entrants and help them engage more deeply in craft, participate further, develop new knowledge of making and build their confidence in terms of what they like, purchase and collect' (MHM, 2020, p. 100). The model in Figure 3.2 reflects this proposed strategy in a ladder or pyramid of deepening engagement with craft consumption.

A series of co-ordinated strategies are needed to help strengthen UK craft businesses as they face multiple challenges. In developing these, it is vital to ensure that UK craft benefits from representing the breadth of expertise and creativity that exists across the population. The Crafts Council recently hosted a number of debates about anti-racism and is working with partners to use craft as a force for good in challenging racism and tackling all forms of inequality.

We are also working with government departments to support the international reach of UK craft (for example, through a UK-wide export programme), studying innovative success factors, new approaches, best practice and innovation in adjacent markets. In addition, efforts are focused on partners and businesses across the market to increase the ability of craft businesses to access appropriate training and relevant government support programmes.

At the same time, we need craft and artisanal products to be visible in the research and policy communities' understanding of the wider creative economy. UK craft is poorly served by the international coding systems for measuring the economy, the basis of the economic estimates produced by the Department for Digital, Culture, Media and Sport (DCMS). Industrial classifications currently only recognise the jewellery trade as craft (SIC code 31.12 – Manufacture of Jewellery). Other craft industries are scattered across the system and in need of aggregation to overcome risks that individual micro-businesses are not identifiable in the data. Working with UK

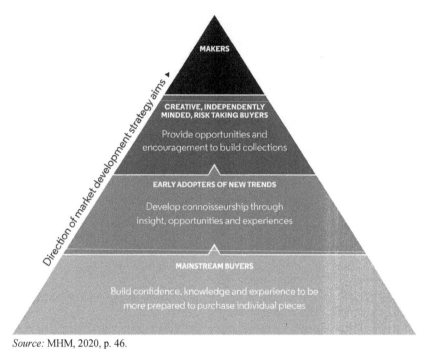

Source: MHM, 2020, p. 46.

Figure 3.2   Strategies for developing the market for crafts

partner organisations such as The Royal Warrant Holders Association and the Heritage Craft Association, the Crafts Council (2020) has proposed a new industrial classification, reflecting heritage as well as contemporary production and the skill sets that craft has in common with other European industries, such as artisan food and drink:

> Contemporary and heritage craft/artisan businesses rely on a creative process about making, often, but not always, through the intelligence of the hand. It involves technical skill and design capability, along with a deep understanding of materials and may involve mechanical and/or digital manufacture on a small scale. These industries are typically, but not exhaustive of: ceramics, design, furniture, glass, jewellery, metalwork, textiles, wood, consumables such as artisan food and drink, and heritage cultural artefacts. Occupational entry routes are likely to be vocational (sometimes through apprenticeships) but may include higher education.

The argument outlined above is set out more fully in a *Creative Industries Policy and Evidence Centre* blog.[18]

The findings have the potential to redefine the place of craft in the UK's entrepreneur economy, enhancing businesses' ability to segment customers and tailor marketing to buyer profiles, a key element in rising to the challenge of the entrepreneurial mindset.

Already viewed as 'the most entrepreneurial of all the creative industries sectors' (Yair, 2012a), craft businesses rely on a tenacity, flexibility and single-minded pursuit of creative and business goals to be sustainable. They face a unique set of challenges in a number of areas: as portfolio workers and sole traders; in a context of declining opportunities in creative education; in setting up in business; in accessing investment; and in locating opportunities to collaborate and obtaining infrastructure support.[19] Smaller than the 47 creative clusters previously identified in the UK (Bakhshi & Mateos-Garcia, 2016), craft businesses are, however, typical of the 709 of distinct creative microclusters identified by Siepel et al. (2020) in that they are more likely to want to grow, and more likely to have grown in the past year than larger ones. In spite of the obstacles they face, craft businesses 'can be seen to situate their work within notions of locality and community to which they add both cultural and economic value, a context that embraces the sustainable as well as the scalable business'. They are often seeking to balance business growth with ambitions for a career that is personally and creatively fulfilling, thus 'asserting their own economic success criteria and making their own meaning, based on a self-defined entrepreneurialism'.[20]

Such a self-defined approach nevertheless still relies on aspects of marketing common to other sectors. Makhitha (2016) argues that craft producers have a weak understanding of the market and are thus open to exploitation by 'the middleman' (Makhitha, 2016).[21] Her evidence shows that too few small and medium-sized enterprises have an understanding of market research beyond advertising and selling and she finds craft producers in South Africa to be no exception. Small craft businesses are therefore even more in need of strategic marketing knowledge – the process of analysing contextual factors that inform strategy to position a business. This positioning is surely dependent on an understanding of the maker's concept and how this is communicated to the consumer and valued in an emotional sense – returning us to discussions of authenticity in craft. The literature explores the relationship between authenticity and marketing (Peterson, 2005; Hartmann & Ostberg, 2013), the latter viewing marketing activity as a social construction within which authenticity is located. Yet they also acknowledge that 'authenticity cannot simply be built into brands: various audiences need to be convinced that the particular market offering is indeed authentic' (p. 884). A deeper appreciation of these audiences and how they position themselves in relation to the values associated with craft (see Jakob, Campbell, and Banks above) would seem to be integral to an understanding of the challenges and needs facing the market for craft and artisanship. MHM's (2020) study offers a significant step towards that.

CONCLUSION

The report's findings demonstrate that craft is a growth industry, with a population of buyers and collectors that is diversifying and flourishing. The marketing of artisanship is becoming as important to the survival and growth of the sector as the sale of its products. There is a growing appreciation of the authenticity, originality and unique provenance of craft items, with buyers and potential buyers keen to understand and experience the skill sets such products entail. The craft sector is demonstrating its ability to flex and innovate in response to changing demand, refining its material knowledge and practice as well as its engagement with audiences and purchasers.

Yet makers and craft businesses face considerable turbulence, potential losses and an unpredictable purchasing environment at this point in time. Those participating in the future market for craft will require resilience and determination in how they cultivate buyers. They will need to be savvy, developing focused strategies to encourage, educate and refine knowledge and understanding to grow occasional buyers into collectors. In order to survive and grow in a changing environment, facing the twin challenges of Covid-19 and Brexit, they will also need government and sector-wide support and advocacy to fulfil craft's economic potential.

NOTES

1. Everyday makers are defined as participants in leisure time craft activities not intending to earn money through selling.
2. MHM (2010). Prior to this, Arts Council England had commissioned the same contractors in 2006 to undertake a study of the market for craft (MHM, 2006), giving us a 16-year historical perspective.
3. The following partners were involved in the study: Arts Council of Wales, Contemporary Visual Arts Network, Craft Northern Ireland, Craft Scotland, Crafts Council, Creative Scotland, Creative United, The Goldsmiths' Company, Great Northern Events/Great Northern Contemporary Craft Fair.
4. MHM (2020).
5. Covid-19 restrictions prevented partners from hosting what would normally have been a face-to-face launch.
6. The value of UK craft exports worldwide was £4.8 billion in 2017 (17% of total Department for Digital, Culture, Media and Sport (DCMS) goods exports). The total value of UK craft exports grew by 31 per cent between 2010 and 2017, from £3.7 billion in 2010 to £4.8 billion in 2017. The value of craft exports includes the export of gemstones and precious metals through the jewellery trade, amounting to around 12 per cent of craft exports. See DCMS (2017).

7.   See Spilsbury (2018). The notion of the craft economy derives from the DCMS definition of the 'creative economy'. The latter includes all those employed in the creative industries and the contribution of those who are in creative occupations outside the creative industries. The 'creative industries' are a subset of the creative economy that includes just those working in creative industries irrespective of their occupation (they may either be in creative occupations or in other roles, e.g. finance). 'Creative occupations' are a subset of the creative economy which includes all those working in creative occupations, irrespective of the industry that they work in.

8.   MHM (2020).

9.   MHM (2020), chapter 5.

10. MHM (2020), chapter 4.

11. Master Craftspeople, Established Professional Makers and Early Career Professionals, according to the market segments set out in the report: MHM (2020), chapter 2.

12. See also O'Leary (2014), HM Government (2016) and Bennett (2020b).

13. The Department for Digital, Culture, Media and Sport's (DCMS, 2020) survey of levels of cultural, digital and sporting engagement during the UK Covid-19 lockdown shows that participation in 'other arts, crafts, or creative activities at home' was the top arts activity (nearly 40% in May).

14. IMRG (2017).

15. ONS (October 2019).

16. See #artistsupportpledge accessed 29 July 2020 at https://artistsupportpledge .com/.

17. The nine buyer profiles are Proto-collector; Adventurer; Early mainstream; Mature mainstream; Millennial mainstream; Gen Z mainstream; New entrant; Nascent group; and Low level traditional (MHM, 2020, pp. 12–27).

18. See Bennett (2020a).

19. See Bennett (2020b).

20. See Bennett (2020b).

21. A charge which one hopes cannot be levelled at the new intermediaries identified by MHM (2020) but for which no data was gathered in *The Market for Craft*.

REFERENCES

Bakhshi, H., & Mateos-Garcia, J. (2016). *Creativity in the UK*, London UK, Nesta.

Banks, M. (2010). Craft labour and creative industries. *International Journal of Cultural Policy*, 16:3, 305–21, http://doi.org/10.1080/10286630903055885.

Bennett, J. (2020a). Counting craft. *Creative Industries Policy and Evidence Centre* blog, June 2020, accessed 29 July 2020 at https://pec.ac.uk/blog/counting-craft.

Bennett, J. (2020b). Towards a new entrepreneurship. In Naudin, A., & Patel, K. (eds), *Craft Entrepreneurship*, London UK, Rowman & Littlefield, pp. 13–28.

Campbell, C. (2005). The craft consumer: culture, craft and consumption in a postmodern society. *Journal of Consumer Culture*, 5:1, 23–42.

Crafts Council (2020). Written evidence submitted by the Crafts Council. *DCMS Committee inquiry into the impact of Covid-19 on DCMS sectors May 2020.* Accessed 14 September 2020 at https://committees.parliament.uk/writtenevidence/ 6061/html/.

DCMS (2017). *Department for Digital, Culture, Media and Sport Sectors Economic Estimates Trade, Table 33: Exports and Imports of Goods by Sub-sector*, London UK, DCMS. Accessed 9 September 2020 at https://www.gov.uk/government/ statistics/dcms-sectors-economic-estimates-2017-trade.

DCMS (2020). Department for Digital, Culture, Media and Sport Taking Part Web Panel COVID-19 Report, London UK, DCMS. Accessed 23 September 2020 at https://www.gov.uk/government/publications/taking-part-web-panel-data -engagement-during-the-covid-19-pandemic/taking-part-web-panel-covid-19-report #arts.

Easton, E., & Cauldwell-French, E. (2017). *Creative Freelancers*, London UK, Creative Industries Federation.

Fine, G. A. (2004). *Everyday Genius: Self-Taught Art and the Culture of Authenticity*, Chicago, IL, University of Chicago Press.

Hartmann, B. J., & Ostberg, J. (2013). Authenticating by reenchantment: the discursive making of craft production. *Journal of Marketing Management*, 29:7–8, 882–911.

HM Government (2016). *Julie Deane's Review of Self-employment*, London UK, HMSO.

IMRG (2017). *The Changing Online Shopping Habits and How to Understand Them.* Accessed 29 July 2020 at https://www.imrg.org/blog/the-changing-online-shopping -habits-and-how-to-understand-them/.

Jakob, D. (2012). Crafting your way out of the recession? New craft entrepreneurs and the global economic downturn. *Cambridge Journal of Regions, Economy and Society*, 6, 127–40.

Makhitha K. M. (2016). Do small craft businesses need strategic marketing to survive? *Investment Management and Financial Innovations*, 13:2, 399–404.

MHM [Morris Hargreaves McIntyre] (2006). *Making it to Market*, London UK, Arts Council England.

MHM [Morris Hargreaves McIntyre] (2010). *Consuming Craft*, London UK, Crafts Council.

MHM [Morris, Hargreaves, McIntyre] (2020). *The Market for Craft*, London UK, Crafts Council.

O'Leary, D. (2014). *Going It Alone*, London UK, Demos.

ONS [Office for National Statistics] (October 2019). How our internet activity has influenced the way we shop. Accessed 29 July 2020 at https://www.ons.gov .uk/businessindustryandtrade/retailindustry/articles/howourinternetactivityhasinf luencedthewayweshop/october2019.

ONS [Office for National Statistics] (2020a). UK Labour market overview, UK: August 2020, estimates of employment, unemployment, economic inactivity and other employment-related statistics for the UK, Figure 3: record quarterly decrease for self-employed workers. Accessed 9 September 2020 at https://www.ons.gov .uk/employmentandlabourmarket/peopleinwork/employmentandemployeetypes/ bulletins/uklabourmarket/august2020#employment-unemployment-and-economic -inactivity.

ONS [Office for National Statistics] (2020b). Vacancies by industry, dataset VACS02, released 11 August 2020. Estimates of the number of UK job vacancies for each industry, based on a survey of businesses. Accessed 9 September 2020 at https:// www.ons.gov.uk/employmentandlabourmarket/peoplenotinwork/unemployment/ datasets/vacanciesbyindustryvacs02.

Oxford Economics (2020). *The Projected Economic Impact of Covid-19 on the UK Creative Industries*, London UK, Creative Industries Federation.

Peterson, R. A. (2005). In search of authenticity. *Journal of Management Studies*, 42:5 1083–98.

Pine, II, B. J., & Gilmore, J. H. (2011). *The Experience Economy*, updated edition, Brighton MA, Harvard Business Review Press.

Siepel, J., Camerani, R., Masucci, M., Velez Ospina, J., Casadei, P., & Bloom, M. (2020). *Creative Industries Radar: Mapping the UK's Creative Clusters and Microclusters*, Creative Industries Policy and Evidence Centre, UK.

Spilsbury, M. (2018). *Who Makes? An Analysis of People Working in Craft Occupations*, London UK, Crafts Council.

Stevens, D. (2011). Validity is in the eye of the beholder: mapping crafts communities of practice. In M. E. Buszek (ed.), *Extra/ordinary: Craft and Contemporary Art*, Durham NC and London, Duke University Press.

Yair, K. (2012a). *Craft & Enterprise*, London UK, Crafts Council.

Yair, K. (2012b). *How Makers and Craft Organisations are Using Social Media Effectively*, London UK, Crafts Council.

4. Social embedding, artisanal markets and cultural fields: quality, value and marketing in the cases of new wave custom motorcycles and boutique guitar pedals

Jon Mulholland and Peter Webb

INTRODUCTION

We have witnessed an exponential growth in 'all things artisanal', of artisanal economies of small-scale making (Ocejo, 2017). According to a recent report from the UK-based Crafts Council, the total value of craft sales in the UK alone has grown from £883 million in 2006 to over £3 billion in 2019 (Crafts Council, 2020). According to the Crafts Council (2020), 'the growth in the public's desire for authenticity, for experiences, for ethical and sustainable consumption have helped fuel an interest in making and in handmade objects' (Crafts Council, 2020, p. 5). In a similar vein, Ocejo (2017) has claimed that 'businesses in the artisan economy … are based on shared understandings of quality, authenticity and the importance of "localness". They thrive on cultural omnivirousness and the idea of connecting people with the products they buy and the people who connect them' (Ocejo, 2017, p. 20). At its heart, artisanship, reflecting the craft upon which it is based, can be understood as 'quality-driven work' (Sennett, 2009, p. 24). The marketing of artisanal goods routinely draws on such associations in its representational practices, and in fact, so productive have such associations become, that corporate manufacturers of mass produced goods have also been eager to 'wash' their products as embodying craft and artisanal qualities.

Artisanal markets face the challenge of establishing, consolidating, and growing themselves within a broader context of hegemonic, globalised neo-liberal capitalism (see Scrase, 2003). Against the manifest pathologies of neo-liberal capitalism, artisanal markets may make legitimate claims to providing a more sustainable, just, locally emplaced, and creative economic model for supporting human flourishing, at least in some contexts (see Korn, 2013). Consumption of artisanal goods in turn may offer alternative relationships to consumption itself, and to the goods that are consumed (Crafts Council, 2020).

Understanding the nature, dynamics and prospects of artisanal markets is not only important intellectually, as these markets present significant challenges to our sociological and economic understanding of markets more generally, but is important to our considerations of what a progressive political-economic and social alternative to the toxicities of neo-liberal capitalism may look like. Artisanal markets offer an effective case study for sociological critiques of neo-classical economic models of the structure and dynamics of markets generally, of economic action within those markets, and of the nature and forms of marketing found therein.

Specifically, this chapter asserts, and explores, the concept of embeddedness as a means to understanding the ways in which artisanal markets are socially enmeshed within, and co-produced by, cultural fields, and in ways that profoundly complicate the economic logic of these markets. Stressing a multi-modal understanding of embeddedness, the chapter draws particularly heavily on the work of Jens Beckert (2003, 2007, 2020; Beckert et al., 2017), understanding embeddedness as a solution to inherent 'problems of coordination' in markets. Rather than thinking of economic actors as 'rational actors' along the lines of neo-classical reductionism, we offer a more fully sociological account of economic actors as engaged in culturally grounded interpretive practices within a context of inter-subjective meaning formation. Again drawing on the work of Beckert, the chapter then goes on to explore the construction of quality as a defining feature of artisanal goods, and specifically the role that field-specific, inter-subjective, symbolic practices play in complicating the ways in which goods are ascribed with properties of 'quality'. Drawing on the ideas of Ravasi and Rindova (2004) we then go on to explore how quality relates to questions of value. In markets of uncertainty, where the 'intrinsic quality' of the good may not always be readily determinable, and where quality itself is in some significant part, symbolically constructed, ideas of both quality and value emerge from complex, inter-subjective processes of meaning formation in fields-as-embedded markets.

The chapter goes on to apply this framework to two selected 'non-typical' artisanal markets, new wave custom motorcycles and boutique guitar pedals, and specifically to two illustrative case studies (Old Empire Motorcycles and Cog Effects) to illuminate the context-specific dynamics of socially embedded artisanal markets, and to demonstrate how such embeddedness goes on to frame how quality and value become variably constructed and marketed. The chapter concludes by arguing that only a substantive and sophisticated *sociological* model of social embeddedness is able to provide a platform for understanding how artisanal markets may function in their profound inter-weavings with cultural fields in the framing of quality and value.

UNDERSTANDING THE SOCIAL EMBEDDING OF MARKETS

Despite the 'fuzziness' (Hess, 2004) of embeddedness as a concept, undergoing its own 'great transformation' within the New Economic Sociology (Beckert, 2007), and notwithstanding important challenges to its very conceptual value (Beckert, 2003; Krippner, 2001), the concept of embeddedness has enjoyed centre stage within the New Economic Sociology, establishing something of a privileged position within this context (Krippner 2001).

Though Karl Polanyi himself made only very limited explicit reference to embeddedness in his ground-breaking *The Great Transformation* (1944), Polanyi's insistence on the need to understand the ways in which economic structures, relations and exchanges are necessarily embedded in social institutions set the scene for the concept's foundational status within the New Economic Sociology (Beckert, 2007). But it was arguably Mark Granovetter's (1985) seminal paper that was to become the 'founding manifesto' of economic sociology (Beckert, 2007). With a particular regard for the role of social networks, Granovetter (2005) argued that economic exchange is structurally embedded in social networks, which in turn serve to shape economic activity through framing the flow of information, facilitating punishment and reward, and crucially serving as a basis for trust.

However, notwithstanding its influence, the limitations of this narrow structural reading of embeddedness have been highlighted by many (Varman and Costa, 2008; Podolny, 2001). Structural models of embeddedness advanced a rather abstracted understanding of how economic action was channelled through the 'pipes' (the connections) provided by social networks (Podolny, 2001). But in so doing, such models failed to appreciate the nature and role of the *social substance* that flowed through these pipes (Krippner, 2001; Podolny, 2001). The structural embeddedness thesis also largely failed to offer a sufficient challenge to the ways in which neo-classical economics understands market actors as pure rational actors (Varman and Costa, 2008; Krippner, 2001).

Reflecting these limitations, the embeddedness concept has developed in multiple directions in an effort to render it more effective and comprehensive, in its grasp of 'the social nature of economic processes' (Hess, 2004, p. 167). One of the most all-encompassing early taxonomies of embeddedness was provided by Zukin and DiMaggio (1990). They considered embeddedness to have political forms (associated with the situatedness of economic processes in a contestation for power involving economic and non-economic actors), cultural forms (concerned with the role played by collective understandings in framing economic action), cognitive forms (the impact of structured regularities of thinking on economic action) and structural forms (the role played by social networks). As a further example of such typological efforts, Hess (2004) proposes a three-category framework of societal (including the cultural, cognitive and political dimensions), network and territorial embeddedness.

Efforts to develop more holistic and comprehensive accounts of embeddedness seek to resist accounts of the market as exogenous, a-social, and defined entirely by the rational-instrumental pursuit of economic gain. They variably seek to illuminate the ways in which 'the social' may *constitute* markets (Krippner, 2001). As Fligstein and Dauter (2007) have insisted, sociological accounts of the market must be 'prepared to unpack the black boxes of exchange, competition, and production' and explore the dynamic roles also played by 'trust, friendship, power, and dependence' (p. 113).

We argue that, at its best, embeddedness invites ways of recognising the dialectic inter-penetration of the economic and the social, such that each may function to *constitute* important elements of the other.

Varman and Costa (2008) assert that where markets are socially embedded, producer and consumer behaviour typically transcends anonymous, atomised, gain-seeking instrumentalism. Within such markets, we generally witness more holistic forms of social action, driven by a normative order that includes moral, emotional and expressive dimensions (Varman and Costa, 2008). From the vantage point of the economic actor, then, the cognitions that inform behaviour must be understood as complex, and social. Dequech (2003) points to the importance of the interconnections between the cognitive and the cultural in informing market participation and behaviour. Whilst some residual cognition might be thought of as beyond the cultural, much cognition is inherently cultural in nature. The beliefs and values that govern the terms of participation itself, the exercising of roles within the market, and the acquisition of the substantive cultural knowledge that makes participation in a marketised culture possible (including the capacity to read the cultural and interpersonal signs that are the basis of trust) are all products of cultural and cognitive embeddedness (Dequech, 2003). Finally, we would also assert, certainly in the context of emergent markets that lack equilibrium (Fligstein and Dauter, 2007), that embeddedness is best conceptualised as fluid, processual and never entirely settled. In stressing the flux of embededdness, as always 'a work in progress', Ryan and Mulholland (2015) have proposed the value of *embedding* as an alternative conceptualisation. This chapter will deploy this idea of *embedding* where the processual, nuanced and contingent nature of embeddedness needs to be foregrounded.

Beckert (2003) argues that given their inherent social embeddedness, markets can only be understood with regard to the particularities of the meanings that flow within given communities of interpretive action, where 'judgments on the relevant parameters of the situation are based on generalized expectancies which are, at least in part, intersubjectively shared' (Beckert, 2003, p. 773). More fully, embeddedness exists to provide 'solutions' to three inherent 'coordination problems' of market exchange (Beckert, 2007); namely the problem of value, the problem of competition and the problem of cooperation, and in so doing providing markets with stability and order. In terms of the *problem of valuation*, 'the embeddedness of economic action is a necessary condition for classifying the material world in terms of the relative value of the products offered' (p. 13). The determination of value is dependent on the cognitive-cultural process of commensuration, whereby actors assess the extent to which a particular good satisfies their needs both technically and socially (Beckert, 2007). The socially embedded dimensions of value-determination lie in the communicative processes through which 'quality markers' are established, but also in the ways in which goods allow owners 'to be positioned and, conversely, to form social identities based on market choices' (Beckert, 2007, p. 12).

In respect of the *problem of competition*, producers are commonly driven to seek out 'imperfect' market conditions, markets where pure price competition is impeded in the interests of economic success (Beckert, 2007). This may be achieved amongst other things through network closure or product differentiation (Beckert, 2007). *Cooperation is a core problem* of market exchange because of the imperfect and unequal nature of market-related knowledge, and the ever-present risk of non-satisfaction. Where conditions of uncertainty and therefore risk prevail, trust becomes a principal resource alleviating the perception and reality of such risk. The facility for trust in market exchanges is made possible 'by cognitive scripts that are culturally anchored' (Beckert, 2007, p. 5). Flowing directly from a recognition of such multi-dimensional embeddedness comes an appreciation of the necessarily variable and context specific nature of markets. As such, a market is a 'product of its own history and socioeconomic milieu' (Varman and Costa, 2008, p. 153), and we might then stress the value of understanding *embedding* as the process by which markets sustain connection with histories and milieus across place and over time.

THE PROBLEM OF QUALITY AND ITS VALUATION

At the heart of artisanal markets is the matter of quality, and how quality is valued in exchange in conditions where the quality of goods may be uncertain for the consumer. Embeddedness provides solutions to the problem of valuing quality in conditions of uncertainty. According to Beckert (2020), whilst there are markets in which the quality and value of goods may be largely determinable by the 'intrinsic' character of the goods themselves, there are markets where quality and value are determined primarily symbolically, through culturally grounded, and hence inter-subjective practices of valuation (Beckert, 2020; Beckert et al., 2017). Whereas, in the first case, quality can be objectively and technically verified (at least in principle), in the latter case ('markets from meaning'), quality assessment is concerned predominantly in respect of the good's 'immaterial' character (Beckert, 2020). The valuation of quality in 'markets from meaning' is an ascriptive practice determined discursively and inter-subjectively, where those markets are best understood, in Bourdieusian terms, as meaning-attributing *fields* in which a plurality of actors compete and contest for position and influence (Beckert, 2020), just as they form contingent, periodic and partial consensus. In many 'real-world' markets, including those that serve as our case studies, a complex interplay of quality measures prevail. In fact, such markets function as 'trading zones' in which competing notions of quality are accommodated, contested and navigated (Dahler-Larsen, 2019) and in a context in which different actors' valuations of quality operate within an unstable, relational and hierarchical order (Beckert, 2020). Hence, the quality and value of a good emerges as an outcome of 'endogenous preferences' emanating from the meso-level social order that is the cultural field-as-market.

In markets with a significant 'autonomy' from corporate mass production and consumption, such as in artisanal markets, there tends to be a meaningful level of homology between producer and consumer, reflecting their shared cultural embeddedness in the field-as-market and the dialectical relation between the two in shaping the regime of taste, quality and value. According to Beckert et al. (2017), the 'capital endowment' of consumers in such markets, that is the basis of their capacity to understand, discern and enjoy the goods associated with that market, is a product of their occupation of a shared field-specific habitus. Field-specific cultural goods serve simultaneously to position producers and consumers through processes of distinction (Beckert et al., 2017) within a hierarchical order, just as they confirm belonging to that order.

The endogenous preferences characterising a cultural field-as-market are framed partly by the role of social and cultural institutions that may perform a function of cultural arbitration, such as in contexts of goods being curated for inclusion in prestigious exhibitions, or success in competitions. The role of such institutions is to instil confidence, defined as 'the belief in the credibility of a narrative of the alleged quality of a product' (Beckert, 2020, p. 292), and to set 'how-to' rules for producers (Beckert, 2020).

Inter-subjectively constructed determinations of quality, within the context of fields as markets, however fragile, partial and temporary those constructions might be, provide sufficient amelioration of uncertainty in the market for consumers to feel enabled to make quality-based valuation judgements (Beckert, 2020). But the fact that such markets as fields are dynamic and pluralistic, and as such unstable, is precisely why the quality valuation of a good, or a producer, can never be established 'once and for all', offering both opportunity and risk in the light of shifting meanings within the field (Beckert, 2020). Producers face a perpetual challenge in deploying their capital successfully in sustaining or augmenting the value of their products (Beckert et al., 2017). In the context of artisanal markets, producers will consistently need to instil confidence amongst consumers regarding the quality of their goods. They may strive do this by stressing the dis-similarity of their goods from that which is mass produced, and confirming their goods' embodiment of current field-specific symbolic valuation criteria, including: their aesthetic quality, their 'authenticity', their use of high quality materials, their 'exclusiveness', and critically their embodiment of artisanal know-how and practices.

Key, then, are questions associated with how value is understood within the production and consumption of artisanal goods, and what differentiates them in value terms from their mass-produced counterparts. As the immaterial elements of the goods circulating in these embedded markets are central to their valorisation, we focus here on the idea of symbolic value. Many writers have sought to conceptualise value or symbolic capital (Porter, 1985; Slywotzky, 1996; Ulaga, 2003; Smith and Colgate, 2007). For our purposes, the work of Ravasi and Rindova (2004) chimes well with the creative production that we find amongst our artisanal producers. For Ravasi and Rindova (2004), symbolic value is understood as the immaterial stock and investments required to produce a good. Symbolic value creation requires three types of capital at the same time: firstly, intellectual or cultural capital, that is, the firm's ability to understand and imbue the product with cultural meaning (aesthetic, artistic, educational, technological); secondly, social capital, that is the network of resources and partners in production, suppliers of parts, informational networks tied to the production of the goods; and thirdly, reputation capital – a symbolic capital associated with reputational prestige. This capital will typically be deployed in the marketing of the product or the self-representation of the artisanal producer within their networks of communication.

Ravasi and Rindova (2004) further deepen an understanding of symbolic value by situating it in relation to functional (or instrumental) value. Symbolic value relates to a cultural space, and a particular culture of knowledge and understanding. Symbolic value relates to a good's ability to generate meaning related to a consumer's social identity, their status and the social networks and cultural environments that they inhabit. Functional value refers to the ability of a product to perform specific tasks in satisfying customer need, drawing on human, physical and technological capital to produce a good that fits the customer's value chain and instrumental needs (Ravasi and Rindova, 2004). As such, functional value is created by resources internal to the physical production process itself.

In contrast to the reductionist, rationalistic, understandings of economic actors characteristic of neo-classical economics, Ravasi and Rindova's (2004) account of symbolic value points to how consumers and producers alike inhabit a world of ethics, and accordingly evaluative ideas about production processes (at times resisting massified or overly mechanised methods) and possess an elaborate capacity to understand a good symbolically. But their account of functional value also enables us to see how artisanal production may reconnect producers and consumers into a social relation that removes some of the fetishisation of commodities, reinstating an understanding of the importance of the material quality of the product (as use value) in addition to its symbolic value, in determining a good's exchange value.

As both complexity and fluidity clearly characterise such 'fields-as-markets', we are better to think about the processual dimensions of social embedding against any fixed condition of embeddedness. At this point we will go on to explore the nuances of social embedding in application to two selected case studies.

OUR PROJECT: RESEARCHING NEW WAVE CUSTOM MOTORCYCLES AND BOUTIQUE GUITAR PEDALS

The data informing this paper were gathered as part of a one-year project funded by the Faculty of Health and Social Sciences, University of the West of England, Bristol, UK (*Being Authentic: Exploring Dynamics of Consumption and Production in the Vintage-Retro Market*), a project which served as the platform for the international conference, *Artisan! Crafting Alternative Economies, Making Alternative Lives* (10–11 September 2018, UWE Bristol). Data collection was via semi-structured interviews with artisans (18 in the case of the hand-built motorcycles and 14 in the case of the boutique pedals) and key stakeholders, along with some observational work, and content analysis of related websites and magazines.

The interviews took place both face-to-face, where viable, and by telephone or Skype where not. The duration of the interviews tended to be between one and one-and-a-half hours. Participants tended to be highly engaged, articulate and enthused in discussing their work. Interviews were recorded, anonymised where requested (rarely requested as the artisans often wanted their name and brand to be known), and coded, using an open thematic coding technique, via NVivo Pro.

NEW WAVE CUSTOM MOTORCYCLES

The 'New Wave Custom' motorcycle scene is commonly credited as having its origins in the hand-crafted motorcycles produced in Go Takamine's workshop, BratStyle, in Tokyo, from the late 1990s. From this point and place, but drawing on multiple related developments, a globalised social network of artisanal builders and connoisseur aficionados quickly emerged, facilitated in large part by the Internet. New Wave Custom motorcycles tend to share in common the practice of making hand-crafted aesthetic and technical modifications to 'donor bikes', the latter typically dating from the 1970s to the 1990s, bikes which were often relatively unremarkable vehicles in their 'first lives'. The cultural objects produced via 'Brat Style' customisation took an aesthetic 'stand' against excess, flamboyance, designed obsolescence, relentless technical progress, and materialist gluttony, and embraced a certain 'trash aesthetic' (see Le Zotte, 2017), often prizing the aesthetic value of the patina of age and decay. This 'stand' took the form of a retro, even nostalgic, aesthetic, asserting the virtue of simplicity in form and function, facilitative of a return to a more authentic and unmediated relationship to a life less encumbered by the cluttering advancements of late modernity. 'Brat-style' motorcycles were stripped of all 'unnecessary' components in pursuit of clean lines, under-statement, and a selective valorisation of the 'ordinary'.

Since the late 1990s, the New Wave Custom scene has grown into an international phenomenon, evolving and diversifying in its forms, and ranging from the grass-roots creativities of the shed-crafter to the internationally recognised accomplishments of 'celebrity' artisan builders producing high-value, two-wheeled 'works of art'. Key to understanding the hand-crafted motorcycle market, then, is its social embeddedness in a cultural field. The cultural field in question, closely related to other fields, displays certain characteristic orientations, including a resurgent valuing of crafting and making; a selective sustainability ethic that stands opposed to a 'throw-away' society; a stylistic and consumed nostalgia; and a host of counter/sub-cultural scenes, including punk/hardcore music, surfing, skateboarding, BMX and tattooing. Reflecting, and in part driving, the marketisation of the new wave custom bike scene, the field-as-market has been penetrated extensively by corporate interests, evidencing the ways in which capitalism is so readily able to digest and then capitalise on criticism (Dahler-Larsen, 2019). In this sense, we can conceptualise the New Wave Custom motorcycle phenomenon as a cultural field first, with an emergent habitus and valuation order, only subsequently evolving into market form.

Alec Sharp, Old Empire Motorcycles (OEM)

> What makes us happy is quality not quantity – Alec Sharp

Alec was captivated as a child by the motorcycle road movie *Easy Rider*, and the influential United States TV series, *American Chopper*. Having had the opportunity to build some experience in a local motorcycle workshop after completing his education, whilst putting himself through welding and metal fabrication courses, Alec set up his own company (OEM) at the age of 23 and crafted his first custom bike; a Royal Enfield. It was at this time that the New Wave Custom bike scene exploded into life in the United Kingdom, and OEM secured a presence for one of its bikes at the inaugural *Bike Shed* show in London in 2013, where the *Bike Shed* was to emerge as a key institutional medium through which the symbolic quality and value of bikes in the market were to be established, and the endogenous preferences of the field-as-market were to become formed (see Beckert, 2020). In this sense, OEM were structurally and culturally *embedding* in the emerging New Wave Custom motorcycle scene from its earliest years, and were in a position to 'sediment' (Beckert, 2020) an early reputation within the market through such institutionalised inclusion.

Alec feels structurally embedded in the New Wave Custom bike market, and the cultural field in which that market is itself embedded. Alec talks extensively about his strong and weak ties within a network of builders and cultural intermediaries. Beckert (2007) argues that embeddedness can best be understood as a solution to the fundamental problems of market exchange, including the problem of competition. Alec's account suggests that some of the more problematic features of competition between makers (such as copying or 'stealing' the artistic ideas of others) are ameliorated by a combination of the market's still small size, by the mutual accountability of builders, and by the significant social ties that connect them, including good friendships. Our data confirm the importance of social networks in facilitating trust between builders (see Fligstein and Dauter, 2007). Many commentators (Beckert, 2003; Varman and Costa, 2008; Krippner, 2001) have challenged the rational choice economism that frames the ways in which all market action is assumed to function within neo-classical economics. Theorists of structural embeddedness (Granovetter, 1985; Uzzi, 1996, 1997) have demonstrated the influence of social networks, and weak and strong ties in shaping market relations and exchanges. Reflecting Sennett's (2009) account of 'sociable expertise', Alec maintains an open attitude to sharing information, and to mutual learning through collaboration: 'if anyone emails me I give them as much information as I can to help them out'. Alec believes that a feature of the contemporary era is a greater openness to sharing and collaboration, suggesting a need to reconsider, through a fully sociological lens, the ways in which markets (at least some markets) work to complicate rational choice assumptions regarding market action (Fligstein and Dauter, 2007).

OEM's cultural embeddedness is manifest in the motorcycles they produce. The cultural field that is the New Wave Custom motorcycle scene functions as a symbolic order of valuation, amongst other things, and the motorcycles themselves sit centre stage within that order. Cultural fields embed discursive, intersubjectively constructed meanings governing the meaning and value of goods (Beckert, 2020; Beckert et al., 2017; Ravasi and Rindova, 2004). OEM's motorcycles expertly navigate a path between reproducing primary elements of that sign order, but also seek to selectively and carefully challenge some of the boundaries of that order, producing distinction (Bourdieu, 2010). Those builders who successfully deploy this strategy succeed precisely because of their cultural embeddedness, and because of their capacity to build homologous relationships with consumers (Beckert et al., 2017). This relationship is the basis of producing goods rich in the signs that instil confidence amongst consumers that the good is one of quality, and is one that will position builders with status vis-à-vis other actors within the field (Beckert, 2020; Dequech, 2003; Bourdieu, 2010).

Given that the cultural field in question is one defined by a certain connoisseur consumption, consumers must be 'confident' in builders' 'narratives of quality' (Beckert, 2020). OEM's business strategy has been to walk a 'middle path' within the market, crafting bikes of distinction marked by high-quality design and building, but informed by a pragmatism that promises a chance of economic viability. The key platform for this strategy has been to build a strong quality reputation in the 'grey area' (as Alec calls it) of the market, namely at what might be thought of as a market centre point, sitting between the twin poles constituted by 'top of the game' one-off motorcycles on the one hand, and high-volume product lines on the other. To this end, OEM committed to building a series of ten unique motorcycles, but each sharing a common aesthetic DNA, and some common hand-crafted components. In this way OEM successfully acquired the quality distinction marker of the bespoke, whilst also taking the opportunity for some carefully considered cost-saving standardisation. The success of Alec's careful judgement in this difficult balance act rests entirely on his cultural and cognitive embeddedness within the field-as-market.

OEM have also recognised the value that can be derived from producing a 'top-of-the-game' 'halo bike' (a highly-expensive impact motorcycle displaying the full technical skill and aesthetic qualities of the builder) in bringing international attention, and enhancing a reputation for quality. Such 'halo bike' strategies appear to evidence the way in which measures of quality may rank goods in relation to a 'golden top' of excellence, where excellence is marked by being 'superior' (Dahler-Larsen, 2019). But whilst OEM's own 'halo bike' (*The Typhoon*[1]) secured much international regard, attention does not last long in the field-as-market. Whist enjoying their day in the sun, it became clear that a business model grounded on building 'halo bikes' was the exclusive preserve of those at the 'top of the game', or with external sources of income. Whilst building 'absolutely amazing motorcycles' that are 'a work of art' remains a preferred option, diversification is a practical necessity. To this end OEM also undertake more modest customisations of contemporary mass-produced motorcycles, producing 'bolt-on parts' for sale to consumers who wish to modify their own machines, in addition to selling merchandise. Beckert (2020; see also Beckert et al., 2017) points to the role of inter-subjectively constructed ascriptions of quality and value within 'markets from meaning'. In artisanal markets such as this, maintaining one's position within a symbolic hierarchy of quality remains a difficult and precarious balancing act.

Underpinning consumer confidence in the quality of cultural goods in artisanal markets is the quality of the artisanal labour invested in the good, or at least the presence of confidence-enhancing narratives about that labour quality (Beckert, 2020). In being largely self-taught, Alec sees himself as typical of artisan building in the new wave custom bike market. Speaking of other young builders he knows, 'I don't think a single one has any formal qualifications as such, not that there is a qualification for building bikes.' In the New Wave Custom bike market, artisans are in the most part self-trained, and via the democratising medium of a world-wide web rich in informational resources. According to Alec, many builders use YouTube 'on a regular basis to effectively teach ourselves how to do these particular things'. Interestingly, rather than such DIY routes to know-how serving to discredit the artisanal credentials of new wave custom bike builders, this DIY logic appears to resonate with the grass-roots, counter-cultural qualities of the cultural field, lending the builders reputational position and credibility. Within the context of specific cultural fields, acquiring know-how through such means may be framed as evidencing provenance within the field, as manifesting an organic embeddedness, in turn furnishing the artisan with a confidence-inspiring narrative to accompany the marketing of their goods.

As a niche artisanal market comprising small producers, marketing budgets are inevitably minimal, and marketing responsibilities fall on the artisans themselves. At the same time, given the highly symbolic nature of these motorcycles' value, the quality threshold for 'marketing' content is necessarily high. OEM hosts a website comprising exceptionally high quality photographic images, and video content, accompanied by evocative narrative and an evidencing of reputation and regard within the field.[2] The site is rich in field-specific symbolic references, evidencing their cultural embeddedness. OEM also appreciate the importance of social media platforms to building and maintaining reputation and position in the market, reflecting the growing importance of social media for selling in craft economies (Yair, 2012). OEM also host highly followed Instagram, Facebook and Twitter sites. The key function of such marketing platforms is the opportunity they provide for a builder to construct a convincing narrative of quality in which the consumer can have 'confidence' (Beckert, 2020). Online platforms provide powerful multi-modal opportunities for artisanal producers to communicate marketised meanings rich in virtual contextualisation, where the quality of the good is brought to life in its symbolic and functional use within narrative-rich video and photographic content (see Elliott and Wattanasuwan, 1998). But of particular importance within the field-as-market is the role played by cultural intermediaries, or brokers, whose de facto gate-keeping does much to govern builders' inclusion and position. Of particular note here are the curated websites Bike EXIF and Pipeburn, and the multi-modal Bike Shed, whose annual curated exhibition in London is a pivot-point of the field's annual calendar. Features in influential field-specific magazines such as *Built: Handcrafted Motorcycles* are also important. Presence at festivals and rallies, participation in build competitions, collaborations with celebrities, corporate entities, motorcycle manufacturers, cool brands associated with linked cultural fields, and inclusion in films, documentaries and TV programmes comprise OEM's broad marketing port-folio. The ongoing work needed to ensure sustained position and profile within the field-as-market, and to continue to attract an ever-moving virtual spotlight on international field attention, is more evidence of the value of the processual-focus of the concept of embedding over embeddedness.

BOUTIQUE GUITAR PEDALS

The term 'boutique guitar pedals' describes the making, design, sound devel-opment and manufacture of guitar effects pedals that are not mass produced in factories using cheap components. The history of the term, like the history of guitar effects pedals generally, is contested, but there are some clear dates, times and companies that demarcate the boutique sector. The first guitar effects pedals were manufactured in the 1930s, as integral to, and part of, the guitar itself, by companies such as Rickenbacker. By the late 1940s to early 1950s the first stand-alone pedals were being produced. From the 1960s to the present day, major companies such as Boss, MXR and Electro-Harmonix dominated the pedal making scene, but as the 1990s developed into the 2000s, small DIY/boutique pedal companies began to emerge. Tom Hughes, writing in his book *Analog Man's Guide to Vintage Effects*, refers to 'boutique' as meaning 'high-quality, handmade effects built in small-scale production runs without the use of automation or mass-production techniques, thus allowing for greater attention to detail and custom-tuning of individual units' (Hughes, 2004, p. 20). In terms of quality, these pedals are usually built using higher grade components. The electronics are sturdier, and often placed differently to mainstream company pedals. The price of such pedals is typically higher, though not always, as the economic and business modelling operates in a more 'ad hoc' way. As Hughes says,

> part of the popularity of boutique may lie in its grassroots, back-to-basics appeal. There is a sense that you have *a product of fine craftsmanship* made by a real person who's into what he's doing, not some faceless corporation cranking them out by the thousands, always with an eye on the bottom line. We want to believe that the boutique pedal we've just purchased is a *labour of love*, made with the *finest ingredients*. It's the difference between fresh-baked, homemade Tollhouse cookies and Chips Ahoy. (2004, p. 22)

For makers and musicians then, the 'boutique' tag signifies 'craftsmanship' or 'artisanal crafting' as a marker of quality, uniqueness and the longevity of the product. It also signifies a certain differentiation from the logic and production values of the mass market. For boutique pedal makers, their craft is a labour of love, that relies on the components used but is measured in its quality and value by the pedal's functionality of sound and sound optionality. The boutique pedal industry is a socially embedded market that relies on connoisseur consumers with a good deal of technical and sound knowledge grounded in music production.

Tom George of Cog Effects

Tom George of the boutique pedal company Cog Effects follows a similar pattern to many boutique pedal manufacturers in a socially embedded market. Tom is embedded in the field of music making, performance and production having played in bands, gigged regularly, toured and recorded. As a bass player he found that there were few pedals aimed at the bass-playing community. He began making pedals for himself around 2009/10, including crafting multiple effects pedals into a single unit. He modified a popular pedal – the Big Muff by Electro-harmonix. As others heard the pedal in use he was asked to make pedals for them. Reassessing his life in 2013 following the birth of his children, he started to take pedal building more seriously, developing new ideas for pedals and worked towards becoming a full-time pedal maker. Work that commenced as a hobby gradually developed into a career over time. Tom progressively reduced his paid employment and became a full-time pedal builder in 2016.

As a networked actor he was well embedded in his social and cultural field, comprising not only pedal builders but also musical producers, consumers and distributers. His understanding was built upon years of music listening, playing in bands and working within the industry. He talks about strong and weak ties (Granovetter, 1973) to certain sectors of the industry, or field. His ties to other pedal makers are strong, but his links now to record labels and touring are weak. Disembedding may occur as readily as embedding. Pedal makers themselves have a strong appreciation of certain sounds, and ways of making those sounds for musicians live and in the recording studio. This appreciation also requires a substantive knowledge, and understanding of, the recorded and live music scene, and particular artists. Tom had a deep appreciation of Soundgarden, Rage Against the Machine, Pearl Jam and Alice In Chains, the studios they used, the effects the guitarists used, and the way they set up live. Such cultural knowledge conforms to the idea of cultural capital within Ravasi and Rindova's (2004) theory of symbolic capital. Consumers and other producers are able to read the cultural, aesthetic, technological, artistic meanings and knowledge embedded and realised in Tom's products. This feeds into his reputational status, and his capacity to build homologous and connected relationships with consumers (Beckert et al., 2017). The quality, design, reliability, sound and cultural knowledge imbued in Tom's pedals enable the consumer-musician to position themselves as a knowledgeable actor in the field. Cog Effects have the symbolic value that chimes with this socially embedded market.

As stated earlier, Beckert (2007) argues that embeddedness can be understood as a solution to the fundamental problems of market exchange, including the problem of competition. Tom values the ways in which the community of pedal builders are willing to discuss their work on a number of online forums and Facebook groups, where innovation is rarely copied directly but rather championed by other builders. Ideas are shared and competition muted by the embedded network of actors, and their common love for their craft. As Varman and Costa (2008) suggest, there are moral, emotional and expressive dimensions to the normative order of these types of socially embedded markets. Tom's account of the culture of this builder network illustrates this idea: 'there's a really good community of pedal builders both here and kind of worldwide … there's a really good community spirit. When people have a good idea, other people, other pedal builders, tend to support and celebrate that fact.'

In respect of how quality is evaluated, we can see that the artisanal pedal and custom motorcycle markets function as complex market hybrids, as 'trading zones' (Dahler-Larsen, 2019) where both 'intrinsic' material properties and inter-subjective symbolic meanings simultaneously frame the valuation of quality (see Beckert, 2020), in a process of complex inter-connectivity. Tom and many builders like him seem to operate in both arenas. His approach, in terms of the 'intrinsic' quality of his pedals, is based on using the best quality components for the price that he charges. He uses components that are the 'highest end that I can reasonably use for the price I charge'. In terms of design, he constructs pedals in ways that the mass manufactured pedals don't. In his popular T-16 pedal, the jack inputs are separately mounted rather than mounted on the PCB (printed circuit board), which makes the pedal much less likely to break. Mass manufactured pedals connect everything to the PCB and slot them into the pedal housing.

But the 'market as meaning' (Beckert, 2020) dimensions of the Boutique pedal market are also evidenced through the role consumers play in their connoisseurship via the testimonials that they leave for the pedal makers, and the ways in which the pedals are discussed on forums, chatrooms, Facebook sites and online magazines (and to a lesser degree within some of the printed press that still survives in the digital era). Quality of sound, and the ways a pedal can be utilised, feature highly in the testimonial feedback for pedal makers, and this reinforces their markers of quality and functionality within the interpretive and discursive arena of the embedded market. Testimonials and discussions from musicians and consumers appear on the Cog Effects site itself,[3] and on websites and forums such as ibassmag.com, notreble.com and scotssbasslessons.com. These, then, are the spaces of interpretive ascription, and the confirmation of the quality of the product.

Boutique pedal makers are excellent examples of the ways in which artisanal craft is embedded in, and co-produced by, cultural fields and markets. The products they make are valued for their quality and technological or artisanal knowledge, and the symbolic value order endogenous to the field-as-market. It is also clear that the economic model followed does not fit one of traditional rational-actor economics, as the builders invest much un-costed time in the pursuit of quality, largely driven by their love of their craft. It is also clear that value is measured through a mix of use, and exchange-value, but with a high level of symbolic value interwoven into the computation (Ravasi and Rindova, 2004). As Tom says, when a customer gets in touch they know they are talking to the guy that 'will design and build their pedal for them' and that the knowledge, technical know-how, design aesthetics, and importantly for effects pedals, the knowledge of sound, are key to Tom's products and persona. Without a model of social embeddedness it would not be possible to understand the strength and character of these forms of connectedness.

CONCLUSION

Artisanal markets may offer a contribution to building progressive alternatives to the pathologies of globalised neo-liberal capitalism, but such markets remain only partially understood. A multi-modal and sociologically rich conceptualisation of such markets' social embeddedness provides valuable resources for illuminating how such markets function. We have argued that (at least some) artisanal markets are deeply embedded in cultural fields, such that we might conceptualise these as cultural fields-as-markets. By understanding the particularities of such cultural fields as markets it becomes possible to discern some of the means by which artisans produce quality and value, and establish successful homologous relations with the connoisseur consumers that typically occupy such fields-as-markets.

Through the use of two 'non-typical' case studies we have shown how some artisanal markets function as 'trading zones', where the quality and value of products are constructed through a complex interplay of use, exchange and symbolic values. Quality and value are invariably constructed discursively and inter-subjectively within such fields-as-markets, where an artisans' social embedding largely governs their capacity to navigate (commonly) complex and shifting taste orders, and in doing so both evidencing and (re)establishing their reputational position. Given the reality of artisanal markets as 'trading zones' for the deliberation of quality and value, artisanal products are also bearers of use values associated with certain 'intrinsic qualities' deriving from the materiality of the object itself. A boutique guitar pedal unable to produce the dynamic sound qualities associated with its specified purpose is less likely to become the object of a connoisseur consumer's valuation. As artisans' navigation of the shifting contours of a field's unstable attributions of quality and value are never complete, never a done deal, the process-focussed conceptualisation of *embedding* may offer greater value as an explanatory tool, over the more static concept of embeddedness.

Our artisan's social embedding takes multiple forms and plays multiple roles. It frames the process by which they have acquired, and successfully communicated, their know-how, as developed not through formal training but through a DIY pathway validated through their organic relationship to the field, and the conventions of quality circulating within that field. It is reflected in their position within social networks of co-artisans and cultural arbiters that show patterns of cooperation as much as they do competition. It is also expressed in the manner in which the artisans successfully navigate the complex and precarious trade-offs inherently associated with the need to balance the pursuit of quality, with economic realism, but in a manner that enhances rather than jeopardises their reputational position. Our artisans have an acute understanding of the quality, functionality, design and use value of their goods. This approach to value and quality is symbiotic with the connoisseur consumer's assessment of these types of product, illustrating the different approach to quality and value that these embedded markets create.

Finally, it is manifested in the ways in which, for our artisans, marketing is necessarily effected through immersion in the institutional and cultural landscape of the field. The material and symbolic quality and value of the products, as these are articulated through the substantive content of our artisans' marketing, 'convince' their target connoisseur consumers only because of the homology of their relations with those consumers. The mediums through which our artisans' marketing takes place (social media platforms, discussion forums, review sites, selection for participation in curated exhibitions, etc.) are all characterised by the integration of such mediums within the cultural field itself.

Future research might usefully explore the similarities and variabilities found across different and particular artisanal markets to enrich our understanding of the multiple ways in which social embedding may function.

NOTES

1. See http://oldempiremotorcycles.com/tag/oem-typhoon/.
2. See http://oldempiremotorcycles.com/.
3. See https://www.cogeffects.co.uk/.

REFERENCES

Beckert, J. (2003). Economic sociology and embeddedness: how shall we conceptualize economic action? *Journal of Economic Issues*, 37(3), 769–87. https://doi.org/10.1080/00213624.2003.11506613.

Beckert, J. (2007). The great transformation of embeddedness. Discussion Paper 07/1. Max Planck Institute. https://www.mpifg.de/pu/mpifg_dp/dp07-1.pdf.

Beckert, J. (2020). Markets from meaning: quality uncertainty and the intersubjective construction of value. *Cambridge Journal of Economics*, 44, 285–301. https://doi.org/10.1093/cje/bez035.

Beckert, J., Rössel, J. and Schenk, P. (2017). Wine as a cultural product: symbolic capital and price formation in the wine field. *Sociological Perspectives*, 60(1), 206–22. https://doi.org/10.1177/0731121416629994.

Bourdieu, P. (2010). *Distinction*. Routledge Press. https://www.routledge.com/Distinction-A-Social-Critique-of-the-Judgement-of-Taste/Bourdieu/p/book/9780415567886.

Crafts Council (2020). *The Market for Craft*. The Crafts Council. https://www.craftscouncil.org.uk/documents/880/Market_for_craft_full_report_2020.pdf.

Dahler-Larsen, P. (2019). *Quality: From Plato to Performance*. Palgrave Press. https://doi.org/10.1007/978-3-030-10392-7.

Dequech, D. (2003). Cognitive and cultural embeddedness: combining institutional economics and economic sociology. *Journal of Economic Issues*, 37(2), 461–70. https://doi.org/10.1080/00213624.2003.11506594.

Elliott, R. and Wattanasuwan, K. (1998). Brands as symbolic resources for the construction of identity. *International Journal of Advertising*, 17(2), 131–44. https://doi.org/10.1080/02650487.1998.11104712.

Fligstein, N. and Dauter, L. (2007). The sociology of markets. *Annual Review of Sociology*, 33, 105–28. https://10.1146/annurev.soc.33.040406.131736.

Granovetter, M. (1973). The strength of weak ties. *American Journal of Sociology*, 78(6), 1360–80.

Granovetter, M. (1985). Economic action and social structure: the problem of embeddedness. *American Journal of Sociology*, 91, 481–510. https://www.jstor.org/stable/2780199.

Granovetter, M. (2005). The impact of social structure on economic outcomes. *Journal of Economic Perspectives*, 19(1), 33–50. https://doi.org/10.1257/0895330053147958.

Hess, M. (2004). Spatial relationships? Towards a reconceptualization of embed-dedness. *Progress in Human Geography*, 28(2), 165–86. https://doi.org/10.1191/0309132504ph479oa.

Hughes, T. (2004). *Analog Man's Guide to Vintage Effects*. For Musician Only Publishing, 2nd edition. https://www.buyanalogman.com/Analog_Man_s_guide_to_Vintage_Effects_p/vintage%20effects%20book.htm.

Korn, P. (2013). *Why We Make Things and Why It Matters*. Vintage. https://www.penguin.co.uk/books/110/1102382/why-we-make-things-and-why-it-matters/9781784705060.html.

Krippner, G. R. (2001). The elusive market: embeddedness and the paradigm of eco-nomic sociology. *Theory and Society*, 30(6), 775–810. https://www.jstor.org/stable/658117.

Le Zotte, J. (2017). *From Goodwill to Grunge: A History of Secondhand Styles and Alternative Economies*. University of North Carolina Press. https://www.jstor.org/stable/10.5149/9781469631912_lezotte.

Ocejo, R. E. (2017). *Masters of Craft: Old Jobs in the New Economy*. Princeton University Press. https://princeton.universitypressscholarship.com/view/10.23943/princeton/9780691165493.001.0001/upso-9780691165493.

Podolny, J. M. (2001). Networks as the pipes and prisms of the market. *American Journal of Sociology*, 107(1), 33–60. https://www.jstor.org/stable/10.1086/323038.

Polanyi, K. (1944). *The Great Transformation: The Political and Economic Origins of Our Time*. Beacon Press. https://inctpped.ie.ufrj.br/spiderweb/pdf_4/Great_Transformation.pdf.

Porter, M. (1985). *Competitive Advantage*. Free Press. https://www.hbs.edu/faculty/Pages/item.aspx?num=193.

Ravasi, D. and Rindova, V. (2004). *Creating Symbolic Value: A Cultural Perspective on Production and Exchange*. https://papers.ssrn.com/sol3/papers.cfm?abstract_id=1265021.

Ryan, L. and Mulholland, J (2015). Embedding in motion: analysing relational, spatial and temporal dynamics among highly skilled migrants. In L. Ryan, U. Erel and A. D'Angelo (eds), *Migrant Capital: Networks, Identities and Strategies* (pp. 135–53). Routledge. https://doi.org/10.1057/9781137348807_9.

Scrase, T. J. (2003). Precarious production: globalisation and artisan labour in the Third World. *Third World Quarterly*, 24(3), 449–61. https://doi.org/10.1080/0143659032000084401.

Sennett, R. (2009). *The Craftsman*. Penguin Books. https://yalebooks.yale.edu/book/9780300151190/craftsman.

Slywotzky, A. (1996). *Value Migration*. Harvard Business School Press. https://books.google.co.uk/books/about/Value_Migration.html?id=0yjJWOmRN7wC.

Smith, J. B. and Colgate, M. (2007). Customer value creation: a practical framework. *Journal of Marketing Theory and Practice*, 15(1), 7–23. https://doi.org/10.2753/MTP1069-6679150101.

Ulaga, W. (2003). Capturing value creation in business relationships: a customer per-spective. *Industrial Marketing Management*, 32(8), 677–93. https://doi.org/10.1016/j.indmarman.2003.06.008.

Uzzi, B. (1996). The sources and consequences of embeddedness for the economic performance of organizations: the network effect. *American Sociological Review*, 61(4), 674–98. https://doi.org/10.2307/2096399.

Uzzi, B. (1997). Social structure and competition in inter-firm networks: the paradox of embeddedness. *Administrative Science Quarterly*, 42(1), 35–67. https://doi.org/ 10.2307/2393808.

Varman, R. and Costa, J. A. (2008). Embedded markets, communities, and the invisible hand of social norms. *Journal of Macromarketing*, 28(2), 141–56. https://doi.org/10 .1177/0276146708314594.

Yair, K. (2012). How makers and craft organisations are using social media effectively. The Crafts Council. https://www.craftscouncil.org.uk/documents/874/How_makers _and_craft_organisations_are_using_social_media_2012.pdf.

Zukin, S. and DiMaggio, P. (1990). Introduction. In S. Zukin and P. DiMaggio (eds), *Structures of Capital: The Social Organization of the Economy* (pp. 1–36). Cambridge University Press. https://www.cambridge.org/gb/academic/subjects/ sociology/political-sociology/structures-capital-social-organization-economy ?format=PB&isbn=9780521376785.

PART II

From tradition to innovation: trends and issues
in artisanal and craft making

5. Neo-artisanal practice and the nostalgic: traditional makers' identities, innovation and sustainability in neo-artisanal production

Laura Quinn

INTRODUCTION

According to Cordoso,

> After two centuries of being conceptually severed, there is once again a convergence between the two terms (Craft and Design). This is chiefly due to the fact that customized and small-batch (rather than homogenous, mass-produced) goods are becoming more and more commonplace. This trend marks the return of the bespoke, a relation between producers and consumers that has not been the norm in industrialised economies since the early nineteenth century. (2010, p. 321)

Though now over a decade old, this quote from Cardoso acknowledges a trend which is growing in importance for the artisan. Over the course of this chapter, I will be using the terms craft, crafts people, and artisans. Though not having the same meaning, the terms are, of course, linked. This chapter draws on my experience in my practice. I myself am a crafts person, specialising in glass making, but I produce work for sale and consumption; therefore I also view my work as artisanal practice. Before we go any further, it is worth attempting a loose definition that differentiates crafts people and artisans, though in many cases these identities exist symbiotically in modern makers. Earle (2018) discusses how artisans have specialist knowledge and practice like crafts people, but produce work to sell. The production method, use of technologies, and distribution methods can alter depending on the needs and demands of the consumer.

As stated by Cardoso (2010), craft is now regularly meeting design within artisanal practice to serve the bespoke needs of the new economy consumer.

Artisanal products are becoming sought after amongst some consumers. This type of consumer is more interested in where the product has come from, who has made it and whether it is part of a culture with which they might want to be associated. Crafts people, or artisans, can be understood as culture creators, but why might this be the case? Is it due to the historical existence of the making method they choose to employ in their work, because it has heritage and lineage? Greenhalgh (1997) discusses how the link between craft and the vernacular ironically positioned itself on the culture scene during the modernisation of European culture, and that its 'authentic' quality is what has made it appeal to a wide audience over such a long period of time, up to the present. So, crafts' claim to culture is not a new phenomenon.

This association with the vernacular and cultural history creates a risk that the true motive of the audience and consumer is to ensure that the nostalgic idea of the craftsperson, as using traditional modes of making, continues to exist. Maintaining heritage is important, but a central issue is whether the new artisanal, or neo-artisanal space is a romantic veneration of the artisan, or a departure into new conceptions of making, appropriate to a more innovative and sustainable future. Does the nostalgia of the artisan hinder the evolution of artisanal production within the contemporary economy? If so, how can we teach the audience to continue to support traditional processes, but to embrace those who combine it with new technologies and processes to create practices that can flourish outside of its right to exist because of heritage?

Neo-artisans need to identify, and understand the significance of, the relationship between culture, perceived authenticity and technology in order to design the evolution of a traditional practice. Otherwise there is a risk that craft may become stagnant and not relevant to contemporary culture. Craft and artisanal making needs to move beyond the nostalgic narrative to be able to understand and work with themes from contemporary culture in order to stay relevant.

> I see the craft world as a kind of lagoon and the art world in general as the ocean. Some artists shelter in this lagoon, because their imagination isn't robust enough to go out into the wider sea. Although there are some very good things being made, the craft world at the moment is set up to preserve something that can't look after itself. (Perry, 2005)

Perhaps this statement from contemporary ceramic artist and writer Grayson Perry is a harsh generalisation, but it prompts a thought of what the main objective of craft is, and whether or not it is in preserving something 'that can't look after itself', like nostalgia, or if it needs to become a more assertive force that guides the audience's perceptions and relationship with material objects and culture.

In this chapter, I will discuss how I use social media as a marketing tactic to educate and guide my audience to develop a more sophisticated understanding of my practice, which mixes traditional glass making processes with digital technologies. I will discuss how the result of using marketing tactics like this can imbue the artisanal object with value for the consumer.

As a glass blower, I explore the way that the fragility and delicacy that has been part of the design language and the luxury status of artisanal glass might be reinterpreted in the context of neo-artisanal practice. I look to creating an emotional connection between the consumer and the glass product to promote care and value for the piece. Presenting it as notes from the neo-artisanal field, I will use my experience as a neo-artisan as a case study, and as a viewing lens in this chapter. I will outline what the neo-artisan is and discuss how 'green-washing' and 'green consumerism' can easily mislead the audience's perception of how environmentally friendly a product is by focusing on an isolated sustainable area of the production or materials used. This can deter someone from looking at the overall environmental impact of the production and use of the product (Huong Nguyen et al., 2019). I will discuss how greenwashing and green consumerism can act as an inhibitive force as they threaten to embed craft in the nostalgic viewpoint because it is seen as inherently good and avoid putting it under the same scrutiny which most industries are under to create sustainable production and products. I will discuss how educating my audience through social media is what will allow my practice to navigate the tensions that come with restrictive binaries of craft being good, and industry being bad, ultimately allowing potential for my artisanal practice to take whatever direction is appropriate for sustainable approaches to making, including directions into technological industries for modes of making.

I will discuss how the neo-artisan differs from the traditional craftsperson and how a broad range of skill sets is needed in order to survive, opposing the romantic, nostalgic view of the master dedicating their life to perfecting one making method. I believe the application of identities like designer, manufacturer, craftsperson and artist serves to constrain, particularly when the identities are seen as binary terms rather than co-existing in the same person. The audience's nostalgic idea of the craftsperson's identity can cause their existence to be embedded in maintaining historic culture, but this chapter will outline how through communication and marketing, the neo-artisan can educate the audience to support the growth of the craftsperson and their practice in the neo-artisanal realm. I will question how varied artisanal identities can help to create more efficient, sustainable, making processes. Through sociological understanding of the audience, the maker can communicate perceived 'authenticity' and enable the audience to accept and embrace a turn towards digital manufacture for the nostalgic craftsperson.

THEORETICAL CONTEXT

In writing this chapter I have looked to my own experience as a neo-artisan. From a theoretical point of view, neo-artisanal practice offers opportunities to be discussed with multiple, varying lenses. This section will offer a brief theoretical background of some aspects on which the chapter relies.

The idea of authenticity, and how it affects the relationship between the neo-artisan, product and consumer, will be discussed as it is one of the key constructs of contemporary marketing, including the marketing of craft goods. Authenticity is a complex idea in itself, and though this chapter does not attempt to detail its complexities, it is important that it is acknowledged. Hartmann and Ostberg state that 'Consumers and marketers alike seem to be united in their quest for the "real" and "genuine"' (2013, p. 882), but go on to say that rather than authenticity already existing in an object or experience, instead the object or experience must be made authentic.

In a similar way, Peterson states that 'Authenticity, like "creativity" … and "Entrepreneurship" … do not inhere in the object, person, or performance said to be authentic … . Rather, authenticity is a claim that is made by or for someone, thing or performance and either accepted or rejected by relevant others' (2005, p. 1086). This chapter won't argue whether or not an object is inherently authentic, but instead will discuss authenticity as a construct and a narrative that can be built in relation to the marketing of artisanal practice.

Consumers are familiar with the construct of authenticity when it comes to craft. Glenn Adamson (2013) even suggests that craft is presumed to be authentic: 'Craft is readily presumed to be direct, forthright, honest, authentic, undisguised, organic, integrated' (2013, p. 140). Why might this be? Perhaps it is to do with the heritage that current artisans and craftspeople are associated with, simply by using their specific skills in their chosen material or medium. That heritage represents an opposition to the aspects of modern living which can leave consumers feeling disheartened. Britton and Margetts discuss this association in relation to ceramic artists, but indeed this is comparable with any artisan skilfully working with a material or ingredient and engaging in slow production:

> Whether or not they realise it, people who choose to work as artists in clay now, are tapping into a twentieth century history of gentle or genteel resistance to some of the larger sweeps of modernisation, standardisation, overproduction, mechanisation, sanitisation, mass-marketing, and other aspects of progress that threaten to crush the human spirit. (1993, p. 10)

If heritage and authenticity are easily associated with the artisan, and are things that the contemporary consumer wants, then it would seem logical to promote nostalgic narratives in order to market artisans. But an issue arises when nostalgic narratives inhibit more developed understandings of how artisans can function in the modern market. As discussed by Britton and Margetts (1993), the terms craft, handmade and slow production are placed in discursive binary opposites to standardisation, mechanisation and modernisation. Does a nostalgic narrative support binary terms that might restrain the neo-artisan in exploring more modern modes of production, including digital design and fabrication?

I will be discussing the possible negative impacts of this nostalgic view of the artisan further in the chapter.

One of the main themes in this chapter is sustainability. I have a personal interest in this theme as I seek to make my artisanal practice more sustainable. Many of the ways I do this is through implementing the use of digital design and modern digital fabrication technologies such as 3D printing, water jet cutting and laser cutting. Because craft is understood as being good and moral, opposing the effects of mass production (Adamson, 2013; Britton & Margetts, 1993), it is easy to market it as sustainable. However, as I will discuss further in this chapter, even if craft and artisanal making has a right to heritage and authenticity, it doesn't necessarily make it a sustainable practice.

That is why it is important to acknowledge greenwashing in this chapter. Greenwashing is a term that is becoming more commonly used within contemporary consumer culture. Lyon and Montgomery write that 'Popular usage of the term greenwash encompasses a range of communications that mislead people into adopting overly positive beliefs about an organization's environmental performance, practices, or products' (Lyon & Montgomery, 2015, p. 225). What is important about my practice is that more than just appearing to be more sustainable, I want to make sure that it actually is sustainable. Greenwashing threatens the authenticity within consumable products (Lyon & Montgomery, 2015, p. 223). The use of online marketing tactics, such as on social media, can help to deliver a more detailed narrative of how the artisanal good is made, who made it, where they made it, and ultimately builds a bigger picture. This tactic is something I use in my own practice in the hope that it empowers the consumer to make more informed choices when trying to support sustainable producers. Even more than this, I also use social media to educate my audience on the nuances of determining the sustainability of what I create by giving them an understanding of the complete life cycle of the object. I will discuss further on how this narrative is a type of consumer education.

If there are opportunities to engage in modern digital technologies, whether for manufacturing or marketing, or work in collaboration with other specialists, or decentralise the artisan's skillset outside of their own specialism, do the linked binaries of artisanal and slow making as 'good', and mass automated production as 'bad', prevent the artisan from exploring crossovers?

How might we come away from this restrictive two-dimensional view of the relationship between artisanal and mass production to develop the sophistication of consumer's understanding of the practice. If the consumer can have a more holistic understanding of the entire life cycle of the artisanal product, then perhaps they will be able to support this industry when the time comes for artisans to venture into new modes of making.

One way to develop the consumer's taste and knowledge of the artisanal practice is through what Richard E. Ocejo terms 'service teaching' (2017, p. 209). This term describes the way that artisans can educate their audience by sharing with them the multiple steps within their craft or service that they are providing. This method is one of the core tactics I apply in my own practice, and will be detailed further in the chapter.

This method is also relevant to sustainability or green marketing. In this way we can also teach consumers to understand the complete life cycle of the object and make more informed decisions about how they consume, and what producers they choose to consume from, based on a more informed decision rather than being marketed on a minor sustainable aspect.

The Neo-artisan

As opposed to the term artisan, for embracing a new economy and its consumer, I will be referring to the neo-artisan throughout the text. To help put a definition on the new economy, I draw on Scott's framing: 'The leading edges of growth and innovation in the contemporary economy are made up of sectors such as high-technology industry, neo artisanal manufacturing, business and financial services, cultural-products industries (including the media), and so on, and that these sectors in aggregate constitute a "new economy"' (2006, p. 3).

Whilst artisanal production is concerned with the creation of a consumable or functional object with a high level of material, ingredient and process knowledge (Upbin, 2013), the neo-artisan is concerned with this production and consumption within the new economy. Where culture is concerned the producer who creates the cheapest item is not necessarily the most competitive as the consumer within the new economy seeks to consumer objects that have qualitative attributes (Scott, 2006). Based on this, I define the neo-artisan as a person involved in the skilled production of consumable items and functional goods with an interest and skill set embedded in material and process-implicit knowledge, whilst using a broader, unspecialised skill set to understand and cater for the new-economy consumer.

The neo-artisan can be a potter, baker, brewer, glass maker, to name a few. Though the variety of neo-artisans' outputs may seem unrelated at first glance, the new economy consumer of these outputs may be similar, consuming products that all have a shared meaning beyond the object itself: from hand-baked sourdough bread to a small brewer's batch ale to hand-blown whiskey glasses. This type of meaning is something Boström discusses: 'an object that one procures can represent a bridge to another person, to a collective with which one is affiliated, or to a more abstract entity such as an idea, ideal, or imagined community' (2020, p. 270). This meaning can then become social; the consumption of such artisanal goods can be used to position the consumer in relation to others.

So, how do you begin to judge the value of the artisanal or crafted object? Tonkinwise attempts to differentiate the output of designers and artists in *Design as Future Making*: 'Designers, as opposed to artists, aim not to create artefacts as ends unto themselves, but artefacts-as-means. Judging the value of a design means judging the value of what it enables more than the artefact itself, what is done with the thing rather than the thing itself' (2014, p. 203). Craft's position, however, is not entirely design, or art. Its position has been elaborated over time, and though not the focus of this chapter, it is necessary to acknowledge the complexity of craft's positioning. Instead of understanding the value of a design object in terms of what you can do with it, as Tonkinwise states, we may look to defining the value of any object for how it connects us to people. Adamson writes that objects are not ends unto themselves, not made to be props to put on the mantlepiece, but instead they serve as a material connection between people: 'every object represents a potential social connection. By better understanding the tangible things in our lives, we better understand our fellow humans' (2018, p. 8).

Neo-artisans create artefacts-as-means whose value goes beyond 'what is done with the thing' (Tonkinwise, 2014, p. 203) because the new economy consumer is interested in the values associated with where the product has come from and who has made it. Take, for example, buying a handmade item of clothing from a local maker. Beyond the item's explicit quality as a usable garment, its purchase and use may also indicate that the consumer is interested in its additional meaning as environmentally conscious, as supporting slow fashion and the local economy.

At what point is this meaning, and value of an object or product, understood? Perhaps there is some implicit understanding gained through the consumer's direct relationship with the object or product, but value that derives from knowing how it is made, who made it, where it came from, the story behind the inspiration, and so on, typically needs to be conveyed through a narrative. The use of marketing is a way to convey this narrative.

More than just a sales tactic, marketing can also benefit the artisan who wishes to educate the consumer of the ethical position of their product, and on ethical consumption, to ensure the consumer can make informed decisions rather than relying on an assumption that because it is craft, it must be a good, moral and sustainable product. As mentioned in the theoretical background section of this chapter, this association is discussed by Britton and Margetts: 'The idea of crafts … is based on a number of myths. The most pervasive and historicist of these is that the making of objects by hand is, in some sense, a moral activity' (1993, p. 7). But the use of marketing, especially via social media, can provide opportunities to develop a narrative of the artisanal product and the artisan; to allow the consumer to decide on the moral position of the practice and product. The following section discusses this in further detail, with a case study of my own glass making practice.

NOTES FROM THE FIELD: TURNING MY GLASS PRACTICE TOWARDS SUSTAINABILITY THROUGH TECHNOLOGY

As mentioned above, artisans making products and objects that have meaning can benefit from new economy consumer interests. For designers, producers and consumers, the sustainability and environmental impact of products is becoming more important. There is an understanding that craft and 'slow' production are an antidote to the climate crisis caused by industrialisation and mass manufacturing (Adamson, 2013). This position is important, but some artisanal production cannot easily defend itself against the accusation that it is highly energy inefficient. For example, hand making a drinking glass takes three kilns heated between 500 and 1200°C. It is an energy-guzzling making method. Recognising this problem, however, allows artisanal glass to become a space to explore key problems in the relationship between the ethical and aesthetic dimensions of neo-artisanal practice.

Within an artisanal craft practice like glass making, there can be a tendency to view the artisan as opposing modern industry and consumer culture. However, it may be a hindrance to continue to perpetuate this standpoint. The binary discourses of craft/automation, artisanal/industrial may be too simplified. A simplified view like this, emanating from crafts people themselves, or their consumers, could constrain artisans' ventures into the use of new technologies and contemporary modes of production. This belief that craft is antithetical to industry is something Glenn Adamson discusses in *The Invention of Craft*: 'craft needs to be liberated from this disengaged position, in which it stands in opposition to the disruptive forces of change' (2013, p. xxiii).

However, there is a space in which craft can still be grounded in a rich historical tradition without opposing innovation. 'Craft's claim to cultural memory can be retained, without fixing it as backward looking or conservative' (Adamson, 2013, p. xiii). One concern would be whether or not the neo-artisanal sphere is an area for the romantic veneration of traditional craft practices, or is it instead an area where craft practitioners can innovate and evolve their practice? If the latter is the case, and I believe it can be, will the audience and consumer's notion of craft authenticity change if there is an introduction of digital manufacturing processes? If the latter can be realised, then craft can truly be enabled to function in the contemporary realm, constantly challenging methodologies and narratives, thus being able to 'look after itself'.

Source: Author's own (2018). 3D printed vortex whiskey tumbler prototype and glass blowing mould positive [3D print].

Figure 5.1   3D printed vortex whiskey tumbler prototype and glass blowing mould positive

Through my own experience as a neo-artisan, I have found that exploring and embracing the use of digital manufacturing in small batch production can have a substantial effect on its efficiency and sustainability. As an example, I have turned to mass production glass blowing systems as an influence for how I model my small batch production methods and processes. In a similar way to how metal moulds are used in mass automated glass blowing factories, I too create handmade moulds for use in my small workshop. Rather than being controlled robotically, however, in my small batch production methods, the process of gathering, shaping and blowing the glass remains firmly a human-powered action.

I first create my object design using computer aided design (CAD). The object is 3D printed, and from this 3D print a plaster cast is made. Finally, molten glass is blown into the plaster mould to create the finished glass piece (Figures 5.1 and 5.2). Not only does the 3D print act as a prototype of the object and help to ensure client satisfaction before entering into the energy hungry glass blowing production stage, it is also that from which the glass blown mould is made. This process reduces the amount of time spent in the production stage, offering a bespoke small batch service to my consumers; something which a large-scale factory would not be able to offer so easily.

Source: Author's own (2018). Vortex whiskey tumbler [handmade glass vessel].

Figure 5.2   Finished vortex whiskey tumbler

More than just helping to ensure that the consumer has an accurate expectation of what the finished object will be like, this bespoke prototyping service enables the consumer to build up a relationship with the object, and perhaps even co-author it. If the consumer has an invested interest in the object from this early stage of the production, it gains an emotional durability that assists in ensuring its extended lifespan due to the care given to it when using the object. I will further discuss this emotional durability later in the chapter. Sharing this progress on social media platforms equally serves as a marketing tool, with reach to a wider audience, who can see the development of the piece in real time. In sharing accounts of the multiple stages of my process, honestly communicating the experimental or early-stage nature of the work, I have garnered much audience support, with comments posted indicating that the audience were willing it to succeed (Figure 5.3).

Source: Author's own [@lauraquinndesign] (30 November 2020).
'600 glass rods cut to 115mm ready to be flame worked and inserted to a framework made up of 900' [photograph]. Instagram: https://www.instagram.com/p/CBfppUJHJI-/.

Figure 5.3   Instagram post discussing an early stage of the process

3D printing, laser cutting, and water jet cutting are no longer new manufacturing technologies; they are contemporary technologies used in a broad range of sectors, including craft. Without the support of consumers, in respect of this exploration in digital innovation, craft may be jeopardised when the time comes for it to embrace newer technologies, such as virtual reality. Rather than the craft producer and consumer just being custodians of heritage, they must also become pioneers of evolution, if craft is to establish a robust right to exist going forward.

Product qualities in which the new consumer is interested, such as those of sustainability, need to be considered beyond the question of mere marketing tactics. In order to make our practice more sustainable as neo-artisans, the objects we produce and consume need to be viewed in a holistic way. As neo-artisans, we cannot think of ourselves as exempt from the responsibilities of transparency. It is neither ethical nor helpful for neo-artisans to lure the new economy consumer in, via their interests in the inherent qualities of artisanal products purely through the adoption of a marginal and insincere sustainability-related framing, such as in the use of recycled packaging. Nor can we continue to rely on craft's moral public profile, assumed as ethically good, to consider ourselves sustainable. Fortunately, the neo-artisan is able to deploy a varied skill set and identity and, if supported by the consumer, is able to make and effectively communicate sustainability-related interventions across the many stages of the product life cycle.

In *New Materialism: How Our Relationship with the Material World Can Change for the Better*, Andrew Simms and Ruth Potts criticise the half-hearted effort of producers to be more environmentally conscious, via the latter's inclusion of only minor sustainable elements to their product:

> The green movement, which works to save conditions for life on the planet, has perversely been made synonymous with a rejection of the material world [...] but, scared of their own shadows, many environmentalists instead took to preaching a green variant of consumerism – it was still about the glitz, and the label, but your Jimmy Choo shoes might have a percentage of recycled content in their soles. (2012, pp. 9–10)

As neo-artisans we are multi-skilled and well equipped to design and make objects that hold better claims to sustainability because we can implement sustainable design tactics at all stages of our small batch production, from design conception to production, distribution, use and end of life. It is vital that we understand the needs of sustainable economies, and design objects and processes accordingly, as well as articulating narratives that guide the audience and consumer to embrace new technologies in traditional craft. We need to encourage the audience's acceptance of the use of mass manufacturing methods in small batch production. By embracing this crossover, by both audience and maker, craft design can evolve, and thrive, in a sustainable way within neo-artisanal manufacturing.

Identity

Identity is a central influence in the production and consumption of artisanal goods. It can be profitable when a selling point of an object is that it was hand-crafted by an artisan with a specified, singular identity, such as master glass blower, master brewer and so on. The notion that the maker has taken years to master their craft imbues the product with a higher emotional value than products made in a non-autonomous, high-production setting. Richard A. Peterson (2005) even goes as far as to say that the value of an object isn't judged by its quality, but the authenticity of the artist, and that in order to understand the value of the object we must know the background of the artist.

Equally, an attachment to a singular identity can be a constraint, preventing the exploration of alternative identities better suited to the success of neo-artisanal production in the new economy. A decentralised identity can help in exploring other ways in which a neo-artisanal practice can adapt to a changeable economic climate: 'smaller decentralised units in large-scale networks can react with greater success to complex problems than large, singular, centralized ones. Dinosaurs are not as nimble as shoals of fish' (Klein, 2015, p. 30). In her article, What Design Can and Should Be Doing in the 21st Century: Ten Proposals, Amelia Klein (2015) states that in a world that is increasingly interconnected, successful artisans can adapt, and master many tools and processes. There is a duality in this, however. Having to adapt and master new skills in order to thrive in the new economy must also converge with the audience and consumer acceptance of just that. We need the audience to distance themselves from the romantic, nostalgic notion of the maker as a sole worker, labouring in their workshop. Rather, they must instead see the maker as a neo-artisan interlaced in the broader manufacturing and technological community, embracing change and innovation and including it in what they produce and how they produce it.

It is worth noting that developing modes of production based on technology and consumer demand for culture is not exclusive to neo-artisans, but is something that artisans throughout history have needed to consider (Earle, 2018). The following section will outline how audience education can be helpful in supporting neo-artisanal claims to authenticity, whilst simultaneously engaging audiences with an enhanced understanding of technological advances.

Audience Education Through Marketing: Maintaining the Nostalgic, Embracing the New

The question is, how do neo-artisans guide their audience to support and embrace the 'new' whilst maintaining the identity of their product as authentic (as steeped in culture); the intrinsic properties that this new consumer values as important? The answer may lie in what Richard E. Ocejo (2017) terms 'service teaching' in *Masters of Craft: Old Jobs in the New Urban Economy*.

Service teaching involves not only the delivery of a product or a service, but a level of teaching alongside it. With a skill in narration and persuasion, the neo-artisan can bring the consumer on the entire product or service journey; educating them, and developing their understanding and awareness of the process, and the decisions made along the way. This narration may not only give the consumer, and audience, the feeling that they are involved, but most importantly, it creates a process and product that is emotionally durable, in which the consumer and audience can invest. If used correctly, the outcome can be that the audience and consumer may come to support techniques that move away from the nostalgia of the traditional, and be enabled to embrace the 'new', precisely because of the consumer's involvement in the process.

This method of neo-artisan and consumer collaborative engagement also builds the notion of authenticity and meaning in respect of the product. I stress the word 'notion' as authenticity in itself can be complex to understand and design, as discussed in the theoretical background section of this chapter. The idea of designing authenticity itself seems paradoxical. If authenticity is designed, fuelled with agenda, reshaped to suit different audiences, can it really be authentic? Yet in developing a narrative of the process and product through service teaching, we are in fact designing authenticity into a process and product from the vantage point of the audience and consumer.

Traditionally made craft objects and products already have authenticity because of the process though which they are made, having historical lineage and a labour-intensive nature. Neo-artisans must work hard to establish such qualities in the new identity of the work they produce if they are using digital technologies in combination with the hand. Without this narrative, the introduction of contemporary innovations and technologies into both process and product may jeopardise their claims to authenticity, heritage and culture, and invite a conflict with established nostalgic views of craft. By involving the audience within the narrative process, the product grows in emotional investment. In *Emotionally Durable Design*, Jonathan Chapman (2009) discusses how this emotional investment can be used as a design tactic to make products more sustainable, but also to design and influence the consumer-product relationship.

One example of service teaching for building a design narrative and a sense of authenticity in my own work is my use of social media platforms as a narration tool. This narration tool has the advantages of being chronological, allowing audience interaction. In other words, the audience can share their views on the product or process in real time. Perhaps the audience involvement can even influence my design decisions, allowing them to co-author the piece to a certain extent. By using service teaching, I expand my audience's understanding of my identity, of the entire glass making process. It is not about mastering glass blowing, and I want them to know that. Crucially, this tactic gives autonomy to the process, and embeds a greater value in the finished piece. Figure 5.4 shows another example from my own practice, where I use social media to add narratives to my work. This sharing of information provides a 'service teaching' function, as discussed by Ocejo (2017), but it also enables the audience to understand that the process is time consuming, well considered and labour intensive, all qualities associated with traditional and authentic craft methods, despite the use of rapid prototyping.

Source: Author's own [@lauraquinndesign] (16 June 2020). 'Plans for my new whiskey tumbler are well underway. This tumbler has a cork base that it pops into' [photograph]. Instagram: https://www.instagram.com/p/CBfppUJHJI-/.

Figure 5.4   *Emotionally durable design through service teaching and narration*

According to Sennett, 'the good craftsman is a poor salesman, absorbed in doing something well, unable to explain the value of what he or she is doing' (2008, p. 117) , but social media now offers the modern craftsman or neo-artisan the opportunity to explain the value of what they are doing. As mentioned earlier in this chapter, a limited understanding of the dynamic identity of a skilled artisan could threaten their ability to exist in a highly competitive market, but the ability to use social media to directly reach their audience gives artisans the opportunity to promote their work and themselves through narrative that shows off their dynamic skill set and identity. Doreen Jakob (2012, p. 134) claims that there is a transformation taking place within some creative occupations, where the traditional agent-artist system is no being longer used. Rather, the artisans themselves are responsible for their own showcasing, distribution and marketing. This now results in artisans using highly sophisticated marketing techniques to promote their products, where such artisans are becoming strongly influenced, and enabled, by web-based technology and social media (Jakob, 2012, p. 135).

CONCLUSION

Traditional makers have a central role to play in neo-artisanal production. Only by maintaining tradition and embracing the new along with the many identities it demands will makers survive in the new economy as neo-artisans. They will no longer be 'looking after something that can't look after itself' as Grayson Perry (2005) stated. Makers will need to pull from a variety of skill sets associated with other professions, such as project manager, salesperson, storyteller, designer, sociologist, anthropologist, engineer, technologist and writer. The identity of a modern artisan, with both specialist and unspecialised skills, needs to be embraced if the maker is to adapt to meeting the demands that the new consumer places on neo-artisanal products, particularly when innovations are necessary or appropriate.

The audience and consumer must engage with this fluidity in the neo-artisan's identity, and divest themselves of the nostalgic idea of the traditional crafts-person, working alone in their workshop, as the anchoring of historically grounded claims to authenticity. One way that this can be achieved is through narrative platforms, such as social media, where service education can assure the audience that both the process and product retain the authenticity, care, precision and expertise associated with traditional craft methods.

This chapter comes from a personal perspective, supported by my own research into ideas of narration, marketing, sustainability, audience education and artisanal identities. Providing my own work as an example in the use of social media to market artisanal practice, I have looked to ground this analysis in a real-world case study. Given the rapid growth of online marketing capabilities via a proliferation of social media platforms, future research may usefully explore the role played by such marketing within the context of the neo-artisanal sector. Further use of case study analysis would help us further understand the techniques and tools used by neo-artisans in their online marketing. Qualitative research on the consumer of neo-artisanal goods, specifically those who have been targeted within neo-artisanal social media marketing, might give an indication as to how successful efforts to communicate authenticity and to offer service education in respect of the product and process might be in practice.

The craftsperson, whether traditional or neo-artisanal, needs to sustain a sense of their relevance if their products are to be consistently in demand, whether that be from a gallery audience or a user in their home. Beyond claims to heritage and nostalgia, artisanal craft can look after itself by appealing to, and exploring the needs of, the new economy consumer. In this way, neo-artisans can produce work that won't be in jeopardy of failing this test of relevance, precisely because they are producing work in a field that can 'look after itself' (Perry, 2005). The commonly constructed binary of heritage custodian versus pioneer can be deconstructed; these need not be mutually exclusive. By understanding the meanings, emotional qualities, and environmental impact of neo-artisanal practices and products, along with consumer relationships, the neo-artisan can prosper and continue to be relevant precisely through their deployment of contemporary and future technologies and processes. The neo-artisan must secure an identity around both elements of this outmoded binary if they are to continue to be relevant.

REFERENCES

Adamson, G. (2013). *The Invention of Craft*. Bloomsbury Publishing.

Adamson, G. (2018). *Fewer, Better Things: The Hidden Wisdom of Objects*. Bloomsbury Publishing.

Boström, M. (2020). The Social Life of Mass and Excess Consumption. *Environmental Sociology*, *6*(3), 268–78. https://doi.org/10.1080/23251042.2020.1755001.

Britton, A., & Margetts, M. (1993). *The Raw and the Cooked: New Work in Clay in Britain*, [exhibition catalogue]. Oxford, United Kingdom: Museum of Modern Art.

Cardoso, R. (2010). Craft Versus Design: Moving Beyond a Tired Dichotomy. In G. Adamson (ed.), *The Craft Reader* (pp. 321–32). Berg Publishers.

Chapman, J. (2009). *Emotionally Durable Design*. Earthscan.

Earle, T. (2018). Artisans, Technologies, and Consumers: A Political Economy Approach to Crafts Specialization. In I. Miloglav, & J. Vuković (eds), *Artisans Rule: Product Standardization and Craft Specialization in Prehistoric Society* (pp.1–19). Cambridge Scholars Publishing.

Greenhalgh, P. (1997). The History of Craft. In P. Dormer (ed.), *The Culture of Craft* (pp. 20–53). Manchester University Press.

Hartmann B. J., & Ostberg, J. (2013). Authenticating by Re-Enchantment: The Discursive Making of Craft Production. *Journal of Marketing Management*, *29*(7–8), 882–911. https://doi.org/10.1080/0267257X.2012.732596.

Huong Nguyen, T. T., Yang, Z., Nguyen, N., Johnson, L. W., & Khanh Cao, T. (2019). Greenwash and Green Purchase Intention: The Mediating Role of Green Skepticism. *Sustainability*, *11*(9), article 2653. https://doi.org/10.3390/su11092653.

Jakob, D. (2012). Crafting Your Way Out of the Recession? New Craft Entrepreneurs and the Global Economic Downturn. *Cambridge Journal of Regions, Economy and Society*, *6*(1), 127–40.https://doi.org/10.1093/cjres/rss022.

Klein, A. (2015). What Design Can and Should Be Doing in the 21st Century: Ten Proposals. In A. Klein, & M. Kries (eds), *Making Africa: A Continent of Contemporary Design* (pp. 26–33). Vitra Design Museum.

Lyon, T. P., & Montgomery, A. W. (2015). The Means and End of Greenwash. *Organization and Environment, 28*(2), 223–49. https://doi.org/10.1177/1086026615575332.

Ocejo, R. E. (2017). *Masters of Craft: Old Jobs in the New Urban Economy.* Princeton University Press.

Perry, G. (2005). A Refuge for Artists Who Play It Safe. *The Guardian,* 5 March. https://www.theguardian.com/artanddesign/2005/mar/05/art.

Peterson, R. A. (2005). In Search of Authenticity. *Journal of Management Studies, 42*(5), 1083–98. https://doi.org/10.1111/j.1467-6486.2005.00533.x.

Scott, A. J. (2006). Creative Cities: Conceptual Issues and Policy Questions. *Journal of Urban Affairs, 28*(1), 1–17. https://doi.org/10.1111/j.0735-2166.2006.00256.x.

Sennett, R. (2008). *The Craftsman.* Yale University Press.

Simms, A., & Potts, R. (2012). *New Materialism: How Our Relationship with the Material World Can Change for the Better.* Bread Print and Roses.

Tonkinwise, C. (2014). Design Away. In S. Yelavich, & B. Adams (eds), *Design as Future Making* (pp. 198–214). Bloomsbury Publishing.

Upbin, B. (2013). Artisanal Manufacturing: Creating Jobs to Produce Things in America Again. *Forbes Magazine,* 11 December. https://www.forbes.com/sites/bruceupbin/2013/12/11/artisanal-manufacturing-creating-jobs-to-produce-things-in-america-again/#:~:text=The%20term%20'artisanal%20manufacturing'%20can,human%20hands%20in%20the%20process.

6. Innovation in craft: creating new value through art

Giacomo Magnani and Laura Bresolin

INTRODUCTION

Murano Island and its artifacts have a significant role in the history of the glass industry. It is important to clarify that firms dwelling in Murano are involved in the creation of the so-called "artistic glass," which represents only a part of the whole industry. The artistic glass niche (Porter, 1985) is a very old typical example of "Made in Italy" (Colombo, 2007) if we think that the sixth most ancient firm in the world is the glassmaker Barovier & Toso (Coad, 2018), which has been appreciated for centuries by people around the world.

In many homes around the globe, it is common to find artistic glass, such as chandeliers, vases, glasses and small sculptures, very often created on Murano. This evidence is also confirmed by the numbers that still show its current diffusion: of the almost 165 million euros in turnover produced by the Murano system in 2013, as much as 40 percent – around 66 million euros – was derived from foreign sales. However, the value of exports has decreased from over 88 million euros estimated for 2008 to 65.6 million for 2014, a loss of 22.7 million euros (which becomes over 31 million if the data are adjusted for inflation, i.e., in real terms) (Confartigianato, 2015, pp. 88–9).

In fact, the state of the art of glass production, which made the small island famous all over the world, today reports a complex scenario in a deep crisis. Insofar as Murano glassworks are concerned, at the end of the 1990s, the tax breaks that reduced energy costs were cancelled, opening a period of economic difficulties for businesses facing a sudden increase in production costs. About 37 percent of companies did not know how to react to this factor, and many companies (27%) responded by reducing their profit margins or by reducing staff (19%). However, very few glass factories have looked for alternative strategies; 12 percent have tried to react to the increase in the cost of energy with entrepreneurial proactiveness by varying their strategies and differentiating production (Confartigianato, 2015, pp. 88–9).

This chapter illustrates how the traditional skills of craftsmen, which characterize this niche, thanks to the contamination with "high" art, can lead to a competitive advantage even under adverse conditions. In other words, the role of artists involved in the production of glass artifacts, which make them artworks, could add new energies to the traditional resources of this industry, generating value for the market. For this reason, we chose to analyze the case of Berengo Studio, where the visionary entrepreneur Adriano Berengo introduced an aspect of innovation, bringing back to light the relationship between craft and art, an element of the past tradition. What Berengo Studio accomplished in the artistic glass industry demonstrates how differentiation and innovation can originate from an entrepreneurial idea based on art. Despite some interpretations in the literature, craft and art are both parts of the greater cultural industry (Gray & McGuinnan, 1993); however, after the Industrial Revolution, these two fields were divided between "art thinkers" and "art makers" (Sennett, 2008).

This chapter shows how the strategic choice implemented by Berengo could be assimilated with the choices of some agricultural firms that reintroduced as a form of innovative crops old "heirloom" types of vegetables grown with traditional and often disused methods called *traditiovation* (a portmanteau of *tradition* and *innovation*) (Cannarella & Piccioni, 2011).

A BRIEF HISTORY OF THE SECTOR

Glass first made its appearance around 4000 BC in Egypt, where some of the oldest known objects of this material originated, such as simple vases and decorated ampoules, which were found in the tombs of the pharaohs. Thanks to Phoenician merchants, glass spread outside the country of production. In the 1st century BC in Syria, the most revolutionary and simple tool was invented: the blowing cane. The consequent technique of "blowing" replaced the previous technique of "pouring" and remained almost unchanged over the centuries, representing one of the fundamental stages in the history of glass art. After the conquest of the eastern shores of the Mediterranean, the Roman Empire played a decisive role in the diffusion of glass and the improvement of its production techniques.

Some centuries later, the relations of the Serenissima with the Orient had a fundamental role in the birth of the Venetian glass industry. The oldest trace in the lagoon known today is a Venetian document dating back to AD 982 (Gasparetto, 1958), in which the name of Domenico Florianus appears as "glass maker", while the news relating to citizen glassmakers became more frequent starting from 1279. In 1291, all the Venetian glassworks were moved to Murano to limit the risk of fires in the city.

During the Renaissance, in Venice, the glassblowers started reorganizing their production in a way that resembles industrial production today. It is interesting to note that this happened 200 years before a similar revolution took place in European ceramics and porcelain factories.

In 1441, the statute that regulates the life of glassmakers and their guild was written in the vernacular. The Murano glassmakers improved and refined glass production and around 1450 invented crystal. In order to protect the primacy of Venice in the processing of the precious artifacts and luxury glass, Murano glassmakers were forbidden to expatriate, but despite this regulation, in the 16th century, several glass furnaces arose in all European countries.

With the Arts and Crafts Movement and during the Art Deco and Bauhaus periods, the medium gained popularity. There are several examples of artists using glass, like Gallé, Daum, Tiffany, Lalique and Argy-Rousseau. At the end of the 19th century, glass factories increasingly employed designers to create new series and new designs to translate into glass, but it was not imaginable that autonomous artists could individually create experimental artworks (Vanderstuckken, 2016). It was only in the 1950s that glass master Egidio Costantini, together with the visionary Peggy Guggenheim, invited such artists as Picasso, Corbusier, Fontana, Braque, Chagall, and many others to collaborate with Muranese glass masters. This initiative encouraged several others on the island of Murano, but over the years, none of the furnaces, except for Berengo Studio, devoted their production exclusively to art in glass.

A STRATEGIC ANALYSIS: THE INDUSTRY'S MAIN CHARACTERISTICS

From the qualitative point of view, we can recognize some relevant aspects of this niche industry:

1. *Craft sector.* Firms are primarily craft firms if we consider both the high degree of handmade output, and the traditional materials and methods (Metcalf, 1997), the production process, and the structure of the firms belonging to this sector, which are almost the same as the ones of the past. Strange as it may seem, the furnaces where glass is made today are still very similar to those of the past, with the difference that the original heat source, timber, has been replaced by gas.
2. *Creative sector.* The role of human resources, as we will see, is strategic. Creative resources are more important than financial ones (McAuley, 1999). Human competencies are as essential as in the past. On average, there are 4.2 employees in a glass factory, divided as follows: 1.4 are the masters, 0.8 the servants, 0.3 the young helpers, 1.6 the employees and workers, and 0.1 the men at night who prepare the mixture

(Confartigianato, 2015). The role of human resources is central (McCray, 1999).

3. *Small size of firms.* Firms operating in this niche focused more on quality connected with their creative resources rather than on quantity, which is why there are mainly small enterprises or micro firms.
4. *Traditional products.* In 40 percent of glass factories, the most wide-spread products are sculptures and lighting fixtures, followed by other objects and tableware. As for the processing style, half of the companies adopt both the classic and the modern styles, but glass factories that have abandoned the classic to dedicate themselves exclusively to modern-style products are less common, only 18.6 percent.
5. *Deep connection with the heritage of the Venetian lagoon.* As craft firms competing in many traditional sectors in Italy – the traditional "Made in Italy" (Cologni, 2007) – are typically linked with the cultural tradition and institutions of the territories where they operate, even Murano's glass-makers are influenced by the relevant cultural context of Venice, the city of the Biennale, museums, exhibitions, and the oldest film festival (the first movie was projected in 1932[1]), and for this reason we can assert that Venice is the natural context where creative entrepreneurs can grow in the border territory where craft touches art (Colombo, 2007).

The great number of small and micro firms does not allow for public data about the finances of the firms' industry. The only available study on the Murano industry comes from Confartigianato in collaboration with Consorzio Promovetro Murano, which analyzes the period 2005–14. Considering the companies of the glass sector in its broadest meaning, including artistic glass, the 436 Venetian active companies at the end of June 2014 represent about 9 percent of all Italian companies in the sector (just over 4,900). The second-largest province is Naples, with about 170 companies and almost 6 percent of national representativeness, while the third position is occupied by Milan with 231 companies and 4.7 percent of the national total.

However, if we analyze Venice under the artistic glass industry production, with its total of 314 active companies in 2014, the city is predominant, with 30 percent of the production of the whole Italian territory (Confartigianato, 2015, p. 33).

A SECTOR IN CONTRACTION

The glass sector overall, in the period 2005–08, including artistic glass, faced a decrease of 5 percent of registered companies, which happened almost exclusively from 2007 to 2008, data that prefigure the advent of a difficult period. The following four-year period, from 2008 to 2011, represents the worst moment for the sector, corresponding to the first phase of the economic crisis, which was thought to be the hardest, with a loss of active businesses of 8.8 percent.

The crisis became even stronger from 2011 to 2013, causing the closure of another 30 active companies (Confartigianato, 2015). But data show that the subcategory of artistic glass has had a less abrupt decrease compared to the macro sector. In fact, according to the data provided by the Confartigianto study, despite the crisis, the total loss in 2013 was limited to 4.4 percent, compared to the beginning of the crisis, reaching a peak of 5.6 percent in comparison with the 1990s. If so, it could be said that the system of artistic glass not only better resisted the crisis but reacted rather well.

Reasons for the Crisis

But what were and are the main reasons for the sector crisis? To briefly summarize some of the main critical issues, we have to take into consideration the complexity of the production process and the competition of artifacts coming from abroad.

Cost of energy

One of the starting points of the origins of the crisis began at the end of the 1990s, with a cut in the incentives on gas that until then had guaranteed that factories would pay energy at 40 percent of the market price. Since then, energy costs have become the main expense, even surpassing that of the staff payroll (Confartigianato, 2015).

Difficulty in finding a workforce

Young people, who traditionally saw an opportunity in the furnace job, have stopped considering employment in glass factories in recent years due to the evident decrease in the number of employees and the increased number of factories in difficulty. Therefore, the sector is facing a lack of generational change and the consequent progressive aging of the workforce.

Linked to this aspect is the professional training of new employees, which has never brought the desired results, even with the relaunch of the Abate Zanetti Glass School, probably because the factors mentioned above have in some way influenced the possible school enrollments.

The Abate Zanetti Glass School is heir to an ancient institution known as the School of Drawing for Glassmakers, founded in 1862 by Abate Vincenzo Zanetti; today, it aims to promote Murano glassmaking and heritage with courses held by some of the best Glass Masters of Murano, renowned around the world. In 2016, the technic-technological high school also opened, with a specialization in graphics and communication and managed by Liceo Parini (high school). In the spring of 2020, the city council approved the donation of the Abate Zanetti Glass School under a nine-year free concession to the Fondazione Musei Civici di Venezia, of which the Murano Glass Museum is part. As Chiara Squarcina, director of the Glass Museum, states, this move will create a glass training center, the only one of its kind in Europe, which will be able to make use of the Murano production tradition, achieving, in the specific field, world-class excellence.

Sudden adaptation to environmental legislation

Until 1998, the issue of environmental and safety rules at work had been neglected throughout Venice, but from this date onward, businesses had to comply with regulations, compelling them to adapt within a few years to adjustments that had never been made before, significantly increasing not only their costs but also the workload due to the numerous requirements (Confartigianato, 2015, pp. 51–2).

Low-cost foreign products

Last but not least, in the late 1990s, an actual invasion of cheap glass products, mainly from China, occurred, flooding the shops of Italian dealers due to the much lower prices and lower quality that afforded higher margins and which often, to the eyes of the tourists, do not appear clearly different from original Murano glass production.

This is typical not only in the case of the glass industry but also is quite pervasive in many craft sectors where, as Fillis (2004) posits, the real craft products "must compete with both domestic and foreign competition where many products appear hand crafted even though mass produced via technological processes."

STRATEGIC RESOURCES

Although much of the literature on the resources-based view is focused on large firms, as Barney et al. (2001) posit, we can recognize the strategic role of resources and competencies in also obtaining a competitive advantage for small enterprises. This is particularly evident in the glass sector, where all kinds of resources can be identified (tangible, intangible and human; Grant, 1991).

The firms of this industry base their activities on physical resources, such as furnaces, which are a fundamental component for creating glass products. These plants are quite simple from a technological point of view and remain virtually unchanged from those used in the past.

Even intangible assets, like brand, business history, and trade network, can be recognized as a relevant key for the success of a few of the firms operating in this industry. In addition, human resources, as we said, are central as well, given that the skills of the different levels of craftsmen are fundamental for the final product. These resources, including brand and business history, are quite common in the firms on the isle of Murano but probably not enough to compete in a globalized world, especially when the focus strategy, based on differentiation, needs an increasingly powerful lever to be recognized and desired by customers.

As many micro firms are more conservative than larger ones from the strategic perspective (Storey & Cressy, 1996), those operating in this niche, for the reasons we underlined about products and the methods of production, tend to be quite inertial. Therefore, the real distinctive competencies are represented by managerial skills, which can lead to various innovations. Speaking about micro firms, as posited by literature (see, e.g., Dutta & Errad, 1999; Simpson, 2001), we observe management and ownership coinciding in the so-called one-person-centered firms, so entrepreneurial skills, as underlined, are the main component for the micro firms' success.

Entrepreneurial orientation is characterized by innovation, risk-taking, and proactiveness (Miller, 1983). Entrepreneurial skills are less imitable than others and could be the basis on which new occasions of differentiation are built that can develop other intangible assets like brand and network. Because of these entrepreneurial aspects we decided to study in depth the case of Berengo Studio – their economic success is clearly marked by the employment proxy (starting from seven employees in 1993, the company today has about 35 workers[2]) with acknowledgment obtained at international level from a cultural and social point of view.

BERENGO STUDIO 1989: A GLASS FACTORY THAT INNOVATES AND DIFFERENTIATES THROUGH ART[3]

Small and micro firms are not always easy to observe under a financial lens for lack of data, but one proxy to measure economic success is a firm's growth, evidenced by the Berengo Studio. Economic growth, of course, is not the only target for a cultural enterprise like this – as we will explain later, the cultural scope is quite important too.

Cultural goals are more difficult to measure than economic success. Nevertheless, the success of Berengo Studio is confirmed by the acknowledgment of major artists, institutions, and press reviews, which can be seen as a qualitative evaluation of its cultural performance. After seeing *Glasstress* New York edition,[4] Philippe de Montebello, former director of the Metropolitan Museum of Art in New York, stated, "For hundreds of years, glass has been viewed by some as simply a decorative or functional medium, *Glasstress* [Berengo temporary exhibition] … shatters those notions."

Ian Findlay from *Asian Art News* wrote: "The quality and diversity of the images of the glass sculptures at Berengo serve to reinforce the idea that glass is truly a contemporary material"; Reinhold Ludwig on Art Aurea said about *Glasstress*: "alongside the Biennale in Venice, for the second time, there is also plenty of art made of glass in this city on the lagoon … Berengo prophesizes [*sic*] the imminent arrival of a new era." Other articles and interviews continued in major magazines and newspapers such as *The New York Times, The Economist* and *Financial Times*.

Further to this, more than 400 artists who have been successful in their attempt to master glass recognize the stunning glass artworks at Berengo Studio. One of these is the star artist Ai Weiwei. On the occasion of his visit to Murano, he said:

> I think that tradition is like an ocean … humans through these long times struggled to come up with some ideas and skills … which generally get lost when today develops so fast … I am always fascinated by classic ways and from that I can learn a lot and I can apply a new concept, a new language …

Today, many barriers that had imprisoned artistic glass for many years have been broken, but as Berengo says:

> *Glasstress* has become more than an exhibition. It is a kind of cultural movement in the world of glass and art. I would like *Glasstress* to inspire new generations of artists, students and visitors about the importance of traditions and cultural identity and show them how those traditions flourish with new and fresh interpretations … but we are still at the beginning of this glass revolution. (Klotz, 2019)

The Entrepreneurial Approach: How It All Started

Adriano Berengo, although being a real Venetian, by coincidence found himself on the Murano "glass kingdom" in the early 1980s. Returning from the United States and seeing it for the first time under a different light, he was dazzled by its magic – he did not imagine that shortly thereafter, he would become one of the main actors on the legendary island of glass. He had the opportunity to start working as a shop assistant in a traditional glass showroom, selling glass artifacts like drinking glasses *à la façon de Venise*, vases, chandeliers, and glass clowns coming from the adjacent furnace to wealthy international tourists. These categories of products represented and still represent, in many cases, the most common items sold on the island.

With a past as a radio telegraphist on commercial ships and a Ph.D. in comparative literature in the U.S.A. that saw him in the role of a teacher for several years, he discovered an inborn entrepreneurial nature and quickly assumed the directorship of that showroom. It was immediately clear to him that those glass products could not represent the glorious tradition of Murano. Murano was taking advantage of its past to sell decorative glass objects to well-off tourists, thanks to its legendary reputation, but the artifacts had not aesthetically evolved over time, with the sole exception of sporadic examples of glass art and design like Venini and Barovier & Toso, but no firm specialized exclusively in the contemporary interpretation of glassmaking. Berengo started thinking about how to elevate the material and revamp the image of the island. The inspiration came from The American Studio Glass Movement, but primarily from Peggy Guggenheim's experimentations in the 1960s. In fact, together with glass master Egidio Costantini, she invited such artists as Picasso, Chagall and Ernst to bring their contemporary approach to the world of glass. With Guggenheim's patronage, these artists were allowed to break the barriers that so far had confined glass to a traditional decorative and functional role.

Adriano Berengo decided he wanted to continue what Peggy Guggenheim had begun. In the late 1980s, he founded Berengo Studio, a glass furnace on the island of Murano, with one goal: to bring contemporary artists and glass-blowers together to produce works of art in glass, dreaming of initiating a new glass renaissance for Murano.

The initial phases were quite difficult, mainly because of cultural resistance to this kind of innovation. As Berengo stated:

> It is necessary to make an introduction. Nowadays we take for granted the contemporary approach to artistic glass, but at the beginning there was a lot of skepticism: artists had to face the physical barriers due to the undeniable limitations of the material, but mostly mental barriers. Glass, especially Murano glass, at the end of the 1980s was anything but a common material for contemporary art. It had a patina of kitsch and decorative stereotype, with only a few exceptions. The first major difficulty I had to face was to make artists understand that together we could break those barriers.

Innovation in Products and Processes

It is important to present a short overview of glass processing and artwork creation because it is common to underestimate the complexity of its production process. Upstream there is the mixture, the set of materials from which the glass will be fused: 70 percent silica sand to which is added the *fondente* (i.e., the soda), to lower its temperature and make it suitable for being processed. Limestone is added to prevent the glass from opacifying on the surface, and nitrate to facilitate the exit of the bubbles.

The mixture is prepared by specialized workers during the night so that the master will find the material ready for processing the next morning. The mixture thus composed is poured into the refractory crucibles where melting takes place at a temperature of 1,400°C, which is gradually reduced to 800°C, with the fire in direct contact with the crucibles, to give the glass the pastiness suitable for processing. This preparation phase lasts 12 hours.

The whole process is powered by gas, which is used in large quantities and, as described at the beginning of the chapter, constitutes a fixed cost of great impact on the balance sheets of the furnaces. Once fusion has taken place, it is possible to take a certain amount of incandescent paste, for example, with the blowing pipe, and start the processing by adding material taken from the oven until it reaches the desired size.

Three figures are involved in the processing. In order of importance, they are *serventin, servants* – assistants – and the master who is responsible for creating the object with the help of the assistants. This configuration, with some possible variations, constitutes in each furnace the production area called the *piazza* (square), composed of at least one crucible and the tools necessary for processing. The Berengo furnace uses up to three *piazze* (squares), depending on the amount of work mainly connected with the preparation of an exhibition.

The formed piece then necessarily needs to cool slowly in an annealing oven at a decreasing temperature to prevent the object from breaking easily. The cooling time depends on the glass mass composing the piece; it can last from a minimum of four hours to even, astonishingly, a month for full sculptures in larger sizes. The production has thus come to an end, and the second processing with the cold piece can begin in areas dedicated to cutting, grinding, sandblasting, decorating, painting and other procedures on the cold and solid piece.

Regarding an overview of the production costs in a traditional glassworks, more than half comprise direct costs, such as energy, which alone represents 27 percent of the total, and staff, which, added to the first, make for half of the total costs. Raw materials cost an additional 22 percent. Environmental requirements constitute at least 9 percent, due to the fact that Murano is located in an extremely delicate area from an ecological point of view, the Lagoon of Venice, followed by expenditure on rent. Residual costs are logistics and product marketing (Confartigianato, 2015, p. 87).

But the level of differentiation that could potentially overcome the high costs was, of course, to completely change both the products and the process of thinking about the project, not the way of production of glass objects. From an entrepreneurial point of view, a commercial glass factory optimizes production costs with a clear return on sales and a marketing plan focused on a specific product or group of products. Berengo, instead, has to carry the huge costs of experimentation and lost production. Furthermore, since the mid-2010s, demand for the casting technique has strongly increased, involving even more time in processing and manufacturing since it starts from prototypes and requires molds and maquettes. As highlighted, the investment in marketing, in its broadest definition, is huge and includes events, exhibitions and promotions through specialized communication agencies, advertising, PR activities, catalogue printing with major publishers, and so on.

From the beginning, it was clear to Berengo that his furnace should not be like the others, and he could not be just a producer. He was an editor and promoter and, for some artists, also a gallerist and dealer. But how was he to engage with prominent international artists who perhaps had already established relationships – not to mention exclusivity – with their own galleries and dealers?

Over the years, Berengo gained the trust of many artists as well as an impressive range of collectors, most of them not just collectors of glass art but passionate about contemporary art. Because differentiation and diversification in products and innovation in production was a must, Berengo surely had to compromise in order to follow the higher dream. Still today, for a small number of artists, he acts as a producer, a role that helps to cover the enormous running costs and to focus on and invest in major names.

To widen its reach, in terms of visibility, and to reach international collectors, from the 1990s until about 2015, the Studio participated in several international fairs, such as Sofa Chicago, Sofa New York and Design Miami.

Since the late 1980s, Berengo started inviting visual artists, especially those who had never worked with glass before, to experiment with the material in his glass furnace. This choice was the riskiest but also the most innovative. He distanced himself from the American Studio Glass Movement because, in his opinion, it focused too much on the technique applied to "glass art" while Berengo wanted to bet on "art in glass." This seemingly subtle difference was the keystone of his revolution and represents the first major innovation related to the process.

In fact, a distinctive factor that differentiates Berengo Studio from other more important and established companies was the production approach. The artists were free to make production trials hand-in-hand with some of the most skilled *maestri* of Murano, challenging the medium as well as the glassblowers' skills. After an initial period of difficulties, the artists discovered the potential of glass with no prejudice and great curiosity.

The consequent second major innovation is related to the product. This production choice broke the stereotypes associated for so many years with a material that was perceived essentially as decorative, kitsch and certainly not suitable for contemporary art expressions. Berengo managed to fight the undeniable intrinsic difficulties of glass processing to create fresh contemporary art pieces.

Such freedom inevitably involves a lot of risks. As Berengo states:

> I believe that the most innovative aspect of my approach was to start from tradition
> to create something absolutely contemporary ... talking about specific projects,
> each of them is a new chapter, a new challenge, a new risk. I do not take projects
> because I know how to realize them, I accept to follow a path because the proposal
> is unexpected, original, and can bring a new interpretation of contemporary glass.

One of the first artists that Berengo managed to convince to approach his
furnace to explore the potential of glass was the Austrian Kiki Kogelnik in the
early 1990s. Inspired by her ceramics, Berengo saw the potentiality of transforming her poetics into glass. Again, the intuition was correct: on Murano,
Kogelnik's love for the material accompanied her throughout her artistic
career.

Also, not all the artists accept the "hands" of the glass master on their work
as, unavoidably, there is an interpretation and touch of the glass master. One of
the biggest challenges is to find the right compromise, a continuous mediation
and learning process on both sides.

After Kogelnik, more than 400 artists were producing at Berengo's premises: "I opened Berengo Studio in the late '80s. At the beginning, the number
of artists was limited. I was proposing a completely new approach to glass
whose result was uncertain, as well as the market demand, but the potentialities
were very clear in my mind."

Berengo's entrepreneurial skills led him to think it was necessary to go
further and start to organize a kind of temporary exhibition, which became
a new product in itself and, of course, a method of promotion too. The year
2009 became pivotal for Berengo. To be able to claim that his vision was right,
he needed visibility at a top international and institutional art event. In 2009,
he conceived and organized a contemporary "art in glass" exhibition under the
name *Glasstress* that was eventually selected as one of the official collateral
events of the Venice Biennale of Art. What emerges from the interview is
that the organization of important cultural events and exhibitions managed to
increase the attractiveness of the Studio, highlighted the projects, and we can
say also closed faster and more numerous deals with artists:

> The *Glasstress* Venice exhibition, since its first edition, has always been the occa-
> sion to focus the work of the furnace with a clear objective and timing. This allowed
> [us] to strongly push the activity in terms of the number of artists invited and works
> accomplished. [...] So I can say that since the foundation of Berengo Studio, more
> than 400 artists realized new projects in glass in my furnace.

The critical ability of the Berengo Studio has been continuous improvement
and development. All the old glass techniques were proposed and put at the

disposal of the artists' experimentation, such as lamp-working, blown glass in all its facets, glass sculpture modeling, and the use of *murrine*; in terms of production requirements for art, Berengo understood and over time adapted production to the artists' needs. In fact, during its 30 years of activity, the Studio has introduced techniques including blowing Murano glass into molds, which limited the free interpretations of the masters and translated the original idea faithfully.

Following the growing demand for this technique, together with casting glass, in recent years Berengo has established an extension of his furnace with a glass casting studio, engaging highly skilled young craftsmen from different parts of the world, alongside local masters, to provide extremely innovative and high-quality casting facilities. Today the Studio can realize almost anything in glass to the point that the world-famous contemporary artist Ai Weiwei, on the occasion of his visit to the Studio in December 2017, said, 'I can do a lot! [...] and I understand, you can do anything!' (Watzl, 2019).

> Today I am working on what will be the biggest accomplishment of my studio: a new unconventional and surprising, gigantic chandelier. It is an extremely complex work realized with the use of many glass techniques, which has required a dedicated team for over two years now. It is a shocking new masterpiece by Ai Weiwei. The difficulty is also to continuously invest resources. When I accepted the work, I could not imagine it would take so long to realize. I am sure that any other furnace would have surrendered months ago. (Berengo)

Berengo Studio 1989 has become a must-stop for top contemporary artists who want to experiment with glass. During the 58th Venice Biennale of Arts, three countries and their pavilions, including France, Austria and Italy, exhibited contemporary artwork in glass realized at Berengo Studio.

The Innovation of Promotion: From the 1990s to the Present

Since the early years of its foundation, Berengo Studio was invited to exhibit – or had pieces made in his furnace exhibited – all over the world. The 1990s passed quickly under a great resonance about the experimental approach of a small studio from Murano, who relaunched the use of artistic glass for contemporary art. The attention of the global media was attracted by the novelty of the approach and the resonance of the Murano world presented under a different light, with projects that ranged from small, unusual sculptures to huge installations breaking any possible barrier, physical and mental, concerning the material.

The 2000s consolidated the path, with the Studio also receiving an invitation to exhibit in 2001 at the European Parliament, Brussels (Belgium) and in 2006 at the Pushkin State Museum of Fine Arts, Moscow (Russia) with the exhibition *Handle With Care*, and *A Transparent History: Glass Sculptures from the Berengo Collection* at the Museum Moderner Kunst Kärnten, Klagenfurt, Austria.

GLASSTRESS

In its first edition, *Glasstress* 2009 presented extraordinary works borrowed from collectors and museums worldwide to offer a historical perspective from the last century to today. The renowned artists were not associated with glass: among them, Albers, Kounellis, Man Ray, César, Bourgeois, Dan Graham, Fontana, Buren, Penone, and Rauschenberg. The new production works were realized by such artists as Anne Peabody, Marya Kazoun, Jan Fabre, Tony Cragg, Jean-Michel Othoniel, Joseph Kosuth and Fred Wilson. Glass had made its surprising debut in the art world. The press and critics gave an extremely positive response to the project.

The exhibition became an ongoing project, initially planned to be presented only every two years in the context of the Biennale. A differentiation strategy that helped Berengo widen his reach and gain access to greater names in contemporary art was to put together a roster of well-known curators for the second edition of *Glasstress* in 2011. And at the moment of the 2011 Biennale, Berengo Studio saw the "birth" of the wonderful and now famous work by Javier Pérez titled *Carroña*: a traditional blood-red chandelier crashed to the floor with stuffed black ravens feasting on its shards that looked like the innards of a dead animal.

This special work has been featured in exhibitions from Paris to New York, and now it is in the permanent collection of The Corning Museum of Glass, the foremost glass museum in the world. Among the prestigious list of names that created brand new works are such artists as Tony Cragg, Vik Muniz, Tony Oursler, Jaume Plensa, Thomas Schutte and Zhang Huan, and also designers such as Jaime Hayon, Patricia Urquiola and Atelier Van Lieshout.

After the 2011 edition, *Glasstress* became a traveling event, invited to the Makslas Muzejs 'Riga Birža' in Riga, the Millesgården Museum in Stockholm, the Beirut Exhibition Center, the London College of Fashion, the Wallace Collection, the Museum of Arts and Design in New York, the Boca Raton Museum, Florida, and the Ptuj City Gallery in Ptuj, Slovenia. The latest invitation was received from the prestigious State Hermitage Museum in Russia.

In 2013, *Glasstress* was organized in Venice in partnership with the London College of Fashion and the Wallace Collection of London. The show included major established visual artists, designers and fashion designers, including Ron Arad, Alice Anderson, Rina Banerjee, Hussein Chalayan, and many of the Young British Artists, among them Mat Collishaw, Gavin Turk and Tracey

Emin. The event was growing enormously, together with more expectations for each new edition. The need for an institutional structure that could attract sponsorship, promote the event, and preserve some of the artwork became increasingly evident.

In 2014, Adriano Berengo founded the Fondazione Berengo to sustain the *Glasstress* project but also to create a leading institutional voice to introduce glass to the world of contemporary art. The foundation promotes the initial vision of Berengo and works to provide a platform for revitalizing the centuries-old traditions of Venetian glass while also working to foster a vibrant community of contemporary art through innovative collaborations and partnerships.

Based in the Palazzo Franchetti, in the heart of Venice, the Fondazione supports and promotes *Glasstress* around the world. As a second home for *Glasstress* and the future permanent collection, the Fondazione opened an exhibition space on Murano in an abandoned glass furnace. The plan for the future is to establish a permanent museum of contemporary art in glass to showcase some of the most impressive works made in over 30 years of activities and to inspire new generations of artists.

Going back to the promotion strategy of *Glasstress* in Venice during the Biennale, the year 2015 saw the prestigious partnership with the State Hermitage Museum of St. Petersburg. Under the curatorship of Dr. Dimitri Ozerkov, artists were asked to respond to a Gothic theme to give birth to *Glasstress Gotika*. An important addition to the show were historical works from the Hermitage collection of medieval glass and objects that were loaned out from the Museum for the first time to be displayed together with the newly commissioned glass artworks. Again, the past was in dialogue with contemporary expressions to sustain and encourage the vision behind the project of Berengo. In the Venice 2017 *Glasstress* edition, the focus was on "the state of the arts" concerning the development of glass as a medium for contemporary art expression, guided by curators Dimitri Ozerkov, Herwig Kempinger and Claire Phyllis Davies.

The year 2019 was the occasion to celebrate 30 years since the foundation of Berengo Studio and ten years of *Glasstress*. The *Glasstress* 2019 exhibition was held in the unique space of Fondazione Berengo Art Space (the abandoned glass furnace). It is evident that the strategy and level of promotion adopted by Berengo Studio went far beyond the activity of a small Murano glass studio. Themed exhibitions, partnerships with some of the most authoritative museums and institutions around the world, selection and involvement of well-known international curators, and a long list of artists, designers, architects, even musicians, such as Pharrell Williams, that approached glass for the first time with Berengo, make clear how the forward-looking attitude is more comparable to an ambitious international studio rather than a provincial workshop.

STRATEGIC INNOVATION: THE BERENGO STUDIO'S BUSINESS MODEL

During the 1990s, and thanks to the rapid growth of the net economy, management literature started speaking about a business model describing how firms can earn money (Afuah, 2004) or, according to Teece (2010), how firms create value for customers. Morris et al. (2006) identified six questions to describe the business model of the firms. Thus, we tried to draw the business model of Berengo Studio to enhance the elements of the strategic innovation he introduced.

How do we create value? Who do we create value for? What is our source of competence or advantage? How do we differentiate ourselves? How can we make money? What are our time, scope, and size ambitions? Answering the first questions, we can summarize the characteristics of the products coming out of the Berengo Studio as unique, realized with cooperation between the furnace and the artists who are engaged with different projects in diverse ways. In some cases, these are editions, but due to the artisan's touch and the complexity of mastering the glass, it is very difficult to reach a series production at an industrial level. This aspect is usually very appreciated by the artists.

Also, the selling channel is quite unique, as we can read from the Berengo interview:

> … it is mainly based on the personal relationships that I have built over the years with some international clients and friends. Then again, Venice offers the occasion to increase and amplify this client base. Some of the tourists that visit my commercial glass galleries in Venice tend to become clients or sponsors because they fall in love with the project and the material.

"For whom do we create value?" Berengo Studio answers the question with a mixed offer: it can be considered a service company when individual artists use the furnace premises to produce their own pieces (a very small percentage of the revenue); a business-to-business strategy happens when artists or other companies commission the Studio to realize specific works; on the other hand, if we look at the products they sell to customers, it can be considered a business-to-consumer operation.

> I had the good fortune to attract the interest of both glass collectors and collectors of contemporary art. And it is not only collectors but also art fairs and museums are showing an appreciation for this material. As I mentioned, today it is becoming

more and more common to find glass works, mostly produced at Berengo Studio, in prominent exhibitions and retrospectives around the world.

[...] Another important aspect is the tourists that visit Venice. Often they are high-net-worth individuals with a considerable purchasing capacity who are not necessarily looking for contemporary art but for something unique, highly aesthetic, innovative and distinctive, and can find this type of product at Berengo Studio.

Therefore, a central source of competence/advantage is to offer products that differentiate from their competitors, both in their aesthetic and economic value. The main competitive advantage is the production expertise – almost any technique is available – and the production approach, based on freedom of expression and experimentation. Over the last 30 years, this approach based on "learning by doing" brought the Studio to a very competitive know-how level on glass use in contemporary art, making Berengo a leader in this niche. To complete the production overview, important investments in new machinery have been made as well as in terms of the increase of space for production.

The supply chain takes advantage of the location, a district where raw materials for production are easy to find and quite generic, making the company's core business autonomous from third parties. Ownership of important buildings designated for exhibition and multiple uses on Murano Island is a competitive advantage.

The competitive strategy adopted is certainly based on high-spending customers, a target without geographical borders. Customers come from over the world and can be people, institutions, or businesses:

> I would rather say that the artworks themselves are marketing, promoters of my vision. I create occasions for visibility, mainly exhibitions; I attended international fairs but over the last five years or so I preferred to focus on Venice's potentiality. I recently sealed a partnership with the St. Regis hotel because we shared the vision that art and beauty have to make a step toward the visitors/clients and outside the 'box' of museums, so a selection of artworks is on temporary display at this beautiful hotel by the Grand Canal.

Recently, Berengo bought the ancient building of Venini. Berengo has always looked at the Venini Company with great admiration. Founded in 1921, Venini has always been strongly intertwined with the art world and contributed to diffuse the excellence of Murano glassworks also, thanks to the invitation to participate in exhibitions nationally and internationally and numerous awards collected over the decades.

Venini, moreover, had the intuition to involve prominent architects, designers and artists, such as Carlo and Tobia Scarpa, Gio Ponti and Fornasetti. In the 1990s, names like Sottsass, Aulenti, Magistretti, Mendini and Boeri realized special projects in the furnace of Murano. However, the production never turned to pure contemporary art production.

> In July 2019, it happened that the walls of the historic Venini glassworks in Fondamenta dei Vetrai in Murano, where my furnace is also located, were auctioned for a very low price if compared to the historical importance of the building. I felt compelled to enter the offer and try to become the owner of a property that consists of over 4,000 square meters that have marked a part of the most beautiful history of Murano glass. The secret dream is now also to acquire the brand ... but that's another story.

Talking about the differentiation aspects, Berengo's personal international network and experience, together with external collaborators, makes networking power a crucial aspect of the business.

The product differentiation consists of the uniqueness of the proposal able to capture the commercial interest not only of a niche of passionate glass but also international collectors and high-net-worth individuals.

And this is the key factor to monetizing the investment. After all, regarding costs highlighted in the present study, to answer the question "How can we make money?" we have to consider the favorable aspect of the possible marginalities on the final sales, which, when dealing with acclaimed artists, can definitely make a consistent return on the investment. Again, the deals are typically based on the personal relationship with the artists: "... each relationship is unique, I do not have a draft contract, I commit a dedicated team in the furnace in exchange for a work, but each situation is per se and depends a lot on the project and investment."

The more we analyzed the company from a business point of view, the more the double soul of the group emerged – commercial and cultural:

> Besides the short-term need of funds – we all agree that selling is important to sustain a vision – I am creating a museum collection, connected to Fondazione Berengo because some of the artworks realized in my studio are witnesses to a historical change, for contemporary art but above all for the Murano artistic glass.

So, to answer the last question about time, scope and size ambitions, Berengo says:

> My goal is to transform what still today seems original and innovative – the presence of glass artworks in the contemporary art field – into a new normal. Most of the time I produce, or I am invited to, exhibitions of contemporary art exclusively in glass. I would like instead that in the near future glass is present in large contemporary art exhibitions and in the most exclusive fairs like any other material [...] It is still a long way off, but some of the most important names in contemporary art have become spokesmen for this possibility.

And to complete the ambition of the vision, "I would like to give a source of inspiration for the new generations, on the power of our traditions, on the need to evolve without losing our roots, and that art has the strength to free us and break many barriers."

CONCLUSION

The case of Berengo suggests that a source of competitive advantage for craft firms can be discovered in the tradition and in particular in relation to the cultural heritage that is represented not only by tangible historical assets but also by intangible heritage. In this way, craft firms can be seen as the place where the art maker and the art thinker can join once again. But the rediscovery of tradition itself is not enough. As this case study has highlighted, it is important to have a renewal project also through mixed forms of innovation: from the product to the production process, for example, with new machinery and expanding techniques like casting to forms of communication that aim to reach different markets with a company's new image and product proposal.

Berengo Studio, furthermore, has not only identified a new market niche but has also managed to generate new demand, that of contemporary glass art, with all the direct and indirect impact that this implies.[5]

NOTES

1. See www.labiennale.org/it/storia-della-mostra-del-cinema.
2. Data collected in 2020 relating to all companies headed by Berengo.
3. The following pages focus on a case study of Berengo Studio, which the authors wrote after collecting public data and conducting an in-depth interview. The authors would like to express their gratitude and acknowledgment to Mr. Adriano Berengo for opening his furnace and the time dedicated to information collection on the present case study and to Doctor Chiara Squarcina for explaining some recent institutional dynamics concerning the Musei Civici di Venezia.
4. *Glassstress* is the name of the temporary and itinerant exhibition conceived in 2009 by Adriano Berengo, whose aim is to establish a new platform for art made with glass. The first edition took place in 2009 as a collateral event of the Venice Biennale. After 2009, a new temporary exhibition was organized in Venice every two years during Biennale of Art, while in the following years, Glasstress was hosted around the world in different important museums.
5. Both authors have contributed to this chapter. In particular, Laura Bresolin authored the "Introduction"; "A Brief History of the Sector"; "A Sector in Contraction"; "Reasons for the Crisis"; "Berengo Studio 1989: A Glass Factory that Innovates and Differentiates Through Art"; "The Innovation of Promotion: From the 1990s to the Present"; and *"Glasstress."* Giacomo Magnani authored "A Strategic Analysis: The Industry's Main Characteristics"; "Strategic Resources"; "The Entrepreneurial Approach: How It All Started"; "Innovation in

Products and Processes"; "Strategic Innovation: The Berengo Studio's Business Model"; and "Conclusion."

REFERENCES

Afuah, A. (2004). *Business Models: A Strategic Management Approach*. New York: Irwin/McGraw-Hill.

Barney, J., Wright, M. & Ketchen, D. J. (2001). The resource-based view of the firm: ten years after 1991. *Journal of Management*, *27*(6), 625–41. https://doi.org/10.1177/014920630102700601.

Cannarella C. & Piccioni V. (2011). Traditiovations: creating innovation from the past and antique techniques for rural areas. *Technovation*, *31*(12), 689–99.

Coad A. (2018). Firm age: a survey. *Journal of Evolutionary Economics*, *28*(1), 13–43. http://doi.org/10.1007/s00191-016-0486-0.

Cologni F. (2007). La mente creativa, la mano intelligente: il codice Cellini. In P. Colombo (ed.), *La Grande Europa Dei Mestieri D'arte*, 12–15. Milano: Vita e Pensiero.

Colombo P. (ed.) (2007). *La Grande Europa Dei Mestieri D'arte*. Milan: Vita e Pensiero.

Confartigianato (2015). *Murano: Un'economia Fragile? I Numeri, Le Problematiche, Le Prospettive*. Confartigianato Venezia.

Dutta S. & Errad P. (1999). Information technology and organization within European small enterprises. *European Management Journal*, *17*(3), 239–51.

Fillis I. (2004). The internationalizing of smaller craft firms. Insight from the marketing/entrepreneurship interface. *International Small Business Journal*, *22*(1), 57–82.

Gasparetto A. (1958). *Il Vetro di Murano dalle origini ad oggi*. Neri Pozza.

Grant, R. M. (1991). *Contemporary Strategy Analysis: Concepts, Techniques and Applications*. Malden, MA: Blackwell.

Gray A. & McGuinnan J. (eds) (1993). *Studying Culture: An Introductory Reader*. London: Hodder Arnold.

Klotz, U. M. (2019). 30 years Berengo Glass Studio & 10 years Glasstress. *Neues Glas/ New Glass: Art & Architecture*, *2*, 42–4.

McAuley, A. (1999). Entrepreneurial instant exporters in the Scottish Arts and Crafts sector. *Journal of International Marketing*, *7*(4), 67–82.

McCray P. W. (1999). *Glassmaking in Renaissance Venice: The Fragile Craft*. Aldershot: Ashgate.

Metcalf, B. (1997). Craft and art, culture and biology. In P. Dormer (ed.), *The Culture of Craft*, 37–82. Manchester: Manchester University Press.

Miller, D. (1983). The correlates of entrepreneurship in three types of firms. *Management Science*, *29*(7), 770–91. https://doi.org/10.1287/mnsc.29.7.770.

Morris, M., Schindehutte, S., Richardson, J. & Allen J. (2006). Is the business model a useful strategic concept? Conceptual, theoretical and empirical insights. *Journal of Small Business Strategy*, *17*(1), 27–50.

Porter, M. E. (1985). *Competitive Advantage: Creating and Sustaining Superior Performance*. New York: The Free Press.

Sennett, R. (2008). *The Craftsman*. New Haven, CT: Yale University Press.

Simpson, B. (2001). Innovation and the micro-enterprise. *International Journal of Services Technology and Management*, *2*(3/4), 377–87. https://doi.org/10.1504/IJSTM.2001.001610.

Storey, D. & Cressy, R. (1996). *Small Business Risk: A Firm Bank Perspective.* The Centre for Small & Medium-Sized Enterprises (CSME), 39, Warwick Business School.

Teece D. J (2010). Business models, business strategy and innovation. *Long Range Planning, 43,* 172–94.

Vanderstukken K. (2016). *Glass: Virtual, Real.* London: Black Dog Publishing.

Watzl, P. (2019). 10 Jahre Glasstress, 30 Jahre Studio Berengo. *Parnass, 2,* 62–5.

7. The innovative logics of digital manufacturing: the case study of 3DiTALY

Daniela Corsaro and Mirko Olivieri

INTRODUCTION

New technologies have revolutionized company business models and entre-preneurship logics in recent decades (Foss & Saebi, 2017). Nowadays, compa-nies have benefited from the advent of the Internet and digital technologies in different ways. For instance, digital infrastructures have significantly reduced the costs traditionally generated by businesses, and new business models based entirely on the development of digital technologies have spread abruptly (Davidson & Vaast, 2010). Moreover, digital technologies played a key role when Italian companies had to revise their business model following the 2008 financial crisis, which shocked the global economy with serious consequences for the manufacturing sector. According to a survey by the Bank of Italy, between 2009 and 2010 some companies suffered a drop in their return on investment (ROI) of 73.9 per cent. In 2017, the ROI of some industries reached new record levels, showing an increase of 16.1 per cent compared to pre-crisis values (Intesa Sanpaolo, 2018). In this scenario, digital technologies repre-sented a driver for the economic recovery of the companies, particularly for craft firms, with a strong impact on their business. In this context, some com-panies of the manufacturing sector adopted digital technologies in their daily activities and interaction between human users and machines (Johannsen, 2009) emerged with consequences on the business models of these companies.

Hence, digital transformation has posed new research questions about the intersection of digital technologies and entrepreneurship, as digital technology characteristics have shaped entrepreneurial activities (Nambisan, 2017). In particular, the advent of direct digital manufacturing will continue to lead to structural changes in added value in the supply chain, requiring scholars to address this topic (Holmström et al., 2017). As a matter of fact, Bonfanti et al. (2018) highlight three strategic directions which craft firms should consider:

(1) entrust their activities to digital technologies which currently represent a great opportunity for their business, (2) consider customers as an active part in the production and business networking phases, and (3) offer handicraft products by providing a wide range of services.

In light of these developments, we pose a question about the recent business directions taken by Italian companies in the craft context, with the aim of understanding the role of digital technologies in these companies, with a particular focus on the new philosophy and consequences of the digital manufacturing processes. To achieve our research objective, we opted for a case study analysis of an Italian company operating a 3D printing business (3DiTALY), by conducting a series of semi-structured interviews. 3DiTALY is a project development centre, where anyone can bring their ideas and see them concretely realized, as it was the first company in the world to create a store network of digital fabrication. Each project is carried out by a professional team and can be inserted in a distribution circuit which is made up of a network of capillary stores throughout Italy. 3DiTALY caters to a very large and varied clientele that includes professionals such as architects, urban planners, designers, makers, students, and also important companies such as Honda Italia, Trellenborg Pirelli, Samsung, and Rai.

This chapter is structured as follows. First, a literature review is provided on the topics of digital transformation in production and the business model innovation. Second, the research question and the adopted methodology are introduced. Third, results of the case study focusing on changes due to digital transformation both for consumers and firms are presented. The final part of this chapter is dedicated to the discussion, conclusions and limitations of the research.

LITERATURE REVIEW

Digital Transformation and Business Model Innovation in the Craft Sector

Digital transformation has been heavily researched in recent decades. In the initial phase of this transformation, companies were worried about the role of the digital in the planning of business resources or the relationship with consumers (Boersma & Kingma, 2005). Indeed, the changes introduced thanks to new technologies are aimed at improving business processes and efficiency, and reducing costs (Li et al., 2018). In particular in the manufacturing sector, according to Westerman et al. (2014), digital technologies can allow companies to reorient their employees on more strategic tasks entrusting repetitive tasks to machines. This allows employees to focus on innovation and creativity rather than repetitive efforts. In fact, as demonstrated by recent studies (de

Vasconcellos et al., 2021), in digitalized contexts technological resources play a key role and can be considered as a source of competitive advantage which stimulates the creative thinking of employees. However, this form of innovation requires an effort on the part of craft sector companies such as opening company boundaries to suppliers, partners, customers and communities in their manufacturing processes (Chesbrough et al., 2006). According to Bonfanti et al. (2018), among the main reasons that would push these companies to adopt new processes are faster and more effective production and growth in the satisfaction of customer needs.

Consequently, digital technologies have been widely adopted by companies in recent years including drastic changes both in business models (Berman, 2012) and in organizational strategy and culture (Cui & Pan, 2015). The business model, which is defined as the formalization of strategic hypotheses that 'tell a story' by aligning all the components of the organization on common values and objectives (Balocco et al., 2019), has been profoundly affected by the digital transformation. For these reasons, according to some scholars (Chesbrough, 2007; Ghezzi & Cavallo, 2018), it is no longer sufficient for companies to look only at product innovation, as it is increasingly important to focus on innovation of the entire business model. Indeed, business model innovation (hereafter, BMI) is a concept linked to management and entrepreneurship (Massa & Tucci, 2013), as BMI is a set of innovative and non-trivial changes to the key elements of the business model and to the architecture of a company (Foss & Saebi, 2017). BMI is therefore a 'phenomenon of change' characterized by novelties and uniqueness with respect to products and services already existing in the market or already adopted business models (Saebi et al., 2017). Consequently, the definition of new business models and innovation processes has become a central topic in the field of entrepreneurship, as the digital component therefore becomes necessary to innovate the business model.

Hence, digital entrepreneurship is considered as a subcategory of entrepreneurship where at least some elements that would have been physical in a traditional enterprise have been digitized (Hull et al., 2007). Ngoasong (2018) defined digital entrepreneurship as the company practice of pursuing new opportunities offered by new media and Internet technologies. Accordingly, the digital entrepreneur is an individual who uses the new information and communication technologies (ICTs) to create key business activities and functions, such as production, marketing, sales and resource management (Hair et al., 2012). Nowadays, entrepreneurs have a wider range of opportunities for two reasons: (1) the gradual infusion of digital content into a wide range of products and services, such as consumer goods, and (2) the consequent growth in the number and diversity of these digital platforms (Nambisan & Baron, 2019). As a matter of fact, a large number of existing studies in the broader literature (Huang et al., 2013) have shown that digital ecosystems offer important advantages to new ventures, such as the achievement of new stakeholders, access to new markets and improvements in reputation.

According to Hull et al. (2007), six factors determine digital transformation in a company: (1) digital marketing, (2) digital sales, (3) the digital nature of the product or service offered by the company, (4) the digital distribution potential of the product or service, (5) potential digital interactions with stakeholders, and (6) the digital potential of the company's internal activities. In this regard, the academic literature distinguishes 'technological entrepreneurship' from 'digital entrepreneurship', even if the boundaries are not exact. According to Giones and Brem (2017), digital entrepreneurship is much closer to the concepts of information systems artefacts, platforms and information infrastructure. For this reason, digital entrepreneurs often do not focus on the technology that underlies the business idea, but simply focus on the service or final product. In this case, technology is just an input factor (Giones & Brem, 2017). Ferreira et al. (2016) proposed a theoretical framework on the subject of technological entrepreneurship, suggesting it is a combination of entrepreneurship and technology-based innovation. Moreover, according to Beckman et al. (2012), technological entrepreneurship is a type of entrepreneurship that aims to exploit related opportunity progress in science, engineering and innovation in general.

Digital Fabrication and 3D Printing

Over the past century, technological evolution of production systems has been able to produce high-quality standardized products thanks to the lean manufacturing development (Womack et al., 2007). Nowadays, a new trend of mass customization is developing (Tseng & Radke, 2011). The most requested products are personalized and include distinctive characteristics associated with consumers, such as labelling the consumer name on the product. In this context, digital technologies and the flexibility of the production system play an important role in the production of customized products (Chen et al., 2015).

In the manufacturing sector, 3D printing or direct digital manufacturing (hereafter, DDM) identify rapidly evolving production techniques which integrate and replace with higher value results the more expensive traditional manufacturing techniques (Holmström et al., 2017). Recently, some scholars (Abdulhameed et al., 2019; Vitorino et al., 2019) have argued that the term DDM first appeared when additive manufacturing (AM) – defined as the process of a product directly from a 3D CAD (computer-aided design) model – and the Internet of Things (IoT) crossed paths. For instance, starting from an original digital design, 3D printing allows direct manufacturing without tooling and set-up (Gibson et al., 2010). This process is called 'digital fabrication', the production of solid and three-dimensional objects starting from digital drawings: 3D printing is the innovative method which allows the production of entire objects created layer by layer by printers under computer control (Wiecek et al., 2019). Espalin et al. (2014) argue that 3D printing leads to the fabrication of unprecedented complex 3D geometric structures. As a consequence, this profound change in production – from remote factories to local 3D printing – will reduce shipping costs and make it easier to customize products.

According to Rayna and Striukova (2016), the possible applications of 3D printing can be collected in four categories: (1) rapid prototyping, that is, the heart of 3D printing, the application that gave birth to this type of production in the late 1980s; (2) rapid tooling, that is, the indirect prototyping that spread in the mid-1990s. With 3D printing it is possible to produce customized tools, suitable for making final objects; (3) rapid manufacturing, which is the direct production of final objects through additive techniques. In this case, no models are made, but directly the final product (Gibson et al., 2010); (4) spare parts: with 3D printing it is possible to reproduce components or spare parts that are difficult to find or that one needs to customize. Companies and individuals can redesign the piece by modelling it in 3D or create a 3D scan and then print it later.

Hence, this innovative method responds to changes in consumers, who today ask to act as value co-creators by engaging with companies in a process of 'joint production' (Ramaswamy & Ozcan, 2018). Therefore, thanks to digitization and new technologies, consumers will be facilitated in the future and their participation in value creation processes will increase significantly (Dellaert, 2019). At the base of the manufacturing process there is an exchange between sellers and buyers (Vargo & Lusch, 2004). However, although this remains the predominant orientation (Rindfleisch et al., 2019), recent digital transformations in the manufacturing sector allow individuals to self-manufacture their own products. Hence, Rindfleisch et al. recently defined 'self-manufacturing as the use of low-cost and widely accessible digital design and manufacturing tools to create (rather than buy) objects' (2019, p. 167). According to Ratto and Ree (2012), the self-manufacture process is characterized by 'the materialization of digital information'. This process can occur due to two forces: (1) the democratization of production tools and (2) the emergence of an online support community that openly shares their creations (von Hippel, 2018).

RESEARCH QUESTION AND METHODOLOGY

The purpose of this chapter is to investigate the recent business directions taken by Italian companies in the craft context. Specifically, our research aim is to understand the role of digital technologies in these companies, with a particu-

Table 7.1   3DiTALY details

Foundation year	2012
Mission	Our mission is to re-evaluate Italian design and craftsmanship, two sectors that have always made our country famous internationally. We are a container that wants to combine tradition and innovation in the widespread field of design, thanks to a technology open to all that offers new possibilities in the creation of prototypes, projects and objects
Sector	3D printing and connected services
Business details	Italian company operating both in B2B [business to business] and B2C [business to consumer]. The first company in the world to create a store network of digital fabrication
No. of local affiliates	5

Source: Compiled by the authors.

lar focus on the new philosophy and consequences of the digital manufacturing processes. Hence, this study seeks to answer the following research question:

RQ: What is the impact of digital transformation on the business model of manufacturing companies? How have digital technologies such as 3D printing contributed to the innovation of these companies?

For this study, an abductive approach was adopted. Data collection, data analysis and the search for complementary theories have constituted parallel processes alternating the study of theoretical concepts and direct observation. This research process allowed us to improve the understanding of both theory and data (Dubois & Gadde, 2002). Indeed, in the abductive approach, theoretical structures and empirical observations develop simultaneously and interactively.

Hence, to achieve our research objectives, we opted for a qualitative case-study method (Yin, 2009) by analysing the company 3DiTALY (Table 7.1). After a literature review, two researchers conducted a series of in-depth semi-structured interviews which allowed the analysis of complex phenomena and the emergence of unexpected issues (Wengraf, 2001).

For this research, 14 key informants were involved in this study (Table 7.2). The semi-structured interviews lasted between 50 minutes and 90 minutes and were conducted face-to-face in January and February 2020. Upon key informants' consent, all interviews were recorded and transcribed verbatim. The interview scheme was divided into three parts. First, researchers asked key informants to describe the context in which the company operates and how it has evolved over time, focusing on digital transformation effects. Secondly, we asked for information on the critical events that occurred with regard to the

Table 7.2   Key informants' profiles

Key informants' role	Years of experience
Founder	Since 2012
Co-founder	Since 2012
New business developer	Since 2013
Marketing manager	Since 2013
Marketing specialist	Since 2015
Customer manager	Since 2016
Sales manager	Since 2016
Reseller	Since 2016
Reseller	Since 2017
Customer 1	Since 2014
Customer 2	Since 2016
Customer 3	Since 2016
Customer 4	Since 2013
Customer 5	Since 2017

Source: Compiled by the authors.

key relations and processes. Once an interesting element emerged, researchers tried to direct the discussion towards episodes that characterize it, such as the actors involved, effects and how these effects influenced other events and future processes.

Data collection and analysis were carried out to obtain insights and original results. The data analysis phase involved a coding process as the main themes that emerged from the interviews were identified and related to our research objectives.

Data analysis was conducted through three phases of systematic coding (Strauss & Corbin, 1998), which are (1) open coding, (2) axial coding, and (3) selective coding. The objective of the three coding phases is to identify emerging topics by considering the research aim of this study. Furthermore, to identify points in common and differences between what emerged from the different interviews, we used the constant comparison method (Goulding, 2005), which provides for a comparison between the transcripts of the interviews as they were carried out.

RESULTS

Overview of 3DiTALY

3DiTALY is the first Italian printing store founded in Rome in 2012. Today, with seven offices throughout Italy, 3DiTALY represents a network of companies specializing in 3D printers and printing services, material consumption, scanners, and training activities. 3DiTALY offers companies and individuals a professional CAD modelling service, rapid prototyping and 3D scanning. It is the showcase of excellence in the 3D world. 3DiTALY's mission is to re-evaluate both Italian design and craftsmanship, two sectors that have always made Italy famous worldwide. The company is a pioneering and experimental laboratory, which wants to be a point of reference for designers who will use revolutionary 3D printing techniques The company's goal is to make a contribution to the rapidly expanding sector of 3D printing, enhancing its cultural proposal and its appeal.

The philosophy of 3D printing and manufacturers is spreading all over the world. In fact, anyone with an invention or a project can send his own file to a 3DiTALY store which will produce the object, in small batches or in large quantities, or make it himself with some digital manufacturing tools, such as 3D printers. According to Ouweneel et al. (2013), this philosophy aims to encourage creativity and the so-called DIY (do-it-yourself) through accessibility for everyone to digital manufacturing machines, building interest groups around ideas and projects. Moreover, this new form of entrepreneurship surpasses the logic of traditional marketing and assumes social values. Hence, 3DiTALY's philosophy aims to subvert industrial production chains, shortening the distance between the inventor and the entrepreneur to zero kilometres. This process implies proximity to the use of ecological materials, and recycling and personalization of objects, eliminating the chain of large retailers.

New Manufacturing Logics

As emerged from the literature review (Li et al., 2018), the digital transformation and new technologies affected strongly the manufacturing sector, by revolutionizing the supply chain process, improving business processes and reducing related costs:

> Digital manufacturing reverses the economic logic of traditional manufacturing. In mass production, almost all costs are to cover the initial equipping of the machine: the greater the complexity of the product and more changes to be made, so the costs rise. With digital manufacturing, it is exactly the opposite: things that are expensive in the traditional production become free. (Chris Anderson, maker)

Hence, our findings highlight that the economic logics of the manufacturing sector have been dramatically impacted by digital technologies. Therefore, the benefits concern both consumers and businesses: (1) consumers have the possibility to customize products according to their tastes and needs, (2) companies have now the opportunity to reduce their own production costs. Indeed, the costs of 3D printers are constantly decreasing, and consumers will be able to independently produce what they need, and when they need it. As a result, personalization levels will increase, and necessary economic resources will be reduced. Consequently, the consumption logics evolve in favour of 'human creativity', which becomes an important factor that the consumer can exploit in new production processes. Indeed, in 3DiTALY, every dealer combines different skills to facilitate cross-creative approaches: architects, designers, engineers, communication experts and marketers. With the spread of the DIY philosophy, consumers will not only exploit their hard skills, but will also develop their imagination and new capacities to independently produce goods and products. As a consequence, the distance between producers and consumers will get shorter and shorter until they completely overlap, bringing out the new profession of 'digital artisan'.

The Overlap Between Producer and Consumer

Thanks to new technologies such as 3D printing, inventors' creativity is stimulated in several contexts. 3DiTALY, in fact, is not only aimed at the business-to-consumer market, but also at stakeholders such as companies and schools by supplying the machinery necessary to produce artefacts and give substance to ideas. The traditional logics of both production and marketing are overcome by these new production processes, which include the use of the equipment and the involvement of the final consumer in the various phases of the supply chain. The consumer is no longer a passive recipient (Vargo & Lusch, 2004), but becomes an integral part of the process and contextualizes its outcomes based on its real interests. The sudden evolution of 3D printing has greatly amplified the personalization desire of consumers. Change in tastes and needs, and the desire for tailor-made ad hoc products, has given rise to a mass customization trend, which is a phenomenon aiming to provide products and services that best meet the needs of individual customers with almost total production efficiency (Tseng & Radke, 2011).

This type of production differs from the mass production introduced in the 20th century, where large quantities of standardized products are made on an assembly line. In this process, a conventional mass production company is often defined as bureaucratic and hierarchical, in which workers under strict control perform repetitive and strictly defined tasks, resulting in low-cost standardized products and services (Womack, 1993). Today, the aim of companies such as 3DiTALY is to offer speed and flexibility to customers to satisfy their desires, at much lower costs. Indeed, anonymous mass-produced products on a large scale, economically accessible homologated objects, no longer meet the changing needs of consumers. Co-production can also have benefits such as the formation of alliances in order to share resources and generate solutions (Elwyn et al., 2020). These networks, formed on the basis of co-production, offer a powerful strategy that has been adopted by many companies such as 3DiTALY to improve the quality of their products, lowering both production and distribution costs.

Furthermore, as previous studies have reported (Dellaert, 2019; Wiecek et al., 2019), the consumer is more evolved than in the past and is increasingly seeking to get closer to the world of production in order to be able to create a product suitable for the satisfaction of his needs. Hence, the clear boundaries that previously separated the figure of the producer from the consumer are vanishing, and the so-called prosumer is born. The term 'prosumer' was originally coined by Alvin Toffler in 1980 and refers to the development of the individual's participation in markets from a passive consumer to an active participant in the production, maintenance and repair of consumer goods (Ritzer et al., 2012). This term creates a crisis by merging the word producer with that of consumer. It means that a person can play both roles at the same time. In addition to playing the role of consumer within the purchase funnel, the person can play an active role as a producer, taking part in the creation of the product or service. With the advent of the Internet, the information asymmetry between customer and company disappears.

Nowadays, there is more transparency and consumers have become informed, being aware of what the markets offer, and they are able to compare more products without being influenced by commercials and marketing in general. Thus, consumers setting up conversations on social networks and blogs, and providing feedback, reveal their wishes and needs. Companies that have understood the importance of listening to the web, opinions and trendsetters develop products based on the requests and needs received through online conversations, giving consumers the opportunity to participate in the creation of products and services and allowing the development of co-production strategies (Elwyn et al., 2020). This phenomenon is visible in 3DiTALY, where the manufacturer and the user overlap completely.

The Value of the Network

3DiTALY recognizes the importance of the value of the network with stakeholders. The company, in addition to addressing individual consumers or other companies for the sale and supply of its machinery, also develops partnerships that consolidate its role in the market and with new projects and ideas: one example is the 3D printer for chocolate born from the partnership with Antica Dolceria Bonajuto, the oldest Modica chocolate factory in Ragusa, Sicily. In 2014, 3DiTALY and Antica Dolceria introduced an important innovation in a traditional industry by developing the first 3D printer for chocolate. The idea was to print chocolate, for the first time in Italy, using a layered 3D printer. For this reason, WASP (a manufacturer of 3D printers), had to intervene in the project as another player; they updated chocolate extrusion on the Power WASP model. The chocolate is produced with an ancient technique that uses low-temperature processing. This process dates back to the ceremonial Aztec civilization and was brought to Modica (Sicily) in the 16th century by the Spanish.

The production technique has not evolved through the industrial stage and has remained unchanged for ingredients and method of preparation. In detail, the chocolate paste is melted at a temperature of about 31 degrees. Subsequently, it is poured into a normal pastry syringe, which is then applied to the mechanical arm of the 3D printer. A stepper motor applies light pressure via a pin on the top of the syringe, so as to allow the extrusion of the choco-late strand from the spout below. By slowly moving the syringe through the mechanical arm on the X, Y and Z axes, the machine is thus able to create small three-dimensional works, layer by layer. In sum, the oldest technique for making chocolate blends with innovative 3D printing.

> Antica Dolceria Bonajuto was thrilled by the invitation to collaborate, always our belief is that old does not mean it is old but rather a wealth of experience constantly in progress starting from essential fixed points – compared raw material and product characteristics – can always be put to the test service. (3DiTALY, sales manager)

Hence, a new value has been co-created through the combination of tradi-tional craftsmanship and digital technologies. 3DiTALY and Antica Dolceria Bonajuto decided to catch the opportunity to reinvent the art of pastry in order to stimulate creativity and thus the attractiveness of this business even for future young generations. The merging of tradition and new technology gave rise to a new profession, the digital artisan, a combination of traditional crafts-manship and digital evolution.

Furthermore, 3DiTALY's initiatives are developed throughout Italy. In 2005 in Milan, the company established the Digital Arts & Manufacturing Academy (DAMA). The academy aims to train future digital fabrication professionals in several traditional sectors. The idea was born from the union of the know-how in the production of 3DiTALY with the combination of training skills from different disciplines. The aim is to integrate the cultural background of craftsmanship with digital manufacturing technologies:

> DAMA is an innovative production space, a place where heterogeneous people meet and exchange knowledge, with an eclectic vision of the production of objects that embraces ancient processes and new. DAMA is experimentation, experience, virtual world of design but also craftsmanship. I don't want to do the same job as my grandfather, I want to start from there and take advantage of the great opportunities offered by new technologies. (DAMA, student)

DISCUSSION AND CONCLUSIONS

The aim of this chapter is to investigate the role of digital technologies in companies operating in the craft sector, by focusing on the new philosophy and consequences of the digital manufacturing processes. Our research revealed an evolution of 3DiTALY's business models on different levels, which involved both consumers and companies. Indeed, this evolution is certainly caused by digital technologies, but also by new consumers' expectations, namely personalization and the 'human creativity', and production democratization.

Personalization and 'human creativity'. Nowadays, 3D printing is part of a new consumer context characterized by personalization and self-production. By producing pieces in small quantities, 3D printing will undoubtedly undermine and destabilize the economies of scale on which manufacturing production is currently based, thus saving materials and costs, and limiting the level of process pollution. Indeed, the industrial production that has prevailed so far is efficient and convenient only in the production of thousands of identical pieces, while producing a single piece with classic systems is difficult and, proportionally, enormously expensive. Hence, the advent of the 3D printing is a cultural revolution that stands in antithesis to a hyper-specialized society where people only perform the activities for which they have the relevant expertise. Our case study shows how anonymous mass-produced products on a large scale, economically accessible homologated objects, no longer meet the changing needs of consumers.

By supporting previous studies (Dellaert, 2019; Wiecek et al., 2019), we found that, today, the consumer is seeking to get closer to production in order to be able to create a product suitable for the satisfaction of her/his needs and wishes. Indeed, digital fabrication has shortened the supply chain by democratizing technology and allowing people to independently produce in a personalized and innovative way what they need and when they need it. In this regard, digital machinery represents a tool that facilitates man's work in the production of the object. Hence, as the manufacturing industry is currently moving from mass production to mass customization (Tseng and Radke, 2011), our findings suggest that digital technologies impact both consumers and firms:

consumers have the possibility to customize and produce themselves what they need and firms to reduce their production costs. In other words, personalization levels will increase and the necessary economic resources will be reduced. Furthermore, 'human creativity' is stimulated by these technologies, as consumers do not have to choose between the products offered by the market, but they can achieve what they want. Indeed, the DIY philosophy of 3DiTALY develops consumers' imagination and capacities to independently produce any object. However, the results also showed that professionals and consumers in general, who are beginning to use these technologies such as 3D printing for the first time, do not have the necessary skills to make the most of these technological tools. The craft sector, in fact, is traditionally linked to production logics which are far from the implementation of these new technologies in its activities. Therefore, the support of experienced professionals in the production phase becomes essential.

Democratization of production. 3D printing and hybrid production have led to a total change in the way we think, design and produce things. If, for large companies, there has always been the possibility of keeping up with great technological discoveries relating to production, for SMEs, start-ups and hobbyists there have been no economic opportunities to manufacture. However, as the democratization of information through personal computers has been a key advance of the 20th century, the democratization of production through improvements in manufacturing technologies will be a central development in the 21st century (Bull & Groves, 2009). Digital fabrication makes a production democratic that has always followed the logic of the economy of scale made possible by the huge volumes that can be produced within production chains. With digital manufacturing, the mechanism of economies of scale is lost. There is no longer a reduction in the unit cost of a product with increasing volumes, but the unit manufacturing cost remains unchanged whether one piece is produced or many.

This self-production of goods is in opposition to the traditional, centralized and vertically integrated production model. The consumer leaves this paradigm and has the opportunity to produce independently in the manner and timing he prefers, overriding space and time boundaries, breaking the rules of the previous system. Therefore, new production models, such as digital fabrication, allow companies to base their business not on the sale of many units of a selection of objects, but on the sale of a few units of almost all of the objects, radically changing the corporate business model.

Furthermore, this chapter offers practical implications for professionals involved in the craft sector. Indeed, from this case study analysis it emerged that there is a need to invest more in technologies, such as 3D printing, to meet the new requirements of consumers. Our results have shown that offering customized products is now key to gaining a competitive advantage in the craft sector. Specifically, anonymous mass-produced products will be in demand less and less by today's consumers, who will instead opt for self-produced products. Craft sector companies should therefore take into account these evolutions of the consumer and society in general, consequently modifying their business model and reviewing their marketing strategies.

As this research has analysed a case study with a qualitative approach and the number of key-informants is limited, it suffers from limitations of generalizability. Furthermore, this study is context- and country-specific as the company involved in this research operates only in Italy. In future research, findings of this case study analysis should be compared to other companies operating in a digitized context and dealing with different product categories. Both qualitative and quantitative studies could explore this topic from a consumer or business perspective.

REFERENCES

Abdulhameed, O., Al-Ahmari, A., Ameen, W. and Mian, S. H. (2019). 'Additive manufacturing: challenges, trends, and applications', *Advances in Mechanical Engineering*, *11*(2), 1–27.

Balocco, R., Cavallo, A., Ghezzi, A. and Berbegal-Mirabent, J. (2019). 'Lean business models change process in digital entrepreneurship', *Business Process Management Journal*, *25*(7), 1520–42.

Beckman, C. M., Eisenhardt, K., Kotha, S., Meyer, A. and Rajagopalan, N. (2012). 'Technology entrepreneurship', *Strategic Entrepreneurship Journal*, *6*(2), 89–93.

Berman, S. J. (2012). 'Digital transformation: opportunities to create new business models', *Strategy & Leadership*, *40*(2), 16–24.

Boersma, K. and Kingma, S. (2005). 'From means to ends: the transformation of ERP in a manufacturing company', *The Journal of Strategic Information Systems*, *14*(2), 197–219.

Bonfanti, A., Del Giudice, M. and Papa, A. (2018). 'Italian craft firms between digital manufacturing, open innovation, and servitization', *Journal of the Knowledge Economy*, *9*(1), 136–49.

Bull, G. and Groves, J. (2009). 'The democratization of production', *Learning & Leading with Technology*, *37*(3), 36–7.

Chen, D., Heyer, S., Ibbotson, S., Salonitis, K., Steingrímsson, J. G. and Thiede, S. (2015). 'Direct digital manufacturing: definition, evolution, and sustainability implications', *Journal of Cleaner Production*, *107*, 615–25.

Chesbrough, H. (2007). 'Business model innovation: it's not just about technology anymore', *Strategy & Leadership*, *35*(6), 12–17.

Chesbrough, H., Vanhaverbeke, W. and West, J. (2006). *Open Innovation: Researching a New Paradigm*. New York: Oxford University Press.

Cui, M. and Pan, S. L. (2015). 'Developing focal capabilities for e-commerce adoption: a resource orchestration perspective', *Information Management*, *52*(2), 200–209.

Davidson, E. and Vaast, E. (2010). 'Digital entrepreneurship and its sociomaterial enactment', paper presented at 43rd Hawaii International Conference on System Sciences, IEEE Computer Society, January.

de Vasconcellos, S. L., da Silva Freitas, J. C. and Junges, F. M. (2021). 'Digital capabilities: bridging the gap between creativity and performance'. In H. Park, M. Perez and D. Floriani (eds), *The Palgrave Handbook of Corporate Sustainability in the Digital Era* (pp. 411–27). Cham: Palgrave Macmillan.

Dellaert, B. G. (2019). 'The consumer production journey: marketing to consumers as co-producers in the sharing economy', *Journal of the Academy of Marketing Science*, *47*, 1–17.

Dubois, A. and Gadde, L. E. (2002). 'Systematic combining: an abductive approach to case research', *Journal of Business Research*, *55*(7), 553–60.

Elwyn, G., Nelson, E., Hager, A. and Price, A. (2020). 'Coproduction: when users define quality', *BMJ Quality & Safety*, *29*(9), 711–16.

Espalin, D., Muse, D. W., MacDonald, E. and Wicker, R. B. (2014). '3D printing multifunctionality: structures with electronics', *The International Journal of Advanced Manufacturing Technology*, *72*(5–8), 963–78.

Ferreira, J. J. M., Ferreira, F. A. F., Fernandes, C. I. M. A. S., Jalali, M. S., Raposo, M. L. and Marques, C. S. (2016). 'What do we [not] know about technology entrepreneurship research?', *International Entrepreneurship and Management Journal*, *12*(3), 713–33.

Foss, N. J. and Saebi, T. (2017). 'Fifteen years of research on business model innovation: how far have we come, and where should we go?', *Journal of Management*, *43*(1), 200–227.

Ghezzi, A. and Cavallo, A. (2018). 'Agile business model innovation in digital entrepreneurship: lean startup approaches', *Journal of Business Research*, *110*, 519–37.

Gibson, I., Rosen, D. W. and Stucker, B. (2010). 'Direct digital manufacturing', in I. Gibson, D. W. Rosen and B. Stucker (eds), *Additive Manufacturing Technologies* (pp. 363–84). New York: Springer.

Giones, F. and Brem, A. (2017). 'Digital technology entrepreneurship: a definition and research agenda', *Technology Innovation Management Review*, *7*(5), 44–51.

Goulding, C. (2005). 'Grounded theory, ethnography and phenomenology: a comparative analysis of three qualitative strategies for marketing research', *European Journal of Marketing*, *39*(3–4), 294–308.

Hair, N., Wetsch, L. R., Hull, C. E., Perotti, V. and Hung, Y.-T. C. (2012). 'Market orientation in digital entrepreneurship: advantages and challenges in a web 2.0 networked world', *International Journal of Innovation and Technology Management*, *9*(6), 1–18.

Holmström, J., Liotta, G. and Chaudhuri, A. (2017). 'Sustainability outcomes through direct digital manufacturing-based operational practices: a design theory approach', *Journal of Cleaner Production*, *167*, 951–61.

Huang, P., Ceccagnoli, M., Forman, C. and Wu, D. J. (2013). 'Appropriability mechanisms and the platform partnership decision: evidence from enterprise software', *Management Science*, *59*(1), 102–21.

Hull, C. E. K., Hung, Y. T. C., Hair, N. and Perotti, V. (2007). 'Taking advantage of digital opportunities: a typology of digital entrepreneurship', *International Journal of Networking and Virtual Organisations*, *4*(3), 290–303.

Intesa Sanpaolo (2018). 'Economia e finanza dei distretti industriali' ['Economics and finance of industrial districts'], *Studies and Research, Annual Report*, *11*, Milan.

Johannsen, G. (2009). 'Human–machine interaction', *Control Systems, Robotics and Automation*, *21*, 132–62.

Li, L., Su, F., Zhang, W. and Mao, J. Y. (2018). 'Digital transformation by SME entrepreneurs: a capability perspective', *Information Systems Journal*, *28*(6), 1129–57.

Massa, L. and Tucci, C. L. (2013). 'Business model innovation', in Mark Dodgson, David M. Gann and Nelson Phillips (eds), *The Oxford Handbook of Innovation Management* (420–41). Oxford: Oxford University Press.

Nambisan, S. (2017), 'Digital entrepreneurship: toward a digital technology perspective of entrepreneurship', *Entrepreneurship Theory and Practice*, *41*(6), 1029–55.

Nambisan, S. and Baron, R. A. (2019). 'On the costs of digital entrepreneurship: role conflict, stress, and venture performance in digital platform-based ecosystems', *Journal of Business Research*, *125*(1), 520–32.

Ngoasong, M. Z. (2018). 'Digital entrepreneurship in a resource-scarce context: a focus on entrepreneurial digital competencies', *Journal of Small Business and Enterprise Development*, *25*(3), 483–500.

Ouweneel, E., Le Blanc, P. M. and Schaufeli, W. B. (2013). 'Do-it-yourself'. *Career Development International*, *18*(2), 173–95.

Ramaswamy, V. and Ozcan, K. (2018). 'Offerings as digitalized interactive platforms: a conceptual framework and implications', *Journal of Marketing*, *82*, 19–31.

Ratto, M. and Ree, R. (2012). 'Materializing information: 3D printing and social change', *First Monday*, *17*(7), 1–21.

Rayna, T. and Striukova, L. (2016). 'From rapid prototyping to home fabrication: how 3D printing is changing business model innovation', *Technological Forecasting and Social Change*, *102*, 214–24.

Rindfleisch, A., Malter, A. J. and Fisher, G. J. (2019). 'Self-manufacturing via 3D printing: implications for retailing thought and practice', *Marketing in a Digital World, Review of Marketing Research*, *16*, 167–88.

Ritzer, G., Dean, P. and Jurgenson, N. (2012). 'The coming of age of the prosumer', *American Behavioral Scientist*, *56*(4), 379–98.

Saebi, T., Lien, L. and Foss, N. J. (2017). 'What drives business model adaptation? The impact of opportunities, threats and strategic orientation', *Long Range Planning*, *50*(5), 567–81.

Strauss, A. L. and Corbin, J. M. (1998). *Basics of Qualitative Research*. Thousand Oaks, CA: SAGE Publications.

Tseng, M. and Radke, A. M. (2011). 'Production planning and control for mass customization – a review of enabling technologies', in F. S. Fogliatto and G. J. C. Da Silveira (eds), *Mass Customization, Engineering and Managing Global Operations* (pp. 195–218). Cham: Springer.

Vargo, S. L. and Lusch, R. F. (2004). 'Evolving to a new dominant logic for marketing', *Journal of Marketing*, *68*(1), 1–17.

Vitorino, J., Ribeiro, E., Silva, R., Santos, C., Carreira, P., Mitchell, G. R. and Mateus, A. (2019). 'Industry 4.0: digital twin applied to direct digital manufacturing', *Applied Mechanics and Materials*, *890*, 54–60.

von Hippel, E. (2018). *Free Innovation*. Cambridge, MA: MIT Press.

Wengraf, T. (2001). *Qualitative Research Interviewing: Biographic Narrative and Semi-Structured Methods*. Newbury, CA: Sage Publications.

Westerman, G., Bonnet, D. and McAfee, A. (2014). 'The nine elements of digital transformation', *MIT Sloan Management Review*, *55*(3), 1–6.

Wiecek, A., Wentzel, D. and Erkin, A. (2019). 'Just print it! The effects of self-printing a product on consumers' product evaluations and perceived ownership', *Journal of the Academy of Marketing Science*, *48*(1), 1–17.

Womack, J. P. (1993). 'Mass customization: the new frontier in business competition', *MIT Sloan Management Review*, *34*(3), 11–14.

Womack, J. P., Jones, D. T. and Roos, D. (2007). *The Machine that Changed the World: The Story of Lean Production.* New York: Simon & Schuster.
Yin, R. K. (2009). *Case Study Research: Design and Methods.* Newbury, CA: Sage Publications.

PART III

Entrepreneurship and business models in craft
and artisanal markets

8. Entrepreneurs in action? Motivations for crafting a career in handmade goods

Victoria R. Bell

INTRODUCTION

More than ever, working from home or running a business from home has become routine and as such has reconfigured how we use our homes, further blurring the boundaries between work, leisure and family. Those working from home prior to the Covid-19 pandemic of 2020 were already acquainted with negotiating these boundaries, but the lockdown enforced by the UK government in March 2020 further increased complexities for those who may have chosen running a business from home, or those whose main market was, up to then, predominately via word of mouth or face-to-face marketing and sales.

Craftspeople, artists and makers are some of those who have traditionally worked from within a space in the home, and as Sennett (2009) states, the workshop-home can be dated back to medieval times. The rise of making and selling of creative handmade goods is reflected in the establishment of online markets such as Etsy in the USA in 2005 and Folksy in the UK in 2008. Folksy showcases work from designer-makers based in the UK and has over 13,000 makers selling goods (Folksy, 2020), a vast increase from 4,000 in 2017 (Folksy, 2017). The emergence of these online markets, the renaissance of craft fairs prior to the pandemic and pop-up shops, collectives and cooperative endeavours, combined with makers' own online profiles, including websites and blogs offers small scale entrepreneurs a 'cheaper, more effective and more efficient [way] to market themselves and their artefacts to a wider customer base' (Woolley, 2010, p. 142; see also Luckman, 2015; Taylor & Littleton, 2012; Dawkins, 2011; Ekinsmyth, 2011; Grace & Gandolfo, 2014). These markets reflect, in one way, the changing nature of craft production and consumption and the pressure for makers to be dynamic in their business approach. However, Woolley (2010) also argues that this virtual environment has the potential to dilute engagement with the sensory, visual and process qualities of the object, especially for the buyer. Furthermore, this dilution could impact at the micro level for the maker, influencing what they produce for this virtual mass market, which may contradict with their initial motivation for producing unique handmade goods.

Being entrepreneurial is synonymous with being creative (Fillis, 2012) and has traditionally focused on new business start-ups and economics (Ekinsmyth, 2011; McRobbie, 2015), but as Fillis and Telford (2020, p. 6) suggest, entrepreneurialism can be regarded 'as an overarching philosophy within businesses'. Research into creative enterprises proposes a shift in how we conceptualise entrepreneurs and entrepreneurial activity into one that places emphasis on social values and the practice of making which intrinsically underpin creative production and the making process as described by Woolley (2010; see also Ekinsmyth 2011; McRobbie, 2015; Gauntlett, 2018). Sennett (2009, p. 125) describes this expertise as the craftsperson being 'engaged in a continual dialogue with materials'. In some ways, we are experiencing a renaissance in the perceived value of craftsmanship, with consumers seeking goods that are sustainable, unique and have a clear provenance (Ocejo, 2017).

This chapter explores entrepreneurialism through the lens of participants that were part of a longitudinal qualitative study of self-identified artists, designer-makers and crafters carried out in the North of England and were first interviewed in 2015 and then again approximately 18 months later in 2016. All of the participants discussed here began making and selling their products from within the home. Throughout the timescale of the study, some transferred their making to a studio or other space, but the majority continued to work from home. This work adds further understanding of entrepreneurship and craftspeople or makers, exploring how those who began their enterprise from within the home negotiate opportunities and constraints in relation to different aspects of their business, including the production and selling of goods, finding a space within a crowded marketplace, product branding and makers' values in relation to their work (Crawford, 2009; Taylor & Littleton, 2012). The chapter uses the notion of opting out and the Kaleidoscope Career Model (KCM) (Mainiero & Sullivan, 2006) to explore participants' motivations for setting up in business, what constitutes success in their enterprise, their everyday creativity, complexities and contradictions of working within the home, and how these factors contribute to sustaining their enterprise. It will be argued here that the intangible added value, distinct from the making process (Woolley, 2010), coupled with the skills value of the making are significant for both the maker and the consumer (Sennett, 2009; Frayling, 2011; Ocejo, 2017). For the maker this is in terms of being productive, personal fulfilment from the creative process (Dawkins, 2011; Gauntlett, 2018; Crawford, 2009; Luckman, 2015) and from validation of selling their creations and, in line with Woolley

(2010), for the consumer the tangible and resulting intangible value of the craft object that they purchase.

The chapter begins with a discussion of the literature on entrepreneurship and craft enterprise, including a further explanation of the KCM (Mainiero & Sullivan, 2006), followed by a section on embodied practice, emotion and values where Luckman's (2015) and Fillis' (2012) typologies are introduced. The methodology sets out how the research was carried out, using a biographical approach to interviewing and includes an introduction to the participants of this study and the approach to analysis. From the analysis, the findings and discussion section is broken down into four sections: Establishing Enterprise; Communities of Craft; Transitions: Business and Self; and Being Creative. The Conclusion also includes limitations of the research and ideas for future research.

ENTREPRENEURSHIP AND CRAFT ENTERPRISE

Artists and craftspeople and makers often establish their enterprise with an aspiration to succeed in the creative industries, the priority being the making of their product, with business planning second (McRobbie, 2015). For others, the stimulus for being enterprising with handmade goods begins as a hobby or a decision to make a change in career, and can involve a complexity of individual push and pull factors (Hughes, 2005). Mainiero and Sullivan (2006) use the concept of the KCM to define modern changes in women's careers, an acknowledgement that people shift career patterns, with motivations changing over time. The main features of these shifts are conceptualised by Mainiero and Sullivan (2006) as ABC: authenticity, balance and challenge. Authenticity can be characterised as being true to self and 'as a quest to find one's true voice' (p. 115), aligning behaviours and attitude with personal values. Balance is balancing work with personal commitments and challenge relates to the individual striving for stimulating work. Focusing on women's career trajectories, the KCM acknowledges that, unlike men, many women do not pursue a linear, corporate career model and seek out further opportunities and possibilities as their career progresses (Mainiero & Sullivan, 2006). An uncertain future is emerging for many industries due to the pandemic. Furthermore, the rise of short-term contracts and changes in work practices, such as the gig economy, are shifting the ways that we work and these will continue to evolve. As such, the KCM is considered to be useful for considering all careers in the twenty-first century, not just those of women, and is used here to explore the careers of those who have 'opted out' (Maineiro & Sullivan, 2006) to embark on their craft enterprise.

Hughes (2005, pp. 54–64) defines the main pull factors into self-employment as: challenge, positive work environment, meaningful work, independence, and flexibility (see also Ocejo, 2017 for a craft-focused discussion), including work–life balance and the option to work from home. Hughes also takes into account the ability for the individual to control both their work environment and their own destiny as significant pull factors; these pull factors map onto Mainiero and Sullivan's (2006) KCM. Push factors into self-employment as defined by Hughes (2005) include factors such as the restructuring or down-sizing of organisations, unemployment, lack of opportunities to progress, and internal organisational bureaucracy. The move into self-employment, in any sector, is more complex than 'entrepreneurial pull and unemployment push' (Hughes, 2005, p. 47; see also Luckman, 2015); individual and wider structural opportunities and constraints exist which will also influence decisions, for example, family commitments, seeking recognition and purposeful activity (Ocejo, 2017). Similarly, the juncture of career can also impact on priorities and shifts in motivations (Mainiero & Sullivan, 2006; Cabrera, 2007).

Creating unique goods and making a living can be precarious, but fulfill-ing (Dawkins, 2011). As highlighted above, motivations are complex and often contradictory (Luckman, 2015), with participants employing different strategies for ensuring that they are able to continue working in a precarious and often low-paid sector. Many are compelled to have 'portfolio careers' or supplement their income with more stable earnings (Yair & Schwartz, 2011; Hackney, 2013; Baines & Wheelock, 2003; Luckman, 2015; Taylor & Littleton, 2012). The outbreak of Covid-19 has placed further pressures on the self-employed and those working in industries that have been shut down or furloughed as a result of the pandemic and this can further destabilise the ability of artists and makers to keep working in this sector, balancing other commitments as set out in the KCM. Portfolio working can involve a diver-sification of business (Hackney, 2013), with the maker using their skills and providing services often linked to their business, such as hosting workshops. Yair and Schwartz (2011) highlight the challenges of portfolio working and the benefits for makers by diversifying as it can create networks and further opportunities for experiential learning (see also Sennett, 2009; Ocejo, 2017). Others have reached a stage in their life where they have financial security and so are able to self-support, or rely on family support (Becker, [1982] 2008; Baines & Wheelock 2003; Luckman, 2015; Taylor & Littleton, 2012). Whilst portfolio working limits the time and creative space that can be spent making, it can also reduce uncertainty and risk (Clinton et al., 2006).

Becker ([1982] 2008, p. xvi) discussed the central ideas of cooperation, process and comparison in the art world and 'the patterns of cooperation among people who make the works rather than the works themselves', high-lighting the value of collective working (see also Ocejo, 2017 and, for further discussion on craft, collective working and 'sociable expertise', Sennett, 2009, p. 248). Becker suggested that those working in the art world tend to cluster together and this can contribute to working more effectively – and creatively – when they are able to network and work alongside others in a similar field; comparison with others can drive ambition. Becker ([1982] 2008, p. 16) also highlighted the importance of and role of the market to 'weed out the talented from the others'. As introduced above, for artists and craftspeople, today's potential marketplace is varied and vast, which comes with the risk of dilution, but independent makers can reach a large customer base quickly via the internet, if they have the skills and inclination to do so.

EMBODIED PRACTICE, EMOTION AND VALUES

Luckman (2015, p. 55) placed craft businesses into seven categories: hobbyists, part-time makers, part-time small business makers, full-time small business makers, part-time design/studio/art/craft makers, professional full-time design/studio/art/craft makers and named artists. Luckman's (2015) categories describe the craft economy as a continuum, and whilst the typology describes individuals in relation to their business, it does so in terms of enterprise, time and level of artistry. Fillis (2000, cited in Fillis, 2012, p. 27; see also Fillis, 2010) 'constructed a typology of craftspeople' which aimed to characterise craftspeople and their business in relation to a range of emotions, including the 'connection' of the work with its customer base and their own embodied emotion to the making and marketing of their work. He used the terms lifestyler, entrepreneur, idealist and late developer to explain approaches to business. Within each 'type', Fillis (2012) acknowledged that craftspeople will also have a philosophical position in relation to the design, production and marketing of their goods, so adding a further level of complexity to the typology. Sennett (2009, p. 21) describes the emotional rewards of gaining skills in craftsmanship as being 'twofold: people are anchored in tangible reality, and they can take pride in their work'. Fillis' (2012) typology recognises the individuality of the maker and the ways that makers identify with their medium and their emotional link with the artefact they produce, often seeing themselves as being irrevocably part of the product; that the process of making and resulting objects are part of their identity as they are an explicit, tangible expression of their creativity (Woolley, 2010; Grace & Gandolfo, 2014, see also Luckman, 2015; Taylor & Littleton, 2012; Ocejo, 2017, for further discussions on craft and identity). Whilst typologies can appear to be restrictive and do little more than pigeonhole or label people, they have been usefully used in combination here for understanding transitions into and aspirations of creative enterprise and how this translates into business practice.

McRobbie (2015, p. 146) refers to creative enterprise as passionate work and, as she suggests, it is useful to consider artistic and creative enterprises in terms of social values. It is argued here that the combination of object and link with the creator is a complex mix of values, as proposed by Woolley (2010; see also Dawkins, 2011). Woolley (2010, p. 136) suggests that further 'understanding of the meaning and significance of craft objects' is required to assist in improved marketing of crafts and in order to sustain the craft market. As already discussed, motivation for seeking to establish a career in selling handmade goods is varied. This variability is also relevant when discussing craft and maker values, with Woolley (2010, p. 143) advocating that these values are linked with those of the individual maker and the tangible values – the making process – and the intangible values – which are conveyed through 'marketing, promotion, personal identity, artistic vision and craft philosophy' of the maker – that are 'absorbed by the public' (see also Crawford, 2009; Gauntlett, 2018). Both McRobbie (2015) and Ocejo (2017) discuss the sense of and search for self-actualisation or realisation through practice. Ocejo (2017, p. 54) considers how different craft businesses 'create and promote a sense of authenticity' via brand identity such as place as visible provenance. As Greer (2008, as cited in Luckman, 2015, p. 155) states: 'Handmade objects are able to resonate deeply with people because craft allows us to transform emotion into a tangible object.' This relationship for the maker with the object, including the process, lifestyle and identity of creative enterprise (Luckman, 2015), alongside the flexibility of home working can sometimes be counter to the nitty gritty of self-employment and sustaining a living and the pressures to be creative.

METHODOLOGY

The research was longitudinal, taking a qualitative, biographical approach to interviewing participants. Participants were contacted individually and via collectives through researcher attendance at craft fairs, inviting artists and crafters to take part both during these events and post-event. Participants were first interviewed in 2015 and then a follow-up interview was carried out approximately 18 months later in 2016. Seventeen participants took part in the first phase of the research and 11 in the second phase. At time of the first interview, participants ranged between 23 and 67 years of age, with the majority being white British and over half were female. Four participants self-identified as having some kind of disability or ill health (this was not explored explicitly unless participants chose to disclose), and for three participants – all female – this was a significant reason why they were working from home in their medium. Participants were making objects using a variety of media, including ceramics, pottery, wood, mixed media, paint, paper and textiles. Gender-neutral pseudonyms are used here and participants described only by the medium they are working in to help maintain anonymity.

The interviews were semi-structured, with the first taking a biographical approach, with the aim to establish the participant's background, including upbringing, career to date, family and how they got to be making and selling work using their specific medium (Grace & Gandolfo, 2014; Baines & Wheelock, 2003). The aim of this interview was to gain an understanding of the life story of participants and an understanding of the journey and often non-traditional path that brought them to being involved in their creative enterprise (Mason, 2017). The aim of the second interview was to catch up with participants, giving them an opportunity to reflect over their previous year in business, their continuing or changing motivations and discuss any developments with their enterprise since the first interview. It also gave the researcher an opportunity to revisit points and seek clarification or more detail on some of the data collected during the first interview (Saldana, 2003). It was interesting to note that many of the participants stated in the second interview that after the first interview they had reflected on their business and it had been an opportunity to stop and take stock of where they were and consider future plans for their enterprise (Saldana, 2003).

Participants in this study came into self-employment in the arts and crafts from a wide range of backgrounds. Unlike other studies (see, for example, Mischler, 2004; Taylor & Littleton, 2012; McRobbie, 2015) most participants had not had any formal training, but were more likely to have attended lifelong learning, adult education, an evening course, or be self-taught in their craft. Many began through experiential learning, making in their medium as a hobby before making the decision to establish an enterprise.

At time of interviews, participants were at different stages in development of their business. For example, some were just embarking on selling, whilst others were more established both within their business and also within their local craft community. They also, as suggested by both Luckman's's (2015) and Fillis'' (2012) typologies, were able to give their enterprise varying levels of commitment, in terms of both time and business approach. This often depended on responsibilities and flexibilities around portfolio work or personal commitments.

Data were analysed inductively, taking a thematic approach. Initial and focused coding was carried out, which led to the development of categories from the data. NVivo software was used to aid management of the data. Links were then made with existing literature, also highlighting any gaps and differences in findings. From the analysis, it was evident that Luckman's (2015) and Fillis' (2012) typologies, alongside Mainiero and Sullivan's (2006) Kaleidoscope Career Model in the context of craft careers were useful for helping to explain motivations for embarking on and continuing in a career in craft.

FINDINGS AND DISCUSSION

Establishing Enterprise

Motivations for participants establishing their venture and continuing to do so are complex, but the main motivations, or pull factors, given by participants were flexibility, opportunity to work for self, agency and control over decisions, health reasons and the inducement of working creatively, and producing work from their chosen medium. This resonates with the findings of Hughes (2005), Mainiero and Sullivan (2006), Sennett (2009), Luckman (2015) and Ocejo (2017). In terms of the KCM, the notion that makers could balance other areas of their life, with making from home fitting into other areas of their life, was significant. Push factors included changes to work practices, physical and mental illness, and end of contractual working.

The most common reason given for making the move to establish a business venture was opportunity, or that it was an opportune time to make the decision. This was usually combined with or due to another factor, such as health preventing continuation of other work, or family circumstances: a mix of push and pull factors. Participants had, overall, decided to take a positive step from, as one of the participants, Bea described it, 'working for the man' to working for themselves, with the flexibility of time and opportunity to be their own boss and the control and agency that this initially brings. Many others echoed this sentiment, including Jac who works with textiles: 'I love the fact that I work for myself, I answer to myself, I am in control and in charge of my own future.' The recognition of control and agency was strong for participants and they maintained this even though many were not making a living solely from their making; the importance to them was that it was their choice how and when they worked. These motivations again resonate with the KCM; makers were striving for stimulating work and to be challenged creatively and the feeling of agency and control gave them the opportunity to balance other commitments. Whilst this was so, makers also described that the reality of making and selling handmade goods in an often saturated market held many challenges, not least the need to make a living.

Flexibility was important in terms of the way that participants worked; this balance of working, as set out by the KCM (Mainiero & Sullivan, 2006; see also Ocejo, 2017), included flexible working hours and the opportunity to plan around other areas of their life, including portfolio work. For some, this flexibility also related to what they were producing: the flexibility of being creative. George, who works in mixed media, said: 'I think the other thing that appeals to me with this is it's flexible in terms of what I do and what space I use to create them in.'

Balancing other jobs to sustain their creative enterprise, or portfolio working, was usual for participants. For those portfolio-working in order to sustain their creative enterprise, most were using their creative skills to teach others through workshops and classes, with only three participants doing an unrelated part-time job. So whilst Mainiero and Sullivan (2006) overall consider balance as a positive, this could also be a challenge for participants. With flexibility of creative enterprise came the pressure to make a living. This could become more of a challenge as the pandemic of 2020 changes the world of work, with more people working from home or on reduced hours, with some industries more at risk than others.

Communities of Craft

The sense of making and connecting (Crawford, 2009; Gauntlett, 2018; Sennett, 2009) came from the pull of working in the medium itself, as one participant said:

> I took that leap in the first place because basically I wanted to do what I enjoy, I enjoy making things, designing things, being creative and seeing someone with something I've made is the best feeling ever. (Paula; recycled and mixed media)

Using one's hands and connecting with the process of making, or the medium, (Woolley, 2010; Crawford, 2009; Gauntlett, 2018; Sennett, 2009) was one of the enduring factors for participants in continuing with their venture and, for some, was without comparison, as Kit an idealist (Fillis, 2012) part-time maker (Luckman, 2015) said:

> There's the sense of getting lost in a process that is very much about the moment in which you are working and following a path that catches your imagination and takes you on a little journey as it were. It becomes a very important thing for you and it becomes a very fulfilling experience and I think once you've experienced that, it's very hard not to want to experience it again.

This individualistic motivation was also found by Baines and Wheelock (2003) who noted that this was only one part of the story and that many social processes were similarly relevant for artists and makers. Likewise, participants in this research discussed the significance of a sense of belonging to a maker's community, building networks with other makers, and interacting and making connections with their customers (Ocejo, 2017). These networks were built and defined in different ways, but most often described by participants as a community, a platform where they could share knowledge of the creative market and a space where they could seek advice, guidance and support (Becker [1982] 2008; Ocejo, 2017; Sennett, 2009). Some gained a mentor from these connections and, as Ocejo (2017) describes, mentors and the community in which a maker works can be central to guiding philosophies of work and practice. The intrinsic value of these networks was a continuing motivation for participants. The opportunity to share experiences assists makers navigating the market and enables them to learn from those working in a similar way, as set out by Becker ([1982] 2008; see also Ocejo, 2017). Paula, an entrepreneur (Fillis, 2012) and part-time small business maker (Luckman, 2015) explained:

> [Working in a collective] immediately sucked me into a whole new world. I had a whole new group of friends, a whole new network of knowledge and you know, craft fairs to go to, suppliers to get this and that from, ways to price your stuff, advice and help and using that as a resource. So I had a really fast learning process which was great, which I wouldn't have had if I'd stayed at home and just sold on Etsy or something.

Whatever the medium or scale that participants' making and selling, as well as the sociality of a makers' community, participants also stressed that one of the most rewarding and fulfilling parts of their work was the validation from customers or consumers of their product. From starting out, and realising that they had a product that people wanted to buy (and so making the decision to embark on an enterprise), to the continued sense of connection that many of them described (both between them and the customers and the customer and the product), participants reported an authentication of self, product and the process of making in their craft working. This also reflects the challenge of the KCM and doing fulfilling and stimulating work (see Ocejo, 2017). This sentiment is epitomised by Frankie, an artist, idealist (Fillis, 2012) and part-time maker (Luckman, 2015) who said:

> Validation is important. Early on in setting up, that's why exhibitions are so important because you are putting your work out there and you are getting feedback, sometimes it's negative feedback but you have to become more thick skinned because not everyone is going to like the same [stuff].

There is a sense that self is bound up with the product:

> That's the thing with the connection with people who like it you see, its, it's there and that's worth more than money ... it's that sense of communication, that sense of, there's no words. It's just, they get it and in a sense, they get you. (Caz; painter, printer, idealist (Fillis, 2012) and professional full-time art maker (Luckman, 2015))

Transitions: Business and Self

Those who did not, or were unable to, build networks were less likely to have developed their business in the time between the first and second interview.

For some this was due personal circumstances such as disability and the initial motivation being driven by being productive from home. With the direct access to a market via the internet, selling from home seems relatively straight-forward, but counter to that, building networks and knowledge of, for example, branding and markets is less accessible, highlighting some constraints of making handmade goods from home.

Working from home as a sole trader can be isolating and lonely, especially for those working in more remote or rural areas. The opportunity to share ideas and discuss the strains of working creatively was valued by participants and often only developed after some time in business. This could be for several reasons including, as highlighted below, that some participants, when they started their business had not made themselves aware of the potential market; similarly, it can take time to tap into networks. For some participants, the fact that they began their enterprise with little or no formal training, coming from careers such as health, data analysis and the hospitality sector, meant that building the confidence to shake off their own impostor syndrome, or learning how to identify themselves, also took time (for an in-depth discussion of crea-tive identities, see Taylor & Littleton, 2012; Luckman 2015). George, idealist (Fillis, 2012) part-time maker (Luckman, 2015), works in mixed media, and aims to be perceived as a legitimate artist and to be successful in becom-ing involved, integrated and accepted into the designer-maker community. Construction of their product was intertwined with the story of (re)construct-ing George's own identity. As part of this construction of artist-self, George discussed their struggle with making a decision about their artistic identity: 'One of the things that I really struggled with [was] what to call myself; I just went through so many names and I have gone for designer-maker, textile artist … so that took me, well months [to decide].'

At the time of the second interview, George's self-identity had shifted again and they self-identified as 'an artist'; this journey might be what Grace and Gandolfo (2014, p. 57) refer to as 'an ongoing process of self-invention'. This process of taking the step from personal pursuit to public enterprise, including marketing and branding, was often intertwined with personal identity and con-veying values that resonate with the customer; makers often saw themselves as an integral part of their product and so part of the brand, or as Dawkins (2011, p. 274) suggests, 'the self [is] completely bound up with the work', reflecting the notion of authenticity in the KCM. However, branding self, being the front line of the business working at craft fairs and other markets, including digital ones, when lacking confidence or battling impostor syndrome can be challeng-ing (Luckman, 2015).

For others, one of the tensions or challenges of working in this sector was, paradoxically, the pressure to be creative. This finding runs in contrast to the KCM; initial motivations for participants were linked to authenticity and being true to self and personal values, and challenge, striving for stimulating work. The reality of making a living puts these values at risk. For those participants who sought to expand their business, those Fillis (2012) would consider to be an entrepreneur, this became more apparent as they attempted to change the balance of income streams, striving to make a living from selling their handmade goods.

Being Creative

Participants were more likely to make their goods and then seek a market, rather than conduct market research and explore gaps in the market prior to deciding what they were going to make to sell. This was sometimes limited by expertise and creative ideas, especially for those who were elevating their hobby to a business venture, or for others it was simply that they were what Fillis (2012) would describe as a lifestyler. Once their enterprise was established, some participants continued to stand by their original products, ignoring the dynamic nature of the market and the need to plan for the next product. It could be argued that these makers were remaining true to self and so authentic (Mainiero & Sullivan, 2006). These participants were most likely to be a lifestyler or idealist (Fillis, 2012) and/or a hobbyist or part-time maker (Luckman, 2015), reflecting the freedom to be creative due to control and agency via self-support (Becker ([1982] 2008). The entrepreneurs recognised the need to diversify in order to increase sales, making and selling what they considered to be goods that were either artistically inferior or that were cheaper to produce, for example, selling prints of originals and/or cards depicting their product. It was these participants who were more likely to be either sustaining a living, or moving towards it via their creative enterprise.

Bea was one of those considered to be entrepreneurial (Fillis, 2012) and a full-time business maker (Luckman, 2015) and admitted feeling the pressure to produce work that would sell, creating a tension between being true to self (authenticity) in relation to the product and working for self on one's own terms. For Bea, as an artist who works with textiles, the space to be creative is compromised by the need to produce work that is more commercially viable than one-off pieces; the pressures of making a living mean creativity is compromised, as they said:

> Initially it was about doing what I wanted to do, then it was about supporting ourselves, but I now realise the pressures of having to be commercially viable, it's not so good for the creativity and I've sort of lost that outlet, you know, it was really pleasurable, and I mean there are times still were I really get into the zone and I really enjoy doing it, but, yeah, I suppose it's more about the money and not having to do a proper job now.

At the time of the second interview, Bea had reflected on their skills and market potential of their goods and as a result taken part in a small-business digital training course, which covered skills such as how to set up a website and using social media effectively for marketing. Their philosophy was 'make what you sell, don't sell what you make' which chimes with Becker ([1982] 2008, pp. 94–5) who stated: '… most artists, wanting their work to be distributed, do not make what the system will not handle'. This does, to some extent, bring the notion of authenticity from the KCM into question: is being true to self more meaningful if you admit to self that the work you are making does not sell, or does doing this mean that you are selling out?

Tracy, a ceramicist (at time of first interview), entrepreneur (Fillis, 2012) and professional full-time studio maker (Luckman, 2015) was initially working on their business venture part-time whilst working in the voluntary sector, with a kiln in the back of the house and selling their work by attending craft fairs at weekends. When their short-term contract ended, Tracy initially worked full-time from home before moving into studio space. On being creative they said:

> There's a tension between batch production and also innovating new work, I am also keenly aware that there's going to come a saturation point for each design or product and you need to have the next innovation up your sleeve, already designed, kind of already photographed and ready to go at the time that happens.

Although also entrepreneurial in their approach, Tracy initially took a different view to Bea about their creative wares:

> It's not about the money, people say you have to make something that is commercially viable, you have to design with a market in mind, I think if you have the seed of something in your heart, if you've got those intuitive whispers, you should make what you want to make and be damned if it's weird, like.

Hence at the time of the first interview, Tracy could be considered authentic in approach and challenged in terms of creative output being fulfilling and stimulating. At the time of the second interview Tracy self-identified as a potter and had moved again into different studio space and was producing domestic pottery as a mainstay alongside their more creative objects. For Tracy this shift was not detrimental to their authenticity or a challenge; it was a transition for them as a potter, shaking off their impostor syndrome, gaining the conspicuous skills of pottery from a mentor. This demonstrates the implications of shifting careers, as highlighted by the KCM, and specifically how the path to opting out into creative enterprise is not always linear or straightforward, or the utopia it may at first appear to be.

CONCLUSION

The research reveals motivations for establishing enterprise that are complex, and whilst there are commonalities, factors vary depending on individual circumstance, with motivations shifting over time, linked with entrepreneurship and identity. This research supports McRobbie's (2015) proposal that the social values, as well as other entrepreneurial characteristics, are relevant and significant when exploring and supporting creative enterprise. It is clear that participants in this study were entrepreneurial in how they use their time, materials and opportunities, whether this be via happenstance or actively sought. Those that actively sought opportunities were more likely to be entrepreneurs and to be making a living from their enterprise. Unlike McRobbie's research, the majority of participants in this study embarked on their venture without formal training in their chosen medium and were more likely to have escalated their hobby or untaken informal rather than formal training. However, whatever the 'level' of working, the social values, the intangible added value (Woolley, 2010) coupled with the skills of the maker are significant. The emotional or affective labour (Dawkins, 2011; Luckman, 2015; Sennett, 2009; Ocejo, 2017) involved in crafting a career in handmade goods results in makers engaging in a 'publicly performed narrative of self' (Luckman, 2015, p. 118). Makers position themselves in relation to others in the space within which they sell, and this can influence the way they promote, present and brand themselves, and their product, in their chosen marketplace. This is reflected here in the transition of makers into enterprise but also, as illustrated by makers such as George and Tracy, the transition to a new self-identity or 'an ongoing process of self-invention' (Grace & Gandolfo, 2014, p. 57).

The diversification of products did not necessarily result in makers losing their sense of authenticity; in some cases it was strengthened as they found their way and became confident in their skills and abilities as artists and makers. For others the pressure to be creative and sell more commercially viable products brought authenticity into question, but participants found other outlets such as networks and collectives where they were able to maintain their personal and social values as well as build knowledge and support for their enterprise. Balancing other commitments whilst maintaining creative enterprise was most possible for those who were able to self-support and as they had the space to be creative. It is likely that the balance for those who are portfolio working will have become more unstable with the pandemic of 2020, increasing pressures on authenticity and challenge of the KCM (Mainiero & Sullivan, 2006). For part-time makers and hobbyists (Luckman, 2015) and idealists (Fillis, 2012), the pandemic lockdown of 2020 will have gifted the space and time to continue to be creatively productive which was fundamental to their everyday existence.

Connections with others (both maker networks and with customers and consumers) and the sociality of making (Mischler, 2004) contributed to participants' search for fulfilment (or challenge) and sense of success. Using networks to aid cooperation between makers, learn skills and processes and to allow for comparison with others (Becker, [1982] 2008) were significant in participants' transition into creative enterprise and as part of the continued motivation. Businesses were more likely to have evolved organically than via rigorous business planning, for some oscillating between labour and leisure (Dawkins, 2011) and whilst many were not able to sustain a living, being productive and connecting with the medium was intrinsic to their sense of control and agency and, as Collier (2011, p. 105) found, gave them the opportunity 'to calm themselves, to feel centered [*sic*], to have control over a small part of their lives, to have social opportunities, and, for some, just to immerse themselves in the sheer pleasure of the creative process.'

This research has demonstrated the motivations and shifts in motivation for those embarking on and continuing a craft enterprise in the North of England. It has highlighted the efficacy and also some of the limitations of the KCM in relation to craft business motivations. Although longitudinal at two points in time, it still only gives an in-depth view of these participants' experiences at and across this time period. From this project it is evident that the wider continued and changing relevance of the KCM could be researched further. More pertinently, it is evident that further research into craft businesses is needed, especially in light of the Covid-19 pandemic and subsequent lockdowns in the UK that have continued into 2021. How have craftspeople negotiated these drastic changes to our working lives, including the impact of balancing home-working with the rest of the household and the internet being, at times, the sole marketplace? There is a strong chance that competition may have increased over this time, as people in lockdown have turned to creative activities as a means of being productive, and so the succession from hobby to business continues.

REFERENCES

Baines, S. & Wheelock, J. (2003). Creative livelihoods: the economic survival of visual artists in the North of England. *Northern Economic Review*, *33*(34), 105–17.
Becker, H. S. ([1982] 2008). *Art Worlds* (25th anniversary edition). University of California Press.
Cabrera, E. F. (2007). Opting out and opting in: understanding the complexities of women's career transitions. *Career Development International*, *12*(3), 218–37.
Clinton, M., Totterdell, P. & Wood, S. (2006). A grounded theory of portfolio working: experiencing the smallest of small businesses. *International Small Business Journal*, *24*(2), 179–203.

Collier, A. F. (2011). The well-being of women who create textiles: implications for art therapy. *Journal of the American Art Therapy Association, 28*(3), 104–12.

Crawford, M. (2009). *The Case for Working with Your Hands.* Penguin Books.

Dawkins, N. (2011). Do-it-yourself: the precarious world and postfeminist politics of handmaking (in) Detroit. *Utopian Studies, 22*(2), 261–84.

Ekinsmyth, C. (2011). Challenging the boundaries of entrepreneurship: the spatialities and practices of UK 'mumprenuers'. *Geoforum, 42*(1), 104–14.

Fillis, I. (2010). Profiling the behaviour of people working with craft. In L. Valentine & G. Follett (eds), *Past, Present and Future Craft Practice* (pp. 124–35). NMS Enterprises.

Fillis, I. (2012). An aesthetic understanding of the craft sector. *Creative Industries Journal, 5*(1–2), 23–41.

Fillis, I. & Telford, N. (2020). Introduction to the handbook of entrepreneurship and marketing. In I. Fillis & N. Telford (eds), *Handbook of Entrepreneurship and Marketing* (pp. 2–16). Edward Elgar Publishing.

Folksy (2017, June 17). The UK's biggest online craft fair. Folksy. https://folksy.com/.

Folksy (2020, August 24). The blog for modern British craft. Folksy. https://blog.folksy .com/.

Frayling, C (2011). *On Craftsmanship: Towards a New Bauhaus.* Oberon Books.

Gauntlett, D. (2018). *Making Is Connecting: The Social Meaning of Creativity, from DIY and Knitting to YouTube and Web 2.0* (2nd edn). Polity Press.

Grace, M. & Gandolfo, E. (2014). Narrating complex identities: contemporary women and craft. *Women's Studies International Forum, 47*(1), 56–62.

Hackney, F (2013). Quiet activism and the new amateur. *Design and Culture, 5*(2), 169–93.

Hughes, K. D. (2005). *Female Enterprise in the New Economy.* University of Toronto Press.

Luckman, S. (2015). *Craft and the Creative Economy.* Palgrave Macmillan.

McRobbie, A. (2015). *Be Creative: Making a Living in the New Culture Industries.* Polity Press.

Mainiero, L. A. & Sullivan, S. E. (2006). *The Opt-out Revolt: Why People Are Leaving Companies to Create Kaleidoscope Careers.* Davies-Black Publishing.

Mason, J. (2017). *Qualitative Researching* (3rd edn). SAGE Publications.

Mischler, E. G. (2004). *Storylines: Craft-artists Narratives of Identity.* Harvard University Press.

Ocejo, R. E. (2017). *Masters of Craft.* Princeton University Press.

Saldana, J. (2003). *Longitudinal Qualitative Research.* Rowman & Littlefield.

Sennett, R. (2009). *The Craftsman.* Penguin Books.

Taylor, S. & Littleton, K. (2012). *Contemporary Identities of Creativity and Creative Work.* Ashgate Publishing.

Woolley, M. (2010). The making: value and values in the craft object. In L. Valentine & G. Follett (eds), *Past, Present and Future Craft Practice* (pp. 136–50). NMS Enterprises.

Yair, K. & Schwartz, M. (2011). Making value: craft in changing times. *Cultural Trends, 20*(3–4), 309–16.

9. New business models for craft: the case of Artemest

Chiara Piancatelli and Alessandra Ricci

INTRODUCTION

The changing role of digital, through the evolution of mobile technologies, is reflected in the increasing use of digital platforms and devices for e-commerce purposes. Big data, social media and e-commerce have become part of our everyday lives, hastening the shift to marketing 4.0 (Guven, 2020). As a consequence, the influence of digitalization is affecting consumer purchase behavior in the online world, as new communication channels emerge (Štefko et al., 2019). E-commerce plays a critical role in this environment and has become one of the most important activities that affects a consumer's purchase decisions (Guven, 2020).

As a result, the way both business-to-business (B2B) and business-to-consumer (B2C) activities are conducted in many sectors has been completely modified. Businesses must now attend to the differences in marketing brought about by these changes in order to create a lasting competitive edge, and effectively adapt to the digital transformations occurring (Guven, 2020).

This chapter provides an overview of how digital technologies might disrupt conventional enterprises by redefining how craft products are consumed in today's market. It focuses on the benefits that a dialogue with technological innovation may provide to the sector, which is fueled by constant renewal. Hence, an explanation of how the concept of craftsmanship has evolved over time is offered in order to showcase more contemporary forms of craftsmanship based on the interaction between craftwork and digital technologies. Indeed, new technologies are being employed to boost the value of traditional craft practices, satiating the contemporary desire for innovation as well as the renewed search for originality, authenticity, customization, and individualization that excessive industrialization has provoked (Dallocchio et al., 2015; Erdogan et al., 2020).

The analysis continues by introducing the potential of digital tools, in particular arguing that the use of digital platforms makes it possible to create ecosystems in which actors collaborate and compete with each other. As a matter of fact, companies should improve their marketing effectiveness in order to survive and surpass the competition (Akkaya &Tabak, 2017). In this sense, information and communication technologies (ICTs) can contribute to increasing the value of craft products and knowledge by implementing relational systems that enable the development of value co-creation practices. Thus, the contribution offered by digital technology is linked to an integrated management of resources which stimulates innovation processes and, at the same time, the transfer of skills and knowledge.

Furthermore, the discussion analyzes the approaches and logics that should be followed in order to support the current evolution of manufacturing production and consumption methods ushered in by the technological revolution. We have also sought to highlight the importance of ICT in the transformation of contemporary society, as well as to assess the new business models that have emerged, and consider the impact of the Covid-19 pandemic in this context.

Finally, the company Artemest, an Italian curated e-commerce platform established to inspire and celebrate the yearning for beauty in the daily lives of its clients, will be presented. The chapter will use the case study of Artemest to examine the critical phase that artisanal goods are going through as a result of digital transformation, examining how these transformations might turn niche activities into viable economic breakthroughs by forming valuable and strategic partnerships.

DEFINITION AND EVOLUTION OF CRAFTMANSHIP

The craft profession has always existed, but the starting point of its historical itinerary goes back to the ancient world. In ancient Greece, there was no definition of craftsmanship as such, as the expression "téchne"[1] encompassed a wide range of specialized knowledge, such as painting or sculpture, but also tailoring, music or geometry (Tatarkiewicz, 2020).

As a result of the new figure of the Renaissance artist, artisanal products began to be excluded from the realm of fine arts (Herzfeld, 2004; Shiner, 2010). Through the prominence of "reason" during the Enlightenment, the belief that art should be regarded as a distinct area from skill and craftsmanship persisted throughout the 18th century. It may be observed from this that the concept of craftsmanship underwent various modifications linked to the evolution of social circumstances. Traditionally, the term "craft" has been used to describe people with manual abilities who can create exceptional and distinctive items, as well as identifying a specialized class of workers (Adamson, 2013; Dallocchio et al., 2015; Garavaglia & Mussini, 2020; Ricci, 2021).

Indeed, Taylorist and Fordist ideologies promoting economic rationality (Smith, 2013) clashed with the traditional values of craft production. In particular, industrial production achieved a "double devastation, due on the one hand to the commercial competition of industrial products, and on the other hand to the most vulgar plundering of its formal models; the machine, imitating handicraft work, humiliated it and cancelled all the expressive values implicitly contained in the handmade product" (Branzi, 1999, p. 12). Indeed, production specialization was used to respond to a broad and changing demand, while on the other hand, uniqueness and personalization were demanded.

In order to survive, or outperform, the competition in the world market (where industry seems to use craft attributes as marketing tools (Leissle, 2017)), craft businesses must enhance their marketing efficacy (Akkaya & Tabak, 2017) by augmenting their strengths. The craft sector brings together different categories of products, markets, types of consumers and professionals who are involved in the development and production of artifacts through manual work that require high levels of technical and professional competence (Ostrom, 1999; Adamson, 2013; Dallocchio et al., 2015; Cavalli, 2017; Antoldi et al., 2017).

In particular, practical and manual skills required to perform different tasks change according to the individual professions, and as such craft products themselves show great variability. For this reason, craft products could be classified according to their degree of innovation compared to tradition, and to their degree of professionalization compared to high-end products (Adamson, 2013; Antoldi et al., 2017). In this sense, craft work is based precisely on manual skills which, in order to produce quality products, require technical preparation to be developed.

Thus, craft activities require specific skills and complex work processes that differ from industrial and mass production (Dallocchio et al., 2015). Indeed, the craft sector is mostly characterized by small enterprises and small individual or family businesses that execute traditional crafts and produce unique and customized products (Micelli, 2011; Guven, 2020).

Further, although craft professions are clearly rooted in tradition (Shiner, 2010; Sennet, 2008; Micelli, 2011; Dallocchio et al., 2015; Cavalli, 2017; Ricci, 2021), they are not static, but constantly evolving. Indeed, the notion of craftsmanship has evolved over time as it depends on external factors such as demand, environment and especially innovation. Nowadays, craftsmanship is passing through a fundamental phase in its strategic development, determined by the new tools and processing techniques that the digital revolution has brought to bear, and by the widespread tendency to rediscover and enhance local craft traditions.

A MATTER OF INNOVATION: CRAFTMANSHIP IN THE DIGITAL AGE

Craft businesses should innovate by offering technologically innovative, and highly customized, products to national and international markets as a way of dealing with the problems of economic, technological, social, and cultural shift (Micelli, 2011; Dallocchio et al., 2015). Annie Warburton,[2] creative director of the British Crafts Council, rethought the link between craft and production, claiming that new technologies, techniques and materials may drive the crafts world to new heights, where cross-pollination with other areas (such as art, science and technology) can give the sector new life.

The term "digital transformation" refers to a set of strategic processes and transformations aimed at implementing organizational changes through digitization projects with the goal of enabling significant business improvements (Verhoef et al., 2021). Even before the boost to digital transformation given by the Covid-19 pandemic, speed of delivery, process execution, and decision-making in general were already established as adding the greatest competitive value to any business (Atti, 2018). In addition, the capacity to speak about a business, and communicate one's value proposition to the market, has become a critical talent for every type of firm in an increasingly competitive environment (Dallocchio et al., 2015). Nowadays, as information becomes readily globalized, the consumer becomes even more important. Thus, the success or failure of products is undeniably determined by the consumer, as the economic system is becoming increasingly customer-centric. Enterprises may capture, or boost, their market demand by growing their turnover through better connecting with customers, and meeting their demands (Atti, 2018). However, for many artisan workshops, the capacity to improve their work, and to create more effective marketing strategies for reaching out to potential customers, is still lacking (Dallocchio et al., 2015).

Therefore, craft businesses should be open to continuous change by embracing digital technologies, rather than seeing them as a danger to their survival. This might involve including customers in design and manufacturing processes. It might also enable the expansion of their network, and the supply of craft items through a wide range of service providers (Bonfanti et al., 2018), including making partnerships with third-party services to facilitate greater marketing effectiveness in an increasingly competitive context (Akkaya & Tabak, 2017). This might occur through the application of processes, tools and technologies to skills and operating methods, or through the development of technological innovation processes to satisfy the need for the uniqueness, authenticity and personalization that embody the core of craft production. Therefore, it is "a new digital revolution [...] this time in fabrication which, from the computer and digital revolution, has determined the concept of 'digital fabrication'" (Gershenfeld, 2012, p. 43).

The Internet of Things, 3D printing, Fab Labs (laboratories for craft production backed by current technology), and a new generation of makers, namely digital craftsmen, are some examples of innovations that have disrupted the manufacturing sector (Anderson, 2013). While, on the one hand, these innovations develop creative languages and collaborative methods typical of the digital age, on the other they support the supply chains to increase their competitiveness in international markets. In addition, digital transformation is more than just investing in information systems; it is more about developing digital skills, both technical and behavioral, that encourage human capital to be proactive in furthering and managing innovation process through the use of digital technologies (Venier, 2017). Therefore, the artisanal tradition, traditionally linked to small- and medium-scale manufacturing processes, needs to incorporate into the production process tools and competences that utilize techniques supported by the digital.

Even though distribution remains a challenge (Dallocchio et al., 2015), the increasing adoption of digital sales strategies and the existence of a favorable relationship between a network of diverse external partners support the innovative performances key to excelling in the global market. As a result, promotion remains the strategic lever that provides for the most maneuverability, and in an increasingly digitalized and global environment, it necessitates competence and capacity to be handled appropriately and successfully. In the case of small artisan workshops, this latter state is frequently jeopardized by a lack of specific skills, particularly in the digital world, as well as the difficulties of enticing and teaching future generations (Dallocchio et al., 2015).

According to major craft foundations such as the Institut National des Metiers d'Art (France), Fondazione Cologni dei Mestieri d'Arte (Italy), and the Crafts Council (United Kingdom), crafts are at a critical strategic crossing point, with the intelligence of *savoir faire* potentially transforming into economically profitable innovations. In addition, the 2016 report by KPMG for the Crafts Council, "Innovation through crafts: opportunities for growth," describes how traditional know-how, driven from the bottom-up and with an open-ended approach, is combining with new tools and processes to drive innovation via the culture of artisanship as "innovation through crafts [...] concerns the spillover effects of craft into other industries" (KPMG, 2016, p. 3). Thus, the craft economy is providing a reconfigured production model that is leading to alternative consumption patterns. Indeed, the craft economy is a space of culturally embedded knowledge. Craftmanship benefits from the emergence of significant trends in contemporary consumption practices, where the "tailor made" responds to an emerging impulse and need, from the customer point of view, for authenticity, sustainability, personalization, individualization, and new expressions of connoisseurship. Through the union of creative potential and new technologies, the digitalization of production makes it possible to realize complex and customized products through accelerated processes. In particular, the 2016 report suggests that the development of craft skills is not only necessary for innovation but also for achieving incremental economic profits. Thus, it is clear that in today's society, defined by the use of ICT, combined with a renewed interest in craftsmanship, the collaboration between crafts and other sectors creates important effects and new possibilities.

According to the KPMG analysis, exploiting the craft sector's potential can result in major economic gains as the economy transitions to a new paradigm of production and consumption.

Indeed, through the development of new products and new production and distribution processes, digital craftsmanship stimulates innovation within other businesses, contributing not only to the implementation of innovative design and production methods, but also to the creation of added value for producers and customers. For this reason, "craft skills and knowledge have a strong economic impact and significant potential to drive further growth and innovation in other sectors" (KPMG, 2016, p. 5). By embracing opportunities provided by technology and innovative ways of producing, craft businesses will be able to survive, reinvent themselves, and strengthen their competitive advantage by pursuing these strategic approaches (Bonfanti et al., 2018)

DIGITAL PLATFORM ECOSYSTEMS

The previous section of the chapter addressed the positive impacts that open digital innovation can have within crafts and other sectors, as in today's society progressive digitalization is shaping not only the way we produce, but also the way we consume. Digital platforms, which constitute technological infrastructures that make use of expanding information technology, are opening up new possibilities for craft and industry in general. They use an ecosystem of independent actors connected by common institutional logics (Hein et al., 2019), and create mutual value through the exchange of services (Lusch & Vargo, 2011). From a technical point of view, digital platforms are software-based platforms that provide basic functionalities, which is why they have a high strategic importance for companies. Indeed, the use of digital platforms can help to further increase market share, to outperform competitors, to stimulate new technological advances, and so on.

These mechanisms of value creation in the ecosystem take place through the main functionalities of the platform. If, on the one hand, the digital platform eases transactions by directly matching supply with demand, on the other hand, it offers affordance to create value-added integrations by exploiting the capacity for innovation. The decision to work with external sources is based on the availability of internal expertise, as well as the desire to control the development and implementation of innovation individually (Schilling & Shankar, 2019). Adopting an integrated omnichannel strategy approach, supported by third-party partners, is crucial for small artisan enterprises. Building strong relationships with external partners can, in fact, contribute to disruptive performance. Through the application of appropriate technology, businesses will be able to better serve consumer requests, resulting in more profitable and efficient business strategies and a greater degree of final customer satisfaction (Lemon & Verhoef, 2016).

New models of emerging B2B platforms, and the practice of value co-creation, have changed the concept of competition between companies (Hein et al., 2019). B2B platforms, through the integration of different types of services, stakeholders and customers, have transformed the individual value creation process and created new business models: that is, a "co-opetition approach" between stakeholders, based on both competition and cooperation, in a process of common value co-creation. Value creation mechanisms are no longer developed within the boundaries of an organization, but by the combined action of a network of different actors; the so-called "network model." In particular, the practice of value co-creation in platforms is based on the "service dominant logic," which "focuses on the exchange of services during which one actor uses a set of skills and capabilities for the benefit of another actor" (Hein et al., 2019, p. 504).

As a consequence, a service dominant logic has gained importance, highlighting both the current transformation in the way organizations perceive innovation, and the importance of the role of ICT in economic development (Lusch & Nambisan, 2015). Among the various factors that determine the growth of services are ICT, and the outsourcing that is the external supply that guarantees lower costs and greater efficiency and specialization. In particular, ICT is influencing demand and consumption patterns, which is why it is "considered as one of the main innovations and productivity drivers in the service economy, narrowing the differences between services and other manufacturing activities" (Maffei et al., 2005, p. 2). Thus, in consideration of the technological potential and of the new behavioral patterns, service design focuses not only on the processing of the product, but also on the design of the user experience. That is, service design represents a "customer-oriented perspective" that reconciles the need for industrialization with the need for personalization through an approach that integrates the relational dimension with the productive dimension. Indeed, the increased importance of the role of services in the contemporary economy has led to the need to align the mechanisms of service design with economic organizational practices. The combination of innovation theory with the contributions of the user-driven approach can result in new, more comprehensive and innovative business models.

This integrated approach to innovation will be reflected in new business models for innovation and competitiveness that are particularly profitable also for the craft sector, which is experiencing a fundamental moment in its strategic development. On the other hand, an institutional Goods Dominant logic (G-D logic) has evolved over time toward a new model focused on information, experience and networking through the use of digital platforms, that is, toward a Service Dominant logic (S-D logic) (Lusch & Nambisan, 2015). In particular, the G-D logic focuses on production and supply, hence on resources and tangible outputs that are exchanged, whereas the S-D logic focuses on service processes and performances that become the basis of exchange. For this reason, given the importance of innovations in today's organizations, the S-D logic provides a better response to the surfacing of new needs.

In addition, S-D logic is much more complex than G-D logic; indeed, it requires collaborative skills, flexibility and the ability to learn and adapt to customer needs for the success of the organization. Organizations that employ operating resources, such as knowledge, relationships, culture, reputation and technology, develop a competitive advantage, which is why they are considered the most valuable. Basically, the use of S-D logic determines many positive effects, not only on the organization of the actors that form the service ecosystems, and on the digital platforms that simplify the exchange of services, but also on the value-creation practices (Lusch & Nambisan, 2015). In particular, given the importance of intangible services over tangible outputs, value is created through the integration of resources, and the collaboration among the various actors in the ecosystem. Thus, both the service providers who offer the resources and the consumers who benefit from them, become part of the value creation process. This leads to the concept of "value co-creation practices," closely linked to the role of ICT in service innovation.

Further, the study of the effects of digital tools on the industry, and in particular on the craft sector, has shifted from value creation in individual companies to value co-creation practices in more complex service ecosystems. The rise of technology has transformed the traditional models of production and consumption of handicrafts, and has therefore highlighted the need for renewed business models for the development of the sector. The evolution of the business model concept, related to manufacturing, encompasses the various tools that have been discussed so far, such as digital platforms, networking, S-D logic, user-design driven approach, mass-customization, e-commerce, and in general the set of ICTs that trigger mechanisms of sharing, collaborating, and exchanging resources and knowledge.

These considerations have emphasized the importance of the synergy between technical skills and technology to open up a "new design horizon [...] that rethinks the concept of 'bottega', small business, laboratory, atelier, to imagine the possible creation of innovative hybrid places in the spirit of the purest contemporary distributed economy" (Maffei, 2016, p. 46). In particular, the technological capabilities of the renewed business models became evident during the lockdown imposed on Italian manufacturing activities in the first half of 2020 as a result of the Covid-19 pandemic.

The emergency measures introduced by the government to tackle the health crisis led many companies, including artisans, to revise their business models, and traditional sales methods, through the use of digital tools, which proved essential to stemming the losses brought about by the emergency. Growth in the use of online sales and communication channels has also had a significant impact on the craft sector, which, in conjunction with service and technical support skills, has injected new lifeblood into the world of e-commerce in this sector.

The words of the president of the Confartigianato Vicenza and Veneto (2020), Cristian Veller, summarize the essence of the concept:

> Selling online for businesses, even before the emergency, represented a recommended step and investment. It is now certain that the post Covid19 will bring with it a change in our consumption habits. E-commerce will tap into new market segments, promote craftsmanship and build consumer loyalty by offering new experiences. Now, the emergency has highlighted how e-commerce can be an important solution to the objective difficulties faced by many entrepreneurs, including those in the B2B sector (e.g. machine manufacturing, contract clothing) since they can find, thanks to some vertical marketplaces, valid alternatives to trade fairs. I would like to remind everyone that it is not too late to get active and take advantage of this business opportunity, which is truly tailored to any type of company, and is also aimed at European and world markets, provided that you know how to rely on competent and prepared people.

In conclusion, the artisan's workshop is generally the primary selling point, where the craftsman is constantly and closely present, able to explain the product's core values to customers (Dezecot & Fleck, 2017). The Covid-19 pandemic contributed to making e-commerce a consistent feature of our purchase method. Thus, craft businesses need to adapt and evolve by digitalizing their shops, as e-commerce has a direct impact on consumers' purchasing decisions. As a consequence, it is critical to react effectively to these changes, and employ appropriate digital marketing strategies and media tools (Guven, 2020).

The so-called "tradition–innovation paradox" is a phenomenon in which traditionally-based businesses, such as craft companies, are forced to innovate in order to be competitive in a global and digital market while retaining their traditional techniques and procedures (Erdogan et al., 2020).

Indeed, ICT enables the creation of a network of value and the sharing and integration of resources and knowledge that lead to value co-creation and innovation. In practice, the gradual evolution of the various mechanisms behind the organizational logics reflects the emerging role of the organization as a network, easing the co-creation of value through the contributions of digitalization. Through these new business structures, based on the network model, not only large companies, but also craft businesses can grow. Actually, the above-mentioned digital tools support the process of value co-creation through the development of innovative organizational mechanisms, the integration of resources and collaboration between the various actors of the ecosystem. Therefore, these new technologies, processes and institutional logics can give a voice to smaller entities, such as the artisan working in a remote village, who can use digital platforms to support their business.

This is the case of the company Artemest, an Italian e-commerce site that presents a worldwide collection of furniture, jewelry and lifestyle art. Artemest preserves and supports the work of the best Italian artisans, who can use the platform to start, sustain and develop their businesses online through the integration of resources and the collaboration of more than 400 partners that form the basis of its ecosystem.

NEW BUSINESS MODELS FOR CRAFTS: THE CASE OF ARTEMEST

This case study provides an account of key understandings of craft in respect of the Italian market. It highlights the fact that Italian experts have a very specific perception of both craft and artisans. Our analysis of the transformations that digital tools have brought to traditional businesses, changing the way in which handmade products are consumed in the contemporary market, is advanced through the examination of Artemest, an Italian e-commerce platform for luxury handmade products. The final section of the chapter will discuss Artemest's experience of utilizing contemporary technological, social and economic innovations to promote the products and knowledge of Italy's excellence in respect of its material and immaterial heritage.

Our research design was exploratory in nature, based on in-depth interviews with the founders of Artemest: Ippolita Rostagno and Marco Credendino. Using an explorative approach is important in studying phenomena that may only be observable through in-depth data collection (Eisenhardt, 1989). Marketing studies have drawn significantly on qualitative research methods, including interviews. Interviews have proved an effective method for obtaining in-depth accounts of another person's experience (Kvale, 1983). Due to Covid-19 restrictions in Italy, interviews were conducted via video-call. We also had the opportunity of accessing the company's internal documents, such as presentations and reports.

The Mission and Values of Artemest

Artemest[3] is a curated e-commerce company dedicated to Italian luxury crafts-manship, founded in 2015 by the jewelry designer Ippolita Rostagno and the entrepreneur Marco Credendino, and has operational headquarters in Milan and New York. Currently, Artemest represents the main online marketplace for Italian handcrafted luxury products, and is therefore considered an ambas-sador of Made-in-Italy across the world, in terms of craftsmanship and design. The company was founded with the aim of revitalizing Italian craftsmanship and preserving the rich cultural heritage of Italian artisans, artists and design-ers, who were late in adapting to the new digital economy. Artemest is devoted to supporting its vendors to compete in the global marketplace, through the use of tech tools and a series of services, built to support the vendors in the process of internationalization and digitalization.

Therefore, its mission is not only to sell online, but also and most impor-tantly, to celebrate and preserve Italian craftsmanship in respect of the follow-ing core values:

1. Heritage: Keeping alive the Italian artistic heritage and wealth of creativ-ity through storytelling and the promotion of one-of-a-kind pieces.
2. Excellence: Offering the highest standard of craft-finished products made by Italian artisans with uncompromised quality.
3. Craftmanship: Believing in the art of creating unique products and com-mitting to a life vision that blends heritage, expertise and passion with art.
4. Curation: Traveling throughout Italy to carefully select the most talented Italian artisans and handpicking their creations for our customers.

The company works with a growing network of 1,100 artisans, artists and small and medium-sized enterprises (SMEs), selling over 40,000 products in the categories of Furniture & Lighting (40%), Decorative Art (30%), Tableware (20%) and Lifestyle (10%). Indeed, Artemest is not only a virtual shop from which one can buy from an extensive catalogue of products, but it is also a medium that, through the creation of content and storytelling doc-umenting the backstage of the various crafts, communicates and spreads the excellence of Italian craft traditions in over 70 countries.

Vendor Services

According to Rostagno, "Artemest was born from the social vocation to save Italian artisans and small businesses by providing them with an international showcase and support for the global distribution of their splendid creations." The idea came from the founder Ippolita Rostagno's great passion for materials and craftsmanship, combined with the intuition that the cause of the gradual disappearance of craft workshops was the lack of communication opportunities. The furniture and design industry had been skeptical in embracing new technologies and online commerce, compared for example to players in the fashion industry, which were quicker in developing a digital strategy. On the one hand, big furniture companies that had the strength and economic power to internationalize preferred to follow a more traditional distribution strategy and develop a deeply rooted international offline presence through showrooms and sales representatives, without investing in a digital strategy, nor in online sales channels. On the other hand, smaller players, such as workshops, craftsmen and independent artists, who are geographically dispersed across the length and breadth of Italy, did not have the resources, both human and economic, to internationalize. The majority of them are family-run businesses, with a few employees undertaking manual work. The businesses typically lack both English-language skills and managerial capabilities. As a consequence, despite the evident quality of their products, they struggled to digitize their businesses, or market their products internationally, weakening their capacity to compete with international brands. Used to manufacturing and selling to a restricted niche of customers, producers were hesitant to embrace the digital tools, and therefore the limitless possibilities provided by access to the Internet. As a result, such businesses were routinely missing significant sales opportunities, limiting themselves to local demand, and excluding themselves from access to global clients with strong purchasing power.

For this reason, Artemest uses new digital technologies applied to traditional areas to preserve and communicate the value of Italian handicrafts, developed over centuries of tradition, as a means of transcending the limiting effects of craft business's geographical dispersion and isolation. Thus, Artemest supports the craftsmen, artists and small businesses that make up its supply base to sell online through various services:

1. A curated marketplace providing a worldwide showcase to support foreign commerce.
2. A logistics team takes care of everything related to the shipment of products, from collection at the supplier's warehouse, to delivery to the final customer, managing duties and customs in over 70 countries.
3. Content and digital production, through videos, articles, photo shoots and interviews, that serve to communicate the production experience.
4. Analytics and supplier support, through a set of tech tools, that support the vendors during the process of product upload, order management and issue resolution. A dashboard function provides aggregate data and market intelligence reports to the vendors to support their performances online.

5.   Credit collection and fraud detection through multi-currency accounts
     able to invoice and collect credit in various currencies, while guaranteeing
     risk-free transactions.
6.   Customer care, through a customer care team located in different time
     zones, intermediates relations with the final customer, managing cus-
     tomization inquiries, order consolidation, and personalized shopping
     recommendations.
7.   Marketing and PR, through product placement in top global design and
     luxury publications. Online and email marketing, social media and events
     organization promote both artists and products.

Basically, Artemest has adopted, as stated by Credendino, a "hands-on
approach to the supply chain," focused on the provision of commercial, digital,
marketing and development services to small Italian artisanal enterprises. In
addition to these services, Artemest has opened a so-called "Designer Lounge"
in New York, a space conceived for the Artemest Trade Team to have meet-
ings with current and potential clients, press members and key stakeholders.
The lounge features a rotating selection of Artemest furnishings and home
décor, where visitors have the occasion to look at the products in person and to
discuss their project needs with a team member. Even though the digital platform will always be the first point of contact for Artemest, the company places
great importance on meeting and getting to know their customers. In a time
when physical encounters are limited and require special safety precautions,
the Artemest lounge is open on an appointment-only basis.

   Today there is a new attitude toward digital and e-commerce platforms, and
suppliers are increasingly reaching out to join Artemest, truly understanding
and appreciating the services offered. In recent years, new approaches to business development have also emerged amongst SMEs, symptomatic of a new
generation of craftsmen and entrepreneurs coming forward. Family-run companies are experiencing a generational change, with sons and daughters taking
the reins of the companies, bringing with them not only knowledge about
manufacturing processes and techniques handed down from their ancestors,
but also higher educational and managerial skills to lead the companies.

Product and Supply Chain

Therefore, Artemest brings together within their online environment a multi-
tude of Italian designers and craft businesses, selected personally by Ippolita
Rostagno from among the many workshops that hand down authentic craftsmanship across the Italian peninsula. These include the productions of Murano
glass artisans, the marble manufacturing of the Carrara quarries and the
ceramics of Caltagirone and Faenza, among others. The network of producers

brought together by Artemest are truly diverse, including companies of greater and lesser renown, and objects of different forms and size; be they works associated with glass masters, goldsmiths, designers or artists.

It is also noted that even though Artemest's supplier base is entirely Italian, Italy is by no means its largest market – in fact, Italy accounts for only 2 percent of its market. Artemest's main markets are the USA (60%), the UK (10%) and APAC (Asia Pacific countries) such as Australia (5%) and Hong Kong (5%) (Figure 9.1).

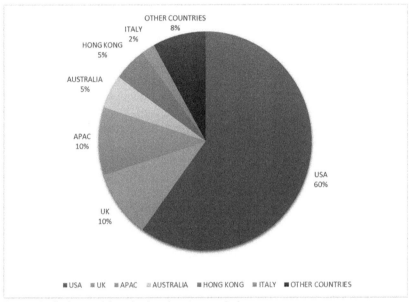

Source: Author's own elaboration based on Artemest's data.

Figure 9.1   Artemest's market

The product assortment is mainly composed of furniture, lighting and home décor, which account for most of the turnover, but also of tableware and lifestyle categories, which are growing rapidly.

Artemest has an offer of more than 40,000 products of extremely high quality (the return rate is below 1%) and of high cost (the average order value is 1,640 euros) which is mainly intended for connoisseurs and HNWI (high net-worth individuals) and trade customers, such as interior designers and architects.

Demand and Identification of Key Personas

The reference market for Artemest is high-end design furniture and home-ware, whose estimated value in 2019 was 43 billion euros (Bain Altagamma Luxury Study, 19th edition).[4] Therefore, Artemest's target audience is mainly composed of private customers with a passion for art and design, educated and wealthy, and in the upper 35–54 age bracket, located in the USA. This market seems to have a stronger propensity for furniture and home décor-related online shopping, thanks to strong e-commerce penetration, and due to the remoteness of the Italian suppliers from the final clients. In addition to private customers (B2C), Artemest sees increasing demand coming from trade professionals, such as interior designers and architects working in hospitality, residential and retail projects, emerging as an important and profitable customer segment. On average, trade professionals spend five times more than private customers on their first purchase on the platform, and repeat-purchase more frequently.

Indeed, having started out as B2C only, the company has progressively developed a B2B logic focused on inter-company relations, with a special selection of products and a dedicated team to support them. B2B clients have access to a dedicated website where they can discover exclusive products and benefits, such as trade prices, CAD files for download, and folders and lists that can be shared with their team and clients. Moreover, trade clients' requests are managed by a dedicated Artemest team that assists them with customization opportunities, renders, sample requests, order management, consolidated shipment and many more. One of the most appreciated features for trade customers is that 75 percent of Artemest product assortment is customizable, in this way embracing the customers' need for exclusivity and bespoke solutions. Recently Artemest has presented a selection of items for contract use, which are available only to B2B clients who register for the trade program, in this way further expanding the choice; products that all have the certifications needed for hospitality use.

Innovation of Artemest's Business Model

Artemest's business success is also based on its dynamic management, which has been able to respond effectively to contemporary developments, in terms of digital innovation, through the use of new technologies in application to Italian artisanal needs. Therefore, the principal contribution made by the website is in its provision of its own digital tools and digital platform oriented not only to the commercialization of products but also to the valorization of the traditions of the Italian craftmanship, connecting artisan and manufacturing production chains (Cianfanelli et al., 2020).

In this sense, Artemest represents a new business model which, using methodologies of service design thinking, aims to develop or improve services and allows for the structuring of relational systems within the ecosystem.

It is an "eco-systemic approach" (Cianfanelli et al., 2020, p. 126) which, through the synergy between the digital medium and the tradition of Made-in-Italy manufacturing, generates new opportunities for collaboration and new value chains. Thus, in this bringing together of technological, social and economic innovation with tradition, it is possible to create an augmented value for Artemest and for the suppliers whose products are promoted via Artemest. As an example of this co-creation of value, having access to data relating to product views, clicks and "adds to cart," suppliers are better supported in respect of ideation and development of future collections, decisions concerning stock levels, and inventory management.

The opportunities provided by digital platforms are well evidenced by the percentage of enquiries and orders that Artemest recorded during the lockdown in the first quarter of 2020. Indeed, despite the limitations imposed by the spread of the Covid-19 virus, sales of online shops, particularly in the furniture and home living segment, accelerated. In addition to consumers shifting spending away from travel, dining and entertainment toward the home, suppliers were leaning extra hard on e-commerce vendors. Specifically, the turnover achieved by Artemest has grown considerably compared to past years, helping more than 1,000 Italian businesses to stem the effects of the lockdown. What was born as a gradual shift from traditional retail to digital, suddenly happened all at once, with a progressive migration of buyers toward online channels, establishing a turning point in this sector. The pandemic has proved a great accelerator, speeding up consumer's adoption of the technology and comfort associated with e-commerce sites. Artemest's online channel skyrocketed in 2020, growing in a single year at a pace equivalent to five years of previous growth. By 2025, online sales will reach one third of total market value (Bain Altagamma Luxury Study, 19th edition).[5] The 2020 pandemic drastically hit the brick-and-mortar channels (−21% in retail; −40% in wholesale, according to the latest Bain Altagamma research), accelerating existing shifts in the distribution ecosystem. Customers in the near future will be less eager to return to brick-and-mortar furniture stores and showrooms, even when this will be a possibility, preferring a more digital approach.

The company's development is also linked to a recent round of financing led by the French private equity fund Olma Luxury Holdings and Swiss holding company Brahma, in addition to the Milan-based Nuo Capital (family office of the Pao Cheng family from Hong Kong), bringing the company's total funding to $11 million. In that regard, the co-founder of Artemest, Marco Credendino, has said that "it was very difficult to find investors who believed in the project. It is hard to sell Italianness to Italians. And indeed today it is the Chinese,

French and Americans who believe in it." Therefore, for the future, Artemest plans to continue to grow and expand its range of services by investing in logistics, customization and augmented reality "to become the leading market-place for contemporary luxury design and the reference point for thousands of customers around the world looking for handmade objects d'art."

In conclusion, our analysis of the case of Artemest has illuminated one example of the current trend in the search for uniqueness and excellence, affirming that craftsmanship is facing an important phase of development directly linked to digitalization through the introduction of a system of inte-grated services oriented not only to the end-customer but also and above all to producers, and to all those actors that make up the ecosystem of Made-in-Italy production.

CONCLUSIONS

This chapter has explored the potential that new technologies offer to the craft sector through an analysis of the tools and processes that have transformed tra-ditional models of production and consumption of manufacturing in the con-temporary market. To this end, a brief overview of the evolution of the notion of craft was provided, in addition to an account of its historical evolution into modern forms of craftsmanship. It has been noted that the transformations of the economic, social and technological context have an influence on the field of craft, which is therefore constantly evolving.

In particular, craftsmanship is facing a new phase in its strategic develop-ment, determined by the fourth Industrial Revolution which, through an accel-eration of innovation, has had effects not only on the world of manufacturing and production, but also on the economic and social system. For this reason, new technologies, combined with traditional operating methods, can generate important impact and new possibilities for the craft sector and for industry in general. Indeed, digital tools are developing new organizational mechanisms based on the integration of resources and on collaboration between stakehold-ers that will enable the co-creation of value by transforming the concept of competition between enterprises to that of "coopetition."

Hence, digital transformation and related changes in management and pro-duction have led to an increase in the complexity of production systems, but at the same time have given new life to craftsmanship. Further, our analysis of the transformations currently taking place in manufacturing has highlighted the development of new business models for innovation and for the sector, transformations oriented toward a customer experience-focused approach. Building on existing literature, this study has accounted for the emergence of new technologies, production practices and institutional logics within the innovation processes of craft products and methods. Digital technologies, applied to traditional craftsmanship, offer economically profitable innovations that give a voice to even the smallest of entities, providing opportunities to develop customer relationships, generate B2B connections, find new solutions and expand communication.

NOTES

1. Téchne (Greek: τέχνη, tékhne, "craft, art") is a term in philosophy that refers to making or doing.
2. Annie Warbuton, New Craft conference at Triennale di Milano, Milan, 2017.
3. The name Artemest derives from the Latin locution "Ars est celare artem" whose literal meaning is "Art consists in concealing art."
4. See https://www.bain.com/insights/the-future-of-luxury-bouncing-back-from -covid-19/.
5. See https://www.bain.com/insights/the-future-of-luxury-bouncing-back-from -covid-19/.

REFERENCES

Adamson, G. (2013). *The Invention of Craft*. London: Bloomsbury Academic/ V&A Publishing.
Akkaya, B., & Tabak, A. (2017). The impact of dynamic capabilities on firm perceived marketing performance of small and medium sized enterprises. *Transnational Marketing Journal*, 5(2), 121–5.
Anderson, C. (2013). *Makers: The New Industrial Revolution*. London: Random House.
Antoldi, F., Capelli, C., & Macconi, I. (2017). Territori che "suonano". I fattori critici di successo della produzione italiana di strumenti musicali. *Quaderni di ricerca sull'artigianato*, 3, 323–50.
Atti, G. (ed.) (2018). *La quarta rivoluzione industriale: verso la supply chain digitale: Il futuro degli acquisti pubblici e privati nell'era digitale*. Milan: FrancoAngeli.
Bonfanti, A., Del Giudice, M., & Papa, A. (2018). Italian craft firms between digital manufacturing, open innovation, and servitization. *Journal of the Knowledge Economy*, 9(1), 136–49.
Branzi, A. (1999). *La casa calda: esperienze del nuovo design italiano*. London: Idea Books.
Cavalli, A. (2017). *The Master's Touch: Essential Elements of Artisanal Excellence*. Venice: Marsilio Editori.
Cianfanelli, E., Giorgi, D., Tufarelli, M., Makki, F., De Gennaro, M., & Soreca, M. G. (2020). Le Italie del saper fare: verso una nuova geografia relazionale del Made in Italy. *Material Design Journal*, 9. https://issuu.com/materialdesign/docs/mdj_09 _issuu/s/10905365.
Confartigianato (2020). *STUDI – In emergenza Covid-19 si modifica il trend di crescita delle MPI con e-commerce: +122 mila imprese (+19,8%)*. https://www .confartigianato.it/2020/05/studi-in-emergenza-covid-19-si-modifica-il-trend-di -crescita-delle-mpi-con-e-commerce-122-mila-imprese-198/.
Dallocchio, M., Ricci, A., & Vizzaccaro, M. (eds.) (2015). *Costruttori di valore: il ruolo strategico del saper fare italiano*. Ricerche.

Dezecot, J., & Fleck, N. (2017). D'artisan traditionnel à marque artisan: quelle perception de l'artisan par le consommateur? In 20ème Colloque International Etienne Thil. https://tel.archives-ouvertes.fr/tel-02886674/document.

Eisenhardt, K. (1989). Building theory from case study research. *Academy of Management Review*, *14*, 532–50.

Erdogan, I., Rondi, E., & De Massis, A. (2020). Managing the tradition and innovation paradox in family firms: a family imprinting perspective. *Entrepreneurship Theory and Practice*, *44*(1), 20–54.

Garavaglia, C., & Mussini, M. (2020). What is craft? An empirical analysis of consumer preferences for craft beer in Italy. *Modern Economy*, *11*(6), 1195–208.

Gershenfeld, N. (2012). How to make almost anything: the digital fabrication revolution. *Foreign Affairs*, *91*(6), 43–57.

Guven, H. (2020). Industry 4.0 and Marketing 4.0: in perspective of digitalization and e-commerce. In B. Akkaya (ed.), *Agile Business Leadership Methods for Industry 4.0* (chapter 2). Bingley: Emerald Publishing.

Hein, A., Weking, J., Schreieck, M., Wiesche, M., Böhm, M., & Krcmar, H. (2019). Value co-creation practices in business-to-business platform ecosystems. *Electronic Markets*, *29*(3), 503–18.

Herzfeld, M. (2004). *The Body Impolitic: Artisans and Artifice in the Global Hierarchy of Value*. Chicago, IL: University of Chicago Press.

KPMG (2016). Innovation through craft: opportunities for growth: a report for the Crafts Council. https://www.craftscouncil.org.uk/documents/876/Innovation_through_craft_full_report_2016.pdf.

Kvale, S. (1983). The qualitative research interview: a phenomenological and a hermeneutical mode of understanding. *Journal of Phenomenological Psychology*, *14*(2), 171–96.

Leissle, K. (2017). "Artisan" as brand: adding value in a craft chocolate community. *Food, Culture & Society*, *20*(1), 37–57.

Lemon, K. N., & Verhoef, P. C. (2016). Understanding customer experience throughout the customer journey. *Journal of Marketing*, *80*(6), 69–96.

Lusch, R. F., & Nambisan, S. (2015). Service innovation. *MIS Quarterly*, *39*(1), 155–176.

Lusch, R. F., & Vargo, S. L. (2011). Service-dominant logic: a necessary step. *European Journal of Marketing*, *45*(7–8), 1298–309.

Maffei, S. (2016). Il superamento della mano. https://www.researchgate.net/publication/313612061_Beyond_hand.

Maffei, S., Mager, B., & Sangiorgi, D. (2005). Innovation through service design: from research and theory to a network of practice. A user's driven perspective. *Joining Forces*, 1–9. http://www.uiah.fi/joiningforces/papers/Maffei_et_al.pdf.

Micelli, S. (2011). *Futuro artigiano: l'innovazione nelle mani degli italiani*. Venice: Marsilio Editori SpA.

Ostrom, V. (1999). Artisanship and artifact. In M. D. McGinnis (ed.), *Polycentric Governance and Development: Readings from the Workshop in Political Theory and Policy Analysis* (pp. 377–93). Ann Arbor: University of Michigan Press.

Ricci, A. (2021). Digital marketing and artisanship: evidence of the conceptualisation of the craftsmanship within craft guilds' websites. Proceedings, Trasformazione digitale dei mercati: il Marketing nella creazione di valore per le imprese e la società XVIII SIM Conference Ancona, 14–15 October 2021, Società Italiana di Marketing, ISBN 978-88-943918-6-2.

Schilling, M. A., & Shankar, R. (2019). *Strategic Management of Technological Innovation*. New York: McGraw-Hill Education.

Sennett, R. (2008). *L'uomo artigiano*. Milan: Feltrinelli.

Shiner, L. (2010). *L'invenzione dell'arte: una storia culturale*. Turin: Piccola Biblioteca Einaud.

Smith, A. (2013). *La ricchezza delle nazioni*. Rome: Newton Compton Editori.

Štefko, R., Bačík, R., Fedorko, R., Oleárová, M., & Rigelský, M. (2019). Analysis of consumer preferences related to the use of digital devices in the e-commerce dimension. *Entrepreneurship and Sustainability Issues*, *7*(1), 25–33.

Tatarkiewicz, W. (2020). *Storia di sei idee: l'arte, il bello, la forma, la creatività, l'imitazione, l'esperienza estetica*. Milan: Mimesis.

Venier, F. (2017). *Trasformazione digitale e capacità organizzativa. Le aziende italiane e la sfida del cambiamento*. EUT Edizioni Università di Trieste.

Verhoef, P. C., Broekhuizen, T., Bart, Y., Bhattacharya, A., Dong, J. Q., Fabian, N., & Haenlein, M. (2021). Digital transformation: a multidisciplinary reflection and research agenda. *Journal of Business Research*, *122*, 889–901.

PART IV

Marketing in craft and artisanal markets

10. The new rise of artisanship in Kenya: evidence from artisan entrepreneurs

Alisa Sydow and Isabella Maggioni

INTRODUCTION

Artisanship in Kenya, as well as in the whole of Africa, has a long history. Goodwin (1958, p. 94) defined art in Africa as "the product of its craftsmen, the raw materials and the canalized inspiration provided by tradition (…)," which "arises from the materials, tools and craftsmen of earlier generations, (…) to create a 'taste' consisting of expected standards." Hence, the concept of artisanship is deeply embedded in the local culture, and represents tradition and heritage (Brown, 2015), strongly linked to Kenyan tribes (Akama, 2002). During Kenya's period as a British colony, its traditions and culture were strongly shaped by the British Empire, thus hiding the local heritage (Tignor, 2015). Yet, in the last decade, Kenya has shown a flourishing economy full of entrepreneurial activities (e.g., it is also called the "Silicon Savannah"; Fingar, 2019). There is also a rising trend of artisanal products, entirely produced in Kenya, presenting key elements of Kenyan traditions (Wright, 2008). However, this rising trend is challenged by negative stereotypical associations towards locally produced products (Maheswaran, 1994).

The literature has extensively discussed the role of country-of-origin (COO) effect from a consumer's perspective (Pappu et al., 2006), and highlighted how in developing economies foreign products are associated with premium brand perceptions, being seen as having higher quality and status value (Batra et al., 2000; Steenkamp et al., 2003; Verlegh & Steenkamp, 1999; Zhuang et al., 2008). This poses numerous challenges for entrepreneurs who offer locally produced products and who would like to leverage the cultural heritage of Kenya. To tackle these challenges, individual entrepreneurs have grouped themselves into a community that strives to develop the brand "made in Kenya," invoking their indigenous traditions and values (Brodie & Benson-Rea, 2016). To shed light on this fascinating phenomenon, we conducted a qualitative field study of 12 artisanal entrepreneurs in Nairobi to explore the new rise of artisanship in Kenya; a new rise that seeks to transform hidden local traditions into high-quality artisanal products that are appealing to an international community. More precisely, we want to understand how artisan entrepreneurs can overcome obstacles to creating a strong brand around "made in Kenya."

Our findings have shown that there are three main practices of creation that account for the rise of artisanship in Kenya: (1) the overcoming of a negative COO effect; (2) the establishment of a strong community; and (3) the improvement of the reputation of local products. In so doing, our study shows that artisan entrepreneurs play an important role as micro-institutional agents (Sydow et al., 2020) that can trigger bottom-up institutional change and facilitate the creation of collective meanings within the country's market network.

The chapter is structured as follows: first, we review the literature on artisan entrepreneurship in Kenya and on the COO effect in developing economies. After outlining the methodology adopted for the study, our key findings will be presented, detailing the principal practices associated with the growth of artisan entrepreneurship in Kenya. In the last section, key findings are discussed, and promising future research trends outlined.

ARTISAN ENTREPRENEURSHIP IN KENYA

Despite its long tradition, there is still a lack of consensus around the definition of artisanship (Igwe et al., 2019). One widely accepted element is that artisanal enterprises are usually deeply connected to their immediate context, including their place and culture (Brown, 2015). Accordingly, some scholars identify artisanship as a cultural form of business venture (Lounsbury & Glynn, 2001). Due to the cultural embeddedness of artisanship, there is a close engagement of the entrepreneur (maker) with the physical world, in its material, spatial and environmental qualities, in crafting items that are highly connected to their locality (Brown, 2015).

However, in the African context, artisan entrepreneurs, and their associated industry, have yet to be widely researched (Igwe et al., 2019). Decades ago, Steel (1979) argued that artisan entrepreneurs, and artisanal manufacturing in developing economies, reveal inherent operational problems in defining, measuring and assisting small-scale activities as most of them take part in the informal economy. Some of the typical artisanal sectors include clothing, food preparation, ceramics, metalwork, hairdressers, shoes, and furniture and wood (Blundel, 2002). Under this definition, artisans are assumed to possess certain technical skills derived from experience or apprenticeship that set them apart from other types of manual worker (Marshall, 1961). Previous studies (e.g., Marshall, 1961; Tregear, 2005) have differentiated between two types of artisan, the first category referring to those who strive for cooperation and community involvement, and the second prioritizing lifestyle goals over growth (Douglas & Shepherd, 2002). Both types are perceived as making fundamental contributions to the economic development of a specific community through their self-organization into formal or informal networks (Tregear, 2005), triggering interest in the local culture, and thus stimulating tourism (Ratten & Ferreira, 2017).

In recent decades we have witnessed the emergence, within the Kenyan economy, of new genres of craft, centered on the innovative reuse of found material. Both the objects and the processes of creating these items are termed *jua kali*, which stands in Swahili for hot sun. In Kenya, the term *jua kali* comprises various types of artisans, such as mechanics, tailors, bakers and other workers, who offer their services and products outside in the heat at street-side tables or open-air markets. Principally, such artisans are self-trained and take part in the informal sector. They reflect the dynamic and ever-evolving network of cultural exchange and artistic innovation within the local culture (Wright, 2008).

COUNTRY-OF-ORIGIN EFFECT IN DEVELOPING ECONOMIES

The concept of COO is well-established in the international marketing literature, with a focus on its influence on consumer perceptions, product evaluations, manufacturers, tourism destinations and places in economic development (Pappu et al., 2006). Since the early 1960s, the literature has explored the complexity of COO influences on branding and consumer behavior (Roth & Romeo, 1992; Maheswaran, 1994; Agrawal & Kamakura, 1999; Verlegh & Steenkamp, 1999; Papadopoulos & Heslop, 2002; Dinnie, 2004). "The little phrase 'Made in' [...] can have a tremendous influence on the acceptance and success of products" (Dichter, 1962, p. 116), and can affect consumers in numerous ways, including product evaluation (Yasin et al., 2007), quality perception and purchase intention (Papadopoulos & Heslop, 2002). Specifically, consumers use the country in which a product is manufactured as an extrinsic cue to inform their purchasing decisions.

From a theoretical standpoint, the influence of COO attributes and associations on product evaluations and consumer behavior has mainly been analyzed as a cognitive process (Bloemer et al., 2009) with consumers using country brand identity and comparing it to a product image or a country image (Usunier, 2011). However, the COO effect also encompasses symbolic and emotional stimuli (Pharr, 2005; Laroche et al., 2005; Pereira et al., 2005), operating through cognitive, affective and normative mechanisms that affect consumer evaluations and behaviors (Verlag & Steenkamp, 1999).

One pivotal construct in the COO literature is brand origin. Although consumer perceptions of origin have been mainly manipulated through the "made in" label information (Thakor & Lavack, 2003), origin information can be communicated in diverse ways. Specifically, strong origin associations could be attached to the brand, which appears to be highly salient to consumers. Thakor (1996) defines "brand origin" as the "place, region or country where a brand is perceived to belong by its target consumers" (Thakor & Kohli, 1996, p. 27). Brand origin associations are among the most salient characteristics of brand identity and personality and a key contributor to brand image (Batra et al., 2000; Thakor, 1996; Thakor & Lavack, 2003), shaping consumers' quality perceptions (Jun & Choi, 2007; Moradi & Zarei, 2012), brand-related attitudes (Ozretic-Dozen et al., 2007) and purchase intentions (Yeong et al., 2007; Prendergast et al., 2010). Andéhn and L'espoir Decosta (2018, p. 890) point out that any objective definition of origin is an inferior predictor as compared to the perceived associations experienced by consumers.

Brand origin has been proven to have a greater impact on consumer purchase intentions compared to manufacturing origin (Papadopoulos & Heslop, 2002), especially in emerging economies. This is because of the positive symbolic meanings associated with foreign brands (Zhou & Belk, 2004; Zhuang et al., 2008). However, the proliferation of hybrid (or multi-national) products sold in international markets has transformed COO into a more complex and multifaceted construct that can be separated into country of design (COD) and country of manufacturing (COM), with COM being more influential in affecting consumer perceptions than COD (Hamzaoui-Essoussi & Merunka, 2006). Moreover, consumers could develop inaccurate brand of origin perceptions due to inaccurate signaling in advertisement or packaging; brand spelling or pronunciation not corresponding to the brand's actual origin; price cues, with low prices usually associated with emerging countries; or deliberate implementation of a foreign branding strategy to convey more favorable associations (Magnusson et al., 2011). These misperceptions could reduce the salience of origin information, and bias consumers' evaluations.

In less-developed economies, consumers tend to prefer foreign brands from more developed countries. Indeed, foreign brands are associated with high quality, and premium status values (Batra et al., 2000; Steenkamp et al., 2003; Verlegh & Steenkamp, 1999; Zhuang et al., 2008). The desirability of foreign brands in developing countries is mainly driven by symbolic motivations, particularly status (Batra et al., 2000). The social distinction achievable through foreign brand consumption outweighs the utilitarian value of such products, and becomes a crucial determinant in the purchase-related decision-making of consumers in developing economies (Zhou & Hui, 2003). Thus, global brands retain a remarkable advantage over local brands in emerging countries, with a market share positively influenced by all components of the brand equity (Zarantonello et al., 2020).

This effect has proven to vary across product types with several authors identifying an interaction effect between COO and product category (Roth & Romero, 1992). For example, Manrai et al. (1998) show that the intensity of the country-halo effect is stronger for consumer packaged/convenience goods, followed by shopping goods, and luxury or premium goods (Manrai et al., 1998). In addition, Ahmed et al. (2004) point out that COO also plays an important role when evaluating low-involvement products. However, this effect is weakened when other extrinsic cues are presented, such as price and brand name (Ahmed et al., 2004). Tseng and Balabanis (2011) highlight how product typicality can help explain COO effects across product categories with ethnically typical products resulting in more favorable consumer attitudes than atypical ones.

COO attributes represent unique features which are used to "support a brand's advantages over competitors" (Papadopoulos & Heslop, 2002, p. 312). Rojas-Méndez provides a comprehensive list of dimensions used to define a nation's brand identity and to begin aligning potential stakeholders' images with the objective of identifying "the relevant nation branding dimensions [...] to help countries [...] when trying to establish a clear and distinctive image" (Rojas-Méndez, 2013, p. 470). Central to the context for research on the COO effect is the heritage associated with a national culture (Lim & O'Cass, 2001). Over time, countries develop a reputation of excellence in particular industries and sectors, often based on resource advantages and expertise that are seen as a part of the country's heritage. The country image is used to guide consumers in their decision-making process, acting as a surrogate for quality (Verlegh & Steenkamp, 1999). Thus, a country's identity and product country image (Rojas-Méndez, 2013) are seen as factors enabling consumers to summarize and collate information associated with a country, based on its people, products and culture.

These inferences are often integrated into stereotypes that are developed for a particular country (Maheswaran, 1994), and can emerge from specific sectors and result in a country being well-known for a specific competency or in a particular product category (Ryan, 2008). A country stereotyping effect is formed by "factual information not subject to change based on consumers' attitudes, sentiments or biases" (Samiee, 1994, p. 581), with reference to the country of manufacture or the country of origin of a specific brand or product. Country reputations and associated stereotypes are generally useful, and relevant to firms that can integrate such competencies into their products.

However, when companies operate in sectors different to those positively affected by these stereotypes, the country product image can have an inverse effect (Roth & Romeo, 1992). In fact, consumers could hold perceptions that such traditional and stereotyped attributes are the only ones that organizations operating in that country can have. Thus, COO positively affects companies and product categories for which a specific country is known, but could generate the opposite effect for those brands that fall outside the country's traditional competencies, resulting in COO detracting from, or preventing, the establishment of the product brand in consumers' minds (Papadopoulos & Heslop, 2002; Roth & Romeo, 1992; Verlegh & Steenkamp, 1999). Thus, consumers may fail to recognize local brands because the existing COO perceptions are so strong that they act as a filter, preventing consumers from including new local brands within their evoked set. However, a country's reputation for excellence in a specific industry becomes a relevant cue only to the extent that it is perceived by consumers, and there is an attitude–behavior gap that limits the accuracy of COO effect measurement, as this may develop through unconscious processing (Andéhn & L'espoir Decosta, 2018). Moreover, Maheswaran (1994) shows how the influence of COO-based stereotypes can vary depending on the level consumer expertise, where novice users appear to rely more on stereotypical information when evaluating a product.

Despite this, several studies have questioned the role and effectiveness of COO as a basis for the development of marketing theory and practice (Bhaskaran & Sukumaran, 2007; Brodie & Benson-Rea, 2016; Andéhn & L'espoir Decosta, 2018). Moreover, although COO brands may be considered an explicit strategy in the pursuit of business goals (Magnusson et al., 2011), few contributions focus on understanding the strategic intent behind the design and marketing of COO brands, or consider the strategic outcomes achieved through this strategy (Usunier, 2011). Specifically, COO branding has been conceptualized primarily as a dyadic relationship between sellers and buyers where the COO brand functions as an identity with an associated image (Brodie & Benson-Rea, 2016). However, firms and consumers do not operate in isolation. They are rather part of relationship networks that influence the development of their strategies, including branding (Håkansson & Snehota, 2006).

Brodie and Benson-Rea (2016) propose a framework for collective country of origin branding that analyses the COO effect, with a focus on the relational processes associated with generating a COO branding strategy, and exploring the role of networks and multiple actors in generating collective meaning within industries and markets. This broader perspective considers relational, social, network, cultural and experiential aspects that jointly co-create collective meaning (Stern, 2006) within a system of relationships.

Underpinning this perspective is a new definition that takes brands to be "complex multidimensional constructs with varying degrees of meaning, independence, co-creation and scope. Brands are semiotic marketing systems that generate value for direct and indirect participants, society, and the broader environment through the exchange of co-created meaning" (Conejo & Wooliscroft, 2005, p. 11). The proposed theoretical framework consists of two phases. The first phase acknowledges the traditional approach to branding in which stakeholder interactions are coordinated by a marketing organization representing the country's industry. The goal of this phase is building the COO brand as identity and image. The second phase introduces a relational approach to COO branding. The COO branding system facilitates an interactive process where collective meaning is further developed and enhanced by firms, trade, consumers and other stakeholders operating in the industry. In this phase, the role of industry association or industry marketing organizations is critical as they orchestrate and facilitate activities within networks around a COO brand to create collective meanings and brand identity built on a set of value propositions. In this phase, the collective brand meaning is shaped and fine-tuned through the development of relationships with customers and leverages the experience of other stakeholders to generate the brand's strategic advantage and financial value (Brodie & Benson-Rea, 2016).

The processes of building a national umbrella brand are enabled by a set of interactions that align a network of stakeholders and relationships to co-create collective meaning for the brand's value propositions. The success of COO branding comes from a strategic understanding and intentional implementation of the umbrella role of branding in the industry (Brodie & Benson-Rea, 2016). It extends beyond developing a distinctive identity and image based on single dimensions; rather, the branding process is developed within the industry network and market, based on a collective interest that generates collective meaning. By aligning this complex set of industry relationships, value is co-created within the network, contributing to the heritage of the national brand.

Drawing on this framework, this study explores the rise of craftsmanship in Kenya, and assesses the COO effect implications for artisanal entrepreneurs in a country whose reputation has suffered from negative associations both locally and globally, but where a series of initiatives are emerging to strengthen the growth of local industries, and encourage the consumption of locally produced goods and services, overcoming deep-rooted stereotypes.

METHODOLOGY

Research Context

Recently, Kenya has become renowned across Africa for its disruptive digital innovations, through strong policy in support of the development of an information and communication technology infrastructure (Ndemo & Weiss, 2017).[1] However, there is a second emerging trend which often remains hidden. Kenya's manufacturing sector contributes 11 percent to its GDP per capita,[2] and includes, for instance, food, furniture, textiles, clothing and soap.

This sector is mainly shaped by small and medium-sized enterprises that represent the idea of craftsmanship rather than mass production. Already in 2013, President Kenyatta stated: "We want to make Kenya Africa's gateway, manufacturing and technology hub." Despite its advancements in relation to African neighbors, Kenya continues to struggle with high rates of corruption,[3] and fragile legal and financial frameworks with deep market imperfections.[4] These factors impact the development of craftsmanship in the manufacturing sector. We used semi-structured interviews to collect data to explore the new rise of craftsmanship in Kenya and, specifically, the ways in which entrepreneurs are triggering this institutional change.

Data

Our research approach was inductive (Thomas, 2006), gathering data on current activity and agents' perception of opportunities, potentials and barriers, from which we developed our theoretical insights. In 2019, we conducted a series of in-depth interviews with 12 artisanal entrepreneurs in Nairobi, along with field observation and the collection of a range of business presentations, business models, performance and mission statements (Table 10.1). We have selected these entrepreneurs because they represent a cross-section of the leading initiators in Nairobi who have recently contributed to building the brand "made in Kenya."[5] We used purposeful sampling (Lincoln & Guba, 1990) to ensure the capture of multiple perspectives, and to achieve theoretical density (Charmaz, 2006). This iterative process of data collection, reduction, representation and verification follows the work of Miles and Huberman (1994). This methodology also allowed us the flexibility to pursue themes as they emerged.

Analysis

Our data analysis is based on the analytical procedures introduced by Gioia et al. (2013), who propose a three-step process that groups responses, develops second-order themes, and ultimately forms an aggregate dimension. According to our study design, we combined this procedure with an abbreviated grounded theory approach (Charmaz, 2006), using coding, categorizing and memo-writing to develop theoretical models. First, both authors independently listened to the interview transcripts, reviewed field notes and analyzed content. Each researcher then developed codes using brief descriptions of the text, highlighting relevant themes that emerged. Secondly, we placed initial codes that conceptually overlapped into developed categories (Gioia et al., 2013). We iteratively referred back to the literature on artisan entrepreneurship and COO effect (Table 10.1). Rather than developing an aggregate dimension (Gioia et

Table 10.1   *Data collection*

# of interviewees	Profile	Type of business	Age of business in years	# of minutes recorded	# of business documents	# of hours of field observation
1	Founder	Natural cosmetics	5	232	24	12
2	Co-founder	Relish & jam	4	176	12	3
3	Co-founder	Leather bags	2	159	23	–
4	Founder	Honey	4	89	4	2
5	Co-founder	Natural cosmetic	3	62	–	1
6	Founder	Fashion	4	43	–	1
7	Manager	Jewelry	5	56	23	–
8	Co-founder	Coffee	3	31	–	4
9	Manager	Leather bags	5	78	25	2
10	Founder	Fashion	2	41	6	–
11	Co-founder	Tea	4	36	12	3
12	Founder	Honey & jam	2	25	10	2
Total				1,028	139	30

al., 2013), we integrated and diagrammed our developed categories (Charmaz, 2006) to illustrate the new rise of craftsmanship in Kenya (Table 10.2).

FINDINGS

In this chapter, we have explored the new rise of craftsmanship in Kenya by investigating artisan entrepreneurs, mainly from Nairobi. Our respondents have participated at least once in the K1 Flea Market, which has become a kind of flagship of their artisan community to sell their products.[6] We found that there are three main practices of creation that account for the rise of artisanship in Kenya: (1) the overcoming of a negative COO effect, (2) the establishment of a strong community, and (3) an increase in the reputation of local products. By doing so, our study shows that artisan entrepreneurs play the role of micro-institutional agents (Sydow et al., 2020) who can trigger bottom-up institutional change. This change has been demonstrated in the transformation of both values and perceptions towards products made in Kenya, and in the creation of a community sharing the same ideas.

Overcome a Negative COO Effect

Whilst Kenya has been formally independent of Great Britain since 1963, the 68 years of colonial rule have impacted Kenya's political, social and economic system (Anderson, 2005). In our study, we have seen that some indigenous

Table 10.2   *Data structure*

Initial coding	Developed category
Historically suppressed indigenous values	
"Actually, it all has something to do with our history. You know, over years we have been taught to lose our indigenous values by the British. Look at the way we still are supposed to wear our hair. Just like the British. So, we are kind of now in a moment, in which people start to re-discover our values. Our tradition. And to understand that we actually do have beautiful things here" (Int. #6).	
"My education has been quite influenced by the British style. When I went to school, they gave you the feeling that we need to adopt the Western lifestyle, with its traditions and culinary characteristic. I guess, that is why, so many people here get crazy about all the stuff that comes from the US or UK" (Int. #5).	Overcome a negative COO effect
Perception of low-quality for local products	
"Most people do not believe that we have high quality ingredients here. And that we have the right skills to turn them into good products. Better then imported" (Int. #11).	
"Even in my family most of them do not believe that Kenyan products can be of high quality" (Int. #4).	
Refuse to consume local products	
"Usually Kenyans would not buy local products. It is not well perceived" (Int. #2).	
"Look at our supermarkets, full of imported products. People do not want to consume local ones" (Int. #7).	
Ambassador to get more people on-board	
"I started in 2010, which was pretty early. So, at the beginning it was actually hard to find people that are willing to go for Kenyan products. However, the ones we got convinced, they helped a lot to convince others. Like influencers, just offline [laugh]" (Int. #12).	
"My customers are really proud of buying local products. That is why they try to convince also their friends. Pretty helpful" (Int. #10).	
Strong feeling of belonging in community	
"The Flea Market is such a wonderful world. I love to be there every Sunday with all my other friends. We became kind of a small family" (Int. #5).	
"Here in the market, we care about each other. We share our thoughts and even problems with each other. It is really nice!" (Int. #3).	Establish a strong community
Perception of partners (no competition)	
"We support each other here. So, when I want to have a break, or a drink, I know that I can just ask my neighbor and she will take care of my business. We are friends here, we trust each other. I mean in the end, we all want the same, we want to make our Kenyan Products strong" (Int. #1).	
"I don't see them as competitors, even if we sell basically similar products. There are so many people outside that need to start using natural cosmetic. Our market is big enough for all of us" (Int. #5).	
Unifying resources and means	
"We actually realized that we kind of struggle with the same problems. And that it could be rather smart to build a brand together to promote Kenyan products made 100 percent in Kenya. You know, people outside need to understand that we are able to make really good products. You know it now [laugh]" (Int. #7).	
"We are in the same boat. So, we started to put our efforts together" (Int. #9).	
Starting off being proud of local products	
"Due to colonization, we do not have a strong perception of 'made in Kenya.' Generally speaking, we are not proud of our products and we are not famous for anything when it comes to handcraft (…) We need to fight for it. We also have the right to have our brand of Kenya. Why not?" (Int. #4).	Increase reputation of local products
"Our products are great. We have so wonderful ingredients that we can use. We should finally start to be proud of it" (Int. #6).	
Interest of government	
"Like always, once we got a little bit famous with our Flea Market and our idea around 'made in Kenya,' the government got interested in us. Because they see the potential to promote Kenya for tourism and to make more money. I don't know what they actually want to do and we will definitely not wait for them as they are always very, very slow. But you know, we are always open. Just skeptical with our government [laugh]" (Int. #9).	
"Now, even the government wants to support us. They heard about our activities" (Int. #2).	

values and traditions are still not socially accepted. For instance, the founder of an emerging fashion brand explained to us:

> Look at the style of our traditional clothes. It is so beautiful, but still, there are so many people that do not want to wear it. They want to imitate Western trends, with Western brands, because they believe that only those brands are high class. (Int. #10).

Another respondent underlined the persistent impact of British values on Kenyan culture:

> You can see it as an initial phase. A young generation of international Kenyans that are proud of where they come from is kind of emerging. They do not have experience [of] the colony period and they do reflect critically the left-overs of this phase. Which are honestly speaking a lot. Look at our education system, so British. Look at the products in the supermarket, so British. We still feel it. (Int. #1)

It is clear that the COO effect heavily influences the perceptions of Kenyan consumers, and results in well-established stereotypes that have critical implications for entrepreneurs operating in this context. One of the main consequences is that local consumers perceive products made in Kenya as low quality. Hence, they generally prefer imported products, as Int. #3 argues: "here, we are used to consuming products from the UK or from the US," and she added, "you only feel trendy if you buy Western products." In most cases, this perception of low-quality Kenyan-made products leads to an in-principal refusal to consume products made in Kenya. "Even so many out of my own family, they would never buy local products. That is totally crazy' (Int. #12). One of the co-founders of a natural cosmetic brand (Int. #5) explained to us, "at the beginning, some people told me that they do not want to use my products, because they are from Kenya. But then, I let them try it, and they have seen that we can produce high-quality even here." Despite the initial challenges to convincing consumers to try the products, he was rather optimistic after having received positive feedback. Most of the respondents in our study outlined how they were able to convince consumers to purchase by letting them try their products.

Establish a Strong Community

Most of the entrepreneurs in our study outlined the relevance of informational institutional support at the beginning of their ventures. The founder of a natural cosmetic brand told us:

> Honestly, I was afraid at the beginning. Because I thought I need to explain a lot to the people, that my products are high-quality products made in Kenya. But thank God, I kind of found some people here in Nairobi that already started to believe in Kenyan products. And they started to spread word-of-mouth [laugh]. You know, a pleasant surprise. (Int. #1)

She highlighted how important it was for her to have the support of those who share with others the values associated with natural cosmetics from Kenya. She continued: "I guess, if it would have been me alone, I would have never been able to grow so fast." Every Sunday, the artisan community in Nairobi meets at the K1 Flea Market to sell their products. One of the respondents described it as: "if you go to the Flea Market, you will feel the atmosphere. We are all very friendly, open and happy to share the products from Kenya. It is like a nice community" (Int. #11).

We visited the Flea Market during our field study, and we felt this sense of being a family and caring about each other (author's personal note) in the interactions between vendors: "first, I was skeptical, because I was afraid that this Flea Market would become just something for tourists" argued one of the artisans producing leather bags (Int. #3). "You know, surprisingly, those are searching for typical Kenya products. Where Kenyans not. But luckily, this market is actually frequented by locals. Finally, it gets a bit more mainstream." He was relieved that there were also local people appreciating the artisan community. Expressing this feeling of being a family at the Flea Market, one interviewee said:

> The best thing between us is that we are not fighting for customers. We do not see each other as competitors. Because at the end of the day, we want the same. We want our people to understand that products made in Kenya are fantastic. So, the more the better. You know? (Int. #6)

Our study shows that there is a relatively strong feeling of community between the artisan entrepreneurs, built on their common goal in promoting natural products made in Kenya.

Increase Reputation of Local Products

In our study, most of the entrepreneurs complained about having limited resources, especially for promoting their products. For instance, one entrepreneur who works in the coffee sector mentioned that "we are all entrepreneurs, so we really do not have a lot of financial resources. That is why we have started to do marketing together. In the end, it is cheaper" (Int. #8). This statement exemplified the fact that the artisan entrepreneurs had started to engage in marketing activities collectively in order to generate synergy effects. As they follow the same goal of promoting local products, they can easily advertise their products together. What began as an informal meeting at the K1 Flea Market has become a more structured channel for promoting craftsmanship in Kenya. "It all started with just a very informal market in which we wanted to sell our cremes," stated one artisan entrepreneur. "But actually, then we got more and more producers and we realized that we all have the same difficulties." She argued that one of the main problems is that

> People do not want to consume Kenyan products. So, we were thinking about what we can do (...) And in the end, we realized, what we need is a strong identity of products "made in Kenya." You know, like your cars from Germany. Made in Germany. Famous worldwide. But we are not famous for anything, if it is not about sport [laugh]. (Int. #1)

Her comment represents well the feelings of most of the artisan entrepreneurs. We found that there was a strong willingness to establish a brand around products made in Kenya, driven by their feelings of pride in their local quality. Over recent years, the artisan entrepreneurs, and the Flea Market, have begun to attract the attention of the government: "the local government is very slow. But when they see an opportunity, because there is some business outside, they get immediately interested in you. That is exactly what has happened with us and our Flea Market" (Int. #11). Another specified: "they want to use it to attract more tourists and maybe even for export. Who knows?" (Int. #7). Both statements stress the role played by the agglomeration of individual ventures, and specifically how such agglomerations may become a catalyst for a new rise of craftsmanship in Kenya, one that might even have an impact on governmental strategy.

DISCUSSION AND FUTURE RESEARCH

In this study we have explored the practices that are contributing to the development of artisanship in Kenya, and understand how artisanal entrepreneurs have addressed key challenges posed by COO-driven stereotypes. Our results show that the COO effect negatively influences Kenyan consumer perceptions of local and artisanal brands, which are consistently perceived as of lower quality compared to foreign alternatives. These stereotypes present challenges for artisanal entrepreneurs, who in turn respond by developing strategies aimed at overcoming the negative associations traditionally linked to Kenyan brands, and educating consumers through the communication of the values stemming from the brand and country heritage. We observe how the role of community-led initiatives is critical. This reflects previous contributions studying the development of national umbrella brands (Brodie & Benson-Rea, 2016) in which an aligned network of stakeholders operates to co-create collective brand value propositions and meaning rooted in the country heritage and traditions. The success of these strategies results in a distinctive brand image and identity. However, in the case of the "made in Kenya" brand, artisanal entrepreneurs are dealing with remarkably negative associations that are widespread in the population.

This specific case study deserves additional attention, as it could provide relevant and actionable insights to counterbalance a negative COO effect and, more generally, negative brand associations stemming from heritage and traditions. Our study preliminarily identifies a series of practices experimented in by artisanal entrepreneurs, such as try-before-you-buy initiatives, and a joint effort to improve the reputation of Kenyan brands through educational activities both online and offline. The artisanal entrepreneurship community has also elected a physical location, the K1 Flea Market in Nairobi, that has become the heart of their community, and the core of their joint activity towards the creation of a relationship network that contributes to the co-creation of collective meanings associated with the "made in Kenya" brand (Price & Coulter, 2019).

However, unlike previous studies of COO branding strategies, our study has shown that, in this case, the initiative originates with individual entrepreneurs creating a "made in Kenya" brand. This behavior reflects a bottom-up approach, rather than the usual top-down approach, to generate change at the institutional level. Prior studies of entrepreneurship in developing economies (cf., Sydow et al., 2020; Battilana et al., 2009) have noted the entrepreneur's function as micro-institutional agents, building formal and informal institutions to achieve their business goals. Yet we have seen in this study that they have also played a significant role in the development of the "made in Kenya" brand, generating cultural as well as institutional changes.

Due to the nascent nature of this research field, we propose that future research should provide additional understanding of the concrete practices and strategies developed by artisanal entrepreneurs to (1) overcome negative COO effect, (2) grow community around the "made in Kenya" brand, and (3) establish a clear and shared brand identity for the country's artisanal production. Moreover, it would be fascinating to better understand the role and impact of artisan entrepreneurs longitudinally. Some possible future research questions might be: how can artisan entrepreneurs overcome the negative COO effect? How may artisanship be mainstreamed? How can artisan entrepreneurs ensure a certain quality standard for made in Kenya brands? How can artisan entrepreneurs work effectively with local government? And how can we measure the cultural impact of artisan entrepreneurs on the local society?

NOTES

1. Kenya has transformed into a dynamic hub which has pushed innovations like M-Pesa (https://www.safaricom.co.ke/personal/m-pesa), Brck (https://www.brck.com), and BitPesa (https://www.bitpesa.co) which have been extremely impactful.
2. See http://www.commonwealthofnations.org/sectors-kenya/business/industry_and_manufacturing/.
3. Kenya was ranked 137th out of 180 in the 2019 Corruption Perception Index; see https://www.transparency.org.
4. Kenya is 77th in *The Economist*'s Business Environment Ranking; see https://www.eiu.com.
5. See http://madeinkenya.brandkenya.go.ke/.
6. For more information, see https://www.safari254.com/vendors-at-the-k1-flea-market/.

REFERENCES

Agrawal, J., & Kamakura, W.A. (1999). Country of origin: a competitive advantage? *International Journal of Research in Marketing, 16*(4), 255–67.

Ahmed, Z. U., Johnson, J. P., Yang, X., Fatt, C. K., Teng, H. S., & Boon, L. C. (2004). Does country of origin matter for low-involvement products? *International Marketing Review, 21*(1), 102–20.

Akama, J. S. (2002). The role of government in the development of tourism in Kenya. *International Journal of Tourism Research, 4*(1), 1–14.

Andéhn, M., & L'espoir Decosta, J.-N. P. (2018). Re-imagining the country-of-origin effect: a promulgation approach. *Journal of Product & Brand Management, 27*(7), 884–96.

Anderson, D. M. (2005). 'Yours in struggle for Majimbo': nationalism and the party politics of decolonization in Kenya, 1955–64. *Journal of Contemporary History, 40*(3), 547–64.

Batra, R., Ramaswamy, V., Alden, D. L., Steenkamp, J.-B. E. M, & Ramachander, S. (2000). Effects of brand local and nonlocal origin on consumer attitudes in developing countries. *Journal of Consumer Psychology, 9*(2), 83–95.

Battilana, J., Leca, B., & Boxenbaum, E. (2009). How actors change institutions: towards a theory of institutional entrepreneurship. *Academy of Management Annals, 3*(1), 65–107.

Bhaskaran, S., & Sukumaran, N. (2007). Contextual and methodological issues in COO studies. *Marketing Intelligence & Planning, 25*(1), 66–81.

Bloemer, J., Brijs, K., & Kasper, H. (2009). The COO-ELM model: a theoretical framework for the cognitive processes underlying country of origin-effects. *European Journal of Marketing, 43*(1–2), 62–89.

Blundel, R. (2002). Network evolution and the growth of artisanal firms: a tale of two regional cheese makers. *Entrepreneurship & Regional Development, 14*(1), 1–30.

Brodie, R. J., & Benson-Rea, M. (2016). Country of origin branding: an integrative perspective. *Journal of Product & Brand Management, 25*(4), 322–36.

Brown, J. (2015). Making it local: what does this mean in the context of contemporary craft? *Arts and Crafts Council*, Islington, London, accessed 29 May 2020 at www.craftscouncil.org.uk/content/files/Crafts_Council_Local_Report_Web _SinglePages.pdf.

Charmaz, K. (ed.) (2006). *Constructing Grounded Theory: A Practical Guide through Qualitative Analysis*, London: SAGE Publishing.

Conejo, F., & Wooliscroft, B. (2015). Brands defined as semiotic marketing systems. *Journal of Macromarketing, 35*(3), 287–301.

Dichter, E. (1962). The world customer. *International Business Review, 4*(4), 25–7.

Dinnie, K. (2004). Country-of-origin 1965–2004: a literature review. *Journal of Customer Behaviour, 3*(2), 165–213.

Douglas, E. J., & Shepherd, D. A. (2002). Self-employment as a career choice: attitudes, entrepreneurial intentions, and utility maximization. *Entrepreneurship Theory and Practice, 26*(3), 81–90.

Fingar, C. (2019). Kenya's reputation for quality leads to choose Nairobi. *Financial Times*, accessed 29 May 2020 at https://www.ft.com/content/367907d0-d558-11e9 -8d46-8def889b4137.

Gioia, D. A., Corley, K. G., & Hamilton, A. L. (2013). Seeking qualitative rigor in inductive research: notes on the Gioia methodology. *Organizational Research Methods, 16*(1), 15–31.

Goodwin, A. J. H. (1958). The art of Africa: an introduction. *Africa South (Cape Town), 2*(4), 94–101.

Håkansson, H., & Snehota, I. (2006). 'No business is an island' 17 years later. *Scandinavian Journal of Management, 22*(3), 271–4.

Hamzaoui-Essoussi, L., & Merunka, D. (2006). The impact of country of design and country of manufacture on consumer perceptions of bi-national products' quality: an empirical model based on the concept of fit. *Journal of Consumer Marketing, 23*(3), 145–55.

Igwe, P. A., Madichie, N. O., & Newbery, R. (2019). Determinants of livelihood choices and artisanal entrepreneurship in Nigeria. *International Journal of Entrepreneurial Behavior & Research, 25*(4), 674–97.

Jun, J. W., & Choi, C. W. (2007). Effects of country of origin and country brand attitude on nonprescription drugs. *Journal of Targeting, Measurement and Analysis for Marketing, 15*(4), 234–43.

Kenyatta, U. (2013). Kenya aims to be Africa's gateway for manufacturing. *Industry Week*, accessed 29 May 2020 at https://www.industryweek.com/the-economy/article/21961212/kenya-aims-to-be-africas-gateway-for-manufacturing.

Laroche, M., Papadopoulos, N., Heslop, L. A., & Mourali, M. (2005). The influence of country image structure on consumer evaluations of foreign products. *International Marketing Review, 22*(1), 96–115.

Lim, K., & O'Cass, A. (2001). Consumer brand classifications: an assessment of culture-of-origin versus country-of-origin. *Journal of Product and Brand Management, 10*(2), 120–36.

Lincoln, Y. S., & Guba, E. G. (1990). Judging the quality of case study reports. *International Journal of Qualitative Studies in Education, 3*(1), 53–9.

Lounsbury, M., & Glynn, M. A. (2001). Cultural entrepreneurship: stories, legitimacy, and the acquisition of resources. *Strategic Management Journal, 22*(6–7), 545–64.

Magnusson, P., Westjohn, S. A., & Zdravkovic, S. (2011). What? I thought Samsung was Japanese: accurate or not, perceived country of origin matters. *International Marketing Review, 28*(5), 454–72.

Maheswaran, D. (1994). Country of origin as a stereotype: effects of consumer expertise and attribute strength on product evaluations. *Journal of Consumer Research, 21*(2), 354–65.

Manrai, L. A., Lascu, D., & Manrai, A. K. (1998). Interactive effects of country of origin and product category on product evaluations. *International Business Review, 7*(1), 591–615.

Marshall, A. (ed.) (1961). *Principles of Economics: Text*. Macmillan for the Royal Economic Society, London: SAGE Publishing.

Miles, M. B., & Huberman, A. M. (eds.) (1994). *Qualitative Data Analysis: An Expanded Sourcebook*, London: SAGE Publishing.

Moradi, H., & Zarei, A. (2012). Creating consumer-based brand equity for young Iranian consumers via country of origin sub-components effects. *Asia Pacific Journal of Marketing and Logistics*, *24*(3), 394–413.

Ndemo, B., & Weiss, T. (2017). Making sense of Africa's emerging digital transformation and its many futures. *Africa Journal of Management*, *3*(3–4), 328–47.

Ozretic-Dozen, D., Skare, V., & Krupka, Z. (2007). Assessments of origin of brand cues in evaluating a Croatian, Western and Eastern European food product. *Journal of Business Research*, *60*(1), 130–36.

Papadopoulos, N., & Heslop, L. (2002). Country equity and country branding: problems and prospects. *The Journal of Brand Management*, *9*(4), 294–314.

Pappu, R., Quester, P. G., & Cooksey, R. W. (2006). Consumer-based brand equity and country-of-origin relationships. *European Journal of Marketing*, *40* (5–6), 696–717.

Pereira, A., Hsu, C. C., & Kundu, S. K. (2005). Country-of-origin image: measurement and cross-national testing. *Journal of Business Research*, *58*(1), 103–6.

Pharr, J. M. (2005). Synthesizing country-of-origin research from last decade: is the concept still salient in an era of global brands? *Journal of Marketing Theory and Practice*, *13*(4), 34–45.

Prendergast, G. P., Tsang, A. S. L., & Chan, C. N. W. (2010). The interactive influence of country of origin of brand and product involvement on purchase intention. *Journal of Consumer Marketing*, *27*(2), 180–88.

Price, L., & Coulter, R. (2019). Crossing bridges: assembling culture into brands and brands into consumers' global local cultural lives. *Journal of Consumer Psychology*, *29*(3), 547–54.

Ratten, V., & Ferreira, J. J. (2017). Future research directions for cultural entrepreneurship and regional development. *International Journal of Entrepreneurship and Innovation Management*, *21*(3), 163–9.

Rojas-Méndez, J. (2013). The nation brand molecule. *Journal of Product & Brand Management*, *22*(7), 462–72.

Roth, M. S., & Romeo, J. B. (1992). Matching product and country image perceptions: a framework for managing country of origin effects. *Journal of International Business Studies*, *23*(3), 477–97.

Ryan, J. (2008). The Finnish country-of-origin effect: the quest to create a distinctive identity in a crowded and competitive and crowded international marketplace. *Journal of Brand Management*, *16*(1–2), 13–20.

Samiee, S. (1994). Customer evaluation of products in a global market. *Journal of International Business Studies*, *25*(1), 579–604.

Steel, W. F. (1979). Development of the urban artisanal sector in Ghana and Cameroun. *The Journal of Modern African Studies*, *17*(2), 271–84.

Steenkamp, J.-B. E. M., Batra, R., & Alden, D. (2003). How perceived brand globalness creates brand value. *Journal of International Business Studies, 34*(1), 53–65.

Stern, B. B. (2006). What does brand mean? Historical-analysis method construct definition, *Journal of Academy of Marketing Science, 43*(2), 216–23.

Sydow, A., Cannatelli, B., Giudici, A., & Molteni, M. (2020). Entrepreneurial workaround practices in severe institutional voids: evidence from Kenya. *Entrepreneurship Theory and Practice,* https://doi.org/10.1177/1042258720929891.

Thakor, M. V. (1996). Brand origin: conceptualisation and review. *Journal of Consumer Marketing, 13*(3), 27–42.

Thakor, M. V, & Lavack, A. M. (2003). Effect of perceived brand origin associations on consumer perceptions of quality. *Journal of Product & Brand Management, 12*(6), 394–407.

Thomas, D. R. (2006). A general inductive approach for analyzing qualitative evaluation data. *American Journal of Evaluation, 27*(2), 237-246.

Tignor, R. L. (ed.) (2015). *Colonial Transformation of Kenya: The Kamba, Kikuyu, and Maasai from 1900 to 1939*, Nairobi, Kenya: Princeton University Press.

Tregear, A. (2005). Lifestyle, growth, or community involvement? The balance of goals of UK artisan food producers. *Entrepreneurship & Regional Development, 17*(1), 1–15.

Tseng, T.-H., & Balabanis, G. (2011). Explaining the product-specificity of country-of-origin effects. *International Marketing Review, 28*(6), 581–600.

Usunier, J. C. (2011). The shift from manufacturing to brand origin: suggestions for improving COO relevance. *International Marketing Review, 28*(5), 486–96.

Verlegh, P. W. J., & Steenkamp, J. E. M. (1999). A review and meta-analysis of country-of-origin research. *Journal of Economic Psychology, 20*(5), 521–46.

Wright, K. D. (2008). Cleverest of the clever: coconut craftsmen in Lamu, Kenya. *The Journal of Modern Craft, 1*(3), 323–43.

Yasin, N. M., Noor, M. N., & Mohamad, O. (2007). Does image of country-of-origin matter to brand equity? *Journal of Product & Brand Management, 16*(1), 38–48.

Yeong, N. C., Mohamad, O., Ramayah, T., & Omar, A. (2007). Purchase preference of selected Malaysian motorcycle buyers: the discriminating role of perception of country of origin of brand and ethnocentrism. *Asian Academy of Management Journal, 12*(1), 1–22.

Zarantonello, L., Grappi, S., Formisano, M., & Brakus, J. (2020). How consumer-based brand equity relates to market share of global and local brands in developed and emerging countries. *International Marketing Review, 37*(2), 345–75.

Zhou, L., & Hui, M. K. (2003). Symbolic value of foreign products in the People's Republic of China. *Journal of International Marketing, 11*(2), 36–58.

Zhou, N., & Belk, R. W. (2004). Chinese consumer readings of global and local advertising appeals. *Journal of Advertising, 33*(3), 63–76.

Zhuang, G., Wang, X., Zhou, L., & Zhou, N. (2008). Asymmetric effects of brand origin confusion: evidence from the emerging market of China. *International Marketing Review, 25*(4), 441–57.

11. Slow production, less consumption: righteous approaches to the paradox of craft businesses

Richard E. Ocejo

INTRODUCTION

The aim of this chapter is to address a simple paradox of the emerging movement of businesses that are based on and promote craft work (Jakob, 2012; Kapp, 2016). These places include traditional brick and mortar retail locations as well as self-employed craftspeople who sell their products directly to consumers online or at a variety of markets with other vendors. On the one hand, these entrepreneurs and craftspeople promote a new elite form of consumption based on culturally 'omnivorous' tastes—that is, tastes that draw from the broad range of the social class spectrum (Peterson and Kern, 1996; Peterson and Simkus, 1992). Empirical evidence shows that it is typically a subset of relatively privileged consumers and producers who demonstrate omnivorousness, or who perform the evaluations and construct the frameworks that determine a product's value based in large part on its provenance (e.g., whether or not a product is 'authentic') (Holt, 1998; Hubbard, 2019; Johnston and Baumann, 2010; Khan, 2010; Ocejo, 2017). Craftspeople make products they feel are superior to or more 'authentic' than those in other cultural strata—that is, those made with other, generally inferior techniques, ingredients, and materials—that they want the consuming public to have. A specific discourse of consumption—or, more specifically, 'good' consumption—is central to their mission (Binkley, 2008; Schor, 1998) as much as 'good' production, or doing something well for its own sake, is (Crawford, 2009; Sennett, 2008).

On the other hand, they also actively (not implicitly) have and promote an agenda of anti-consumption, or resistance to consumption (Kozinets et al., 2010). Anti-consumption can take several forms, from minimalism (Zalewska and Cobel-Tokarska, 2016), or the reduction of material goods for the purposes of achieving some notion of a 'good' life, to more extreme displays of anti-capitalism, anti-globalization, and anti-corporate branding (Hollenbeck and Zinkhan, 2010; Klein, 1999). It has also been linked to the individual's search for authenticity and an authentic identity in an inauthentic world filled with 'non-righteous' forms of consumption (Cherrier, 2009; Zavetoski, 2002). Indeed, craftwork itself has often been seen as anti-capitalistic and anti-modern (Crawford, 2009; Gibson, 2016; Henderson, 2012; Krugh, 2014; Thrift, 1997). As this broad range suggests, being anti-consumerist was once the province of political radicals (think Abbie Hoffman's countercultural treatise *Steal This Book* from 1971) or religious ascetics. Today it is just as often a lifestyle choice of the privileged, with messages that are firmly situated in the mainstream (think lifestyle guru Marie Kondo) (Chayka, 2020; Holt, 1998, 2002).

While not necessarily antithetical to these forms, modern craftspeople possess and use a distinct anti-consumption discourse that reinforces their practices of value-making (that is, the craft work itself and its techniques, ingredients, and materials). They do not just caution consumers against consuming the more popular versions of their own products, which often means the consumption of mass-produced, corporately branded products, because of their inherent problems and inferiority (e.g., craft brewers who define their own businesses and products against those of the big brands; see Thurnell-Read, 2019). Their discourse also entails less consumption of *their own* products. Craftspeople in business tell their consumers to consume their product if they are to consume their category at all, but not to consume it too much or very often. In other words, they are critical of and take aim at consumer capitalism, but they do so by using its tools *and* in ways that seem to harm their own position in the capitalist structure. How can we make sense of this paradox from the perspective of the craftspeople who regularly grapple with it, sometimes unwittingly and sometimes quite consciously?

The following discussion addresses this paradox through an analysis of two dimensions to this distinct anti-consumption discourse, as expressed through craftspeople in a variety of industries and disciplines. The first stems from how craftspeople discuss this discourse directly to consumers and concerns craft consumption as a form of righteous consumption. They frame it as such by emphasizing what consuming their product *should* look like in light of its superiority. In short, craft products should be consumed moderately, but not because of an anti-materialist or radical reason, but because doing so enhances a consumer's appreciation of it. The second stems from how craftspeople show consumers how to do their craft work—the specific skills and techniques involved—both formally, through hands-on instruction, and informally, through tours of their facilities and impromptu conversations in the workplace. This dimension concerns craft production as righteous production, and in effect these consumers are consuming production as most will not go on to become professional craftspeople. Learning to produce better, craftspeople claim, *should not* be pursued for the sake of having more material objects or consuming more overall, even if the production and products are 'better'. But again, this view is not because of an anti-consumption stance. Rather, it serves to reinforce the high regard they hold craft in. Understanding the process of making *should*, again, encourage appreciation toward the products being made. Both dimensions are part of a larger social project in the craft business world of shaping material production and consumption by transforming both into highly reflexive activities.

RESEARCH METHODS

I base my empirical analysis on nearly 150 interviews and many years of ethnographic field work for two separate research projects in the United States, mostly in the New York City metropolitan area. The primary strength in combining these two qualitative methodological approaches is to reveal and analyze the discrepancies between what people *say* about what they do in interviews and what they *actually* do in their everyday lives and natural settings (Jerolmack and Khan, 2014). Ethnographic data collection in research on craft work is especially important because of the emphasis placed on physical actions, interactions and settings within craft worlds. Pairing fieldwork with interviewing in studies on craft practitioners allows researchers to discover how stated meanings diverge from and converge with practiced ones.

The first project (2007–13) focused on four low-status, undesired, blue-collar jobs that have been transformed into cool, highly desired, cultural taste-making occupations: cocktail bartenders who practice mixology and work at specialized craft cocktail bars; craft distillers who make small batches of spirits in distilleries that have become consumer destinations; upscale men's barbers who use traditional and modern barbering techniques to make stylish haircuts for urban professional men in hip barbershops; and whole animal butchers and butcher shop workers who use artisanal butchery to make rare cuts of meat and meat products in specialized shops (Ocejo, 2017). This shift occurred in part through the incorporation of craft-based philosophies and practices into the everyday tasks and identities of these workers.

The second (which began in 2017 and is ongoing) looks at the small city of Newburgh (population 30,000), located about 60 miles north of New York City, where a group of displaced middle-class creatives from New York City are moving and gentrifying (Ocejo, 2019a, 2019b, 2020). Among the occupations of the newcomers are a wide variety of craftspeople and artisans: carpenters, woodworkers, weavers, bookbinders, letterpressers, coffee roasters, and makers of skin products, craft beer, craft cider, craft spirits, craft cocktails, candles and soap. In most cases they are self-employed or own their own small business in this small city, where they have constructed a local creative economy from scratch. While this latter project touches on other topics besides these craftspeople's work and businesses, my data collection has also included them.

Most interviewees range in age from their early 20s to their late 30s, with some in their 40s and up. Each interview lasted at least an hour and was audio-recorded and transcribed. I used the NVivo qualitative data software coding program for my analysis, which was highly inductive. The purposes of using such a program in qualitative work are to both organize lengthy textual data (that is, interviews and notes) and create analytical categories from it that is easy to reference. Much of the field work on craft businesses and workers for the first project was in-depth, sustained and occasionally hands-on. I regularly went to multiple cocktail bars and barbershops as a consumer and served as an intern at a craft distillery and whole animal butcher shop. I also attended a variety of events related to these industries. Because the second project's focus is gentrification and economic growth and not craft work as a path or practice, I have not conducted sustained field work in craft businesses in Newburgh. The following analysis only includes interview data from that project.

THE GOOD AND THE BAD

In his well-known discussion of the subject, Sennett (2008) defines crafts-manship as 'the skill of making things well' (8) and 'doing a job well for its own sake' (9). His definition extends beyond the prosaic notion of physically working with materials—that is, using one's hands to make an actual object—to include any activity, like parenting and being a citizen. He's interested in the abstract idea of craftsmanship, not specifically craft itself. Similarly, Thorlindsson et al. (2018) define craft as 'intrinsic motivation, engagement in the task at hand, holistic understanding, emphasis on informal learning, and the honing of skills that are needed to accomplish the task at hand' (18). These parameters are useful for theories of purposeful action, whether work-related or otherwise. But any notion of craft or craftwork does not exist apart from social structures of power and systems of evaluation (Bourdieu, 1993). People can 'do citizenship' well and parents can parent well, and both can do so for the sake of doing so and society and children can benefit from their efforts. But not all active citizens and parents, not to mention the set of skills they employ, are regarded equally. Judgments abound, and they can have real consequences (see Beaman's 2017 analysis of how non-white French are made to feel like outsiders, and Lareau's 2003 analysis of working-class parents). Craft is not a value-neutral activity.

The craft brewers and craft beer enthusiasts who compose local scenes, for instance, have constructed their own hierarchies of taste constituting bounda-ries of inclusion and exclusion (Borer, 2019). In addition, beer consumption and production have always been intertwined with race, racial identity and racism, and today's craft beer movement not only lacks diversity but has been shown to reproduce the ideology of whiteness (i.e., systemic exclusion) (Chapman and Brunsma, 2020).

Critiques about what 'is' and 'is not' craft, or what is 'good' or 'bad' about a particular activity, are found within communities as much as they are levied at them. In other words, craftspeople and workers in craft businesses—that is, those who follow the more prosaic definition of craft—have their own definitions of what is 'right' and 'wrong' in what they do, what they make and how they make it. Fine (1992) refers to workers' attitudes toward the practices they engage in as their 'occupational aesthetic', or the 'sense of superior production' (1268) they possess that elevates their approaches over those of others. Cocktail bartenders use the 'best' version of a recipe for a cocktail. Craft distillers know when their mash bill leads to a distinct product. Men's barbers can visualize what a proper hairstyle will look like on someone's head compared to someone else. Whole animal butchers know which seams in a carcass will lead to the most flavorful muscle groups. Book repairers feel materials to recreate a vintage text. Potters apply techniques to cultivate a signature style. All of them *know*, or have faith in, the quality and particularity of what they do. Others may perform their tasks differently and make different products, and others may indeed do it 'wrong' entirely, which could have an impact on their status within the occupational community.

In reference to workers at craft businesses, for whom interacting with customers and clients is central to their work, we can also include in this set of aesthetical considerations the 'right' and 'wrong' ways that consumers consume. Their central aim when dealing with consumers is to teach them about their tastes, the products and techniques they use, and the provenance of their ingredients for the purposes of educating them and—hopefully—drawing them into their taste community (Ocejo, 2017). These workers' usual approach is 'the customer is always right'. If people order something that falls a bit outside of their taste community's boundaries, they'll usually make it without any fuss or challenge. But they look for opportunities to adjust a consumer's taste, and even sometimes find sneaky strategies for doing so. As Mike,[1] a cocktail bartender, explains:

> For the most part, you just try to make customers happy. You kind of have to feel out a person to see if they're interested in maybe trying something else. Get them to change, and even if they don't want to change, I still change it for them: 'I'll have a Pegu Club [cocktail], but can I have it with vodka?' You're just like, 'Yeah, sure. Here you go.' And I'll make it with gin and give it to them. They're like, 'Wow this is really great,' I'm like, 'Yeah, it's gin.'

Vodka falls outside of the boundaries of mixology, and cocktail bartenders will try to direct a customer away from it, if they can.[2] Workers can also be critical of consumers' tastes, preferences and requests, sometimes telling them so directly. Noah, a barber, reflects on a client of his:

> There's things I could do and there's things I couldn't do. I think I'm pretty good at being able to relay that, but some people don't want to hear it. Some people *do not want to hear it*. I'll give you a specific example. I have an Asian guy who comes in. He shows me a picture of Ryan Gosling every single time he comes into the shop. I'm like, 'My man, that's going to be really tough because he's got thin white guy hair, like *thin*, Caucasian hair. You have fishing line.' Like, he has literal fishing line coming out of his head, which is totally fine. He's got thick, beautiful, black hair. It will never bald, it will never do anything, it will be jet black until the day he's 110 years old. But he's never going to have that head of [white person's] hair. Never. And he tries every time. I'm like, 'Alright, I'll give it a shot,' you know? But it's impossible, it's impossible. I try to make him happy with what I'm doing. Technically I should just convince him to do something else, that it's just not going to work, but he doesn't want to hear it.

Wearing a hairstyle that fits who you are—physically, and in terms of personality, occupation and life stage—is an important lesson of masculine performance that barbers try to impart on their clients. Not receiving that lesson, or getting the 'wrong' haircut—like constantly ordering vodka, the 'wrong' spirit—are examples of 'wrong', or problematic, consumption. Consumers who do so only become irredeemable when they refuse to listen to a craft worker's knowledge and explanation of that preference. Stephen, a butcher shop worker, describes customers who react negatively when they hear the shop doesn't always carry certified organic products: 'If they hear we don't have [organic products], they leave. They just don't get it. Some people are receptive, if they're into cooking. Some you know are not, and they're just going to roast the shit out of it [the meat they bought]. Those people are hopeless.'

Still, even 'hopeless' consumers, who are unwilling to hear why being certified organic does not mean the animals have not been raised ethically, will get served. They can still consume a craft product, even without the knowledge behind it. In the end, by sneaking in vodka, breaking down someone's hair logically, and labeling someone as 'hopeless', craft workers exert their cultural authority as arbiters of good taste and style.

But craft workers employ other, counterintuitive strategies for reinforcing the value of their work. These strategies come in the form of teaching consumers about consuming less of their product, and both attempt to bestow feelings of righteousness upon the consumer. Consumers—even knowledgeable ones—can become 'righteous consumers' by reducing or slowing down their consumption for the sake of added appreciation. And they can come to understand 'righteous production' through their own practice or knowledge of the craft.

JUSTIFYING SLOW PRODUCTION (AND HIGH COST)

Righteous Consumption

It should be noted that these craft-based anti-consumption strategies simultaneously serve to reinforce the value of craftwork as well as justify the actual value, or cost of their products and services, which is typically higher than their more conventional, widely available, or mass-produced versions. Asserting a product's quality because of its handmade origins and the provenance of its materials and ingredients makes good business sense. Craftspeople often get their materials and ingredients from particular sources and usually pay more for them. Furthermore, their very production methods—that is, crafting mostly by hand—are slow, yielding fewer products. Add these two factors together, and you have craft businesses that must charge more for their products to make a profit. To give a quick example, for craft distillers, aging a spirit is inherently slow, because it takes time. And for those craft distillers who wish to promote local agriculture and support sustainable supply chains, which is most of them, ingredients will cost more and be riskier, because they often come from a single, independent source. Chris, a distiller who advocates for strong local food economies, explains how this works:

> Farmers are always going to be beholden [to the market]. The farmer is only going to make profit above what he would normally expect—and sometimes not even that—if the market at that point has its price point set higher than what he expected. [But] if he is selling directly to us at the same cost that we're buying it, he's cutting out the middleman. That's really just one more thing that's going to help direct everything to more holistic and sound practices, more genetic diversity [in agriculture], and all those things. It's just going to benefit the farmers directly through us. We're making alcohol, [so] we're going to benefit no matter what. We could make [spirits] out of sugar, the lowest available cost to us, and make garbage just like most of the people do, and make profit.

Craft distillers typically do not use low-cost ingredients. They use more expensive ingredients, such as those from a small local farmer. They therefore have to make a profit by raising the price of their bottles.

However, to consumers who are still suspicious of paying that much more for a bottle of alcohol, a cocktail, or a cut of meat compared to the brand name or those at the corner bar or supermarket, promoting less consumption can be additionally effective. As Danny, a cocktail bartender, explains:

> I ask customers who I can tell are bothered by the price: 'how much do you normally spend when you go out [to other kinds of bars]?' They say, '$50.' 'And how many drinks do you normally have?' 'Like 6.' 'Well, here you can have 4 drinks for $50, but they're going to be the best drinks you've ever had. You're going to wait longer for them than you're used to, but your night here will be just as long. And it's going to be a better evening.'

Of course, this perspective is the workers' own. They perceive that customers need such justifying of the products' cost, whether they are actually looking for such justification or not. Either way, craft workers try to ease their concerns by invoking quality of the product and of the experience. In the case of craft cocktails, both the taste of the drink and the experience of being out at a bar will be better, if you choose craft. Doing so means you will consume less, but feel better about your decision (in terms of having a more visceral experience, not necessarily sobriety).

Whole animal butchers and butcher shop workers face the same dilemma. As Jerry breaks down the reality of many families:

> The classic example is, say you need to feed a family of four. You're working two jobs. Say you have $20—which is probably a lot, an over-estimate—but you have $20 to feed that family of four. You could go and you could get one head of broccoli for $4.99, and a pack of chicken breasts or something. If you're getting organic stuff, you're pretty much at your budget there. Or you could go to McDonald's, you could get four double cheeseburgers, four fries, and four drinks. It's 20 bucks, maybe less. Then you have $4 left to pay for the bus to go home. At some point, we have to figure out a way to make good food desirable, accessible, and the norm. Because I still think that going to the farmer's market is the exception.

Perhaps because they sell food, a human necessity, out of the craftspeople I have studied butchers were the most likely to think about how the cost of their product relates to the larger market as a concern for consumer accessibility. They know the expense of their products creates a moral dilemma, because most people cannot afford this basic necessity when it's both crafted at such a high quality and promotes sustainability. Like Jerry, many advocate for reforms in the food industry to make such ethical consumption the norm. But they also have another, simpler response, as Gary articulates: 'You should eat less meat, but when you do it should be really nice meat.' In other words, if you consume less meat, the money you typically spend on meat for your weekly groceries could go toward more expensive, but better-quality meat. You'll eat and feel better, it won't cost you more, and you'll be supporting a craft business and the sustainable, local food system it's a part of. Everybody wins.

But craft workers aim to inspire righteous consumption through consuming less in ways that do not just justify cost but emphasize quality and the value of craft as benefits of consumer choice. One early afternoon a tall, thin man named Chris sits in Anthony's chair:

Anthony: So what are we doing?
Chris: I'm looking for a clean look. Cut the sides and back closely, and
             thin out the hair on top. It's too clumpy.

Anthony looks at him through the mirror while standing behind the chair and putting on an apron. After running his fingers through the top of Chris's hair, he immediately asks, 'Do you use shampoo every day?'

Chris: Yes.
Anthony: That's why it's clumping up. That's not your hair. Your hair
             is coarse and curly, and it's like a Brillo pad on top since you
             shampoo it every day. What I'm going to say to you, if I said the
             opposite, I'd make $10. But it's about making your life easier,
             which is what I'm going to do.

Anthony then provides Chris with a history of shampoo and shampooing, and explains that since he has curly/wavy hair with a cuticle layer that comes up like fish scales he should avoid using shampoo because it removes its natural oils. He also describes hair as 'alive or dead', or alive when it is left on its own, and dead when you use too much shampoo. He ends with a question:

Anthony: Do you have dandruff?
Chris: Yeah.

Anthony moves Chris's hair from the crown of his head.

Anthony: Your head is bright red from the chemical burn from the
             ammonium, the alcohol, the ether, the lye, the sulfates. So in
             about three days when you stop shampooing, which I highly
             recommend you do …
Chris: Stop *altogether*? [incredulous].
Anthony: *Stop altogether*! You never have to shampoo for the rest of your
             life. But in three days your head's going to itch like crazy. And
             in about four days, you're going to have flakes. Light flakes,
             not that kind of chunky, where with your fingernail you could
             take a chunk of head out. You're going to have a little bit of
             flaking, for the most part. You're going to have a little bit of

scabbing because your head is so damaged from it. You've probably been using the dandruff shampoo, right?

Chris: Head and Shoulders.

Anthony: Right. You use Head and Shoulders because you have dandruff, which is dry skin. All Head and Shoulders is is shampoo times two. Instead of taking off what normal shampoo takes off, it takes off twice as much and *really* dries your scalp out. That's why your head gets so red, because you're using twice the amount of shampoo. But in a month, your hair is going to be perfect. You're never going to have to wash it again. You can go twice as long between haircuts. You don't have to worry about thinning it out—you have thick hair, which is great, but it's going to sit down, it's going to look perfect, and it's going to feel great and moisturized. It's going to feel like hair, as opposed to the Brillo. Now, you can wash your hair once a week, if you feel like it. But with your hair I don't recommend it.

Chris: Believe me, it's not something I'm telling *you*. It's something we say all day, every day, and it's why we have the clientele we have. It's because we're here to help, not sell you products. A lot of places are just set up to sell products, because they could make more money selling products than cutting hair. Because it's free money—cutting hair we actually have to work for—and we're telling you not to buy the products.

Once the haircut is over, Chris says he will consider giving up shampooing.

Anthony: You gotta commit; it's not a one-week thing.

Chris: I'll try.

This excerpt shows a simple, common scene at a new upscale men's barbershop. Anthony, who is in service and sales as a barber, is counterintuitively trying to convince Chris that he doesn't need hair products because of his hair texture and the style he desires. He also points out that without using these products he could reduce the number of haircuts he would need to get. Both pieces of advice mean less business for him (the shop sells some independent brands, and offers them to clients depending on their hair type and desired style). Anthony is fine with this result, because, yes, it will hopefully mean Chris will come to trust him and then become a loyal client of his. He would be trading many years of business for a quick, immediate sale. But the main reason is because he wants to impart a central cultural lesson of these barbershops which is intertwined with their craft work: their idea that 'doing' masculinity (West and Zimmerman, 1987) well among culturally savvy elites in the twenty-first century city entails minimal bodily self-care. For barbers, then, being a righteous consumer goes hand-in-hand with being a successful man, at least in terms of one's appearance.

Righteous Production

Transparency, in terms of the processes and materials used in making, is central to the new craft movement. Owners design businesses to showcase as much of how products get made as possible. Even small-scale manufacturing businesses, like breweries, distilleries and coffee roasting plants, which historically have rarely been hospitable to consumption and tourism, have opened their doors to the public through tasting rooms and tours that are often led by actual producers. These initiatives certainly represent new revenue streams for these businesses. But they are also opportunities for craft workers to share their knowledge and show the techniques and tools involved in the process of making with the public. Meanwhile both these manufacturing businesses and workers and other retail-based craft businesses regularly offer formal educational programs and opportunities for consumers to actually learn how to do these crafts themselves. Again, another revenue stream, but also a chance to inculcate cultural knowledge and create righteous producers: people who will consume less by both self-producing more and coming around to better appreciate these products.

Being better producers aligns with the philosophies that undergird these craft occupations and businesses, which include sustainability in some form among their priorities. For example, the whole animal butcher shop I studied ran an internship program in addition to butchery and sausage-making demonstrations for educational and entertainment purposes. I served as an intern as part of my field work. One day I cut bottom round into thin slices to make beef jerky. I am careful to only remove fat from the cut and not any meat. After a few minutes I have a solid pile of fat on the table. Marcus, one of the butchers, walks over to inspect.

Marcus: Is this pile trim or trash?
Richard: Um, both? I haven't separated them yet.
Marcus: There's too much meat you're cutting off with the fat. You don't want to waste that meat. Do you know how much grain and grass a cow has to eat to gain one pound?

I shrug, sensing the rhetorical nature of his question.

Marcus: A lot. We want to waste as little as possible. Make sure we only
               cut fat.

In this simple example, Marcus, stressing the ethical importance of using the
whole animal in the craft of artisanal butchery, instructs an intern (me, in this
case) to be careful about wasting meat. Once again, doing so is better for the
shop's bottom line (meat is money, especially when the owner bought and now
has to sell the whole thing, even the less popular parts). But the main thrust
is to show the important role of craft production in the performance of ethical
practices and ethical products. Being a righteous producer is essential to the
entire philosophy.

More important than teaching cost savings is to impress the importance
for craft workers to get consumers to appreciate the objects they consume
through an appreciation of production. An example of this approach is Joseph,
a 30-year-old potter, who in 2018 moved to Newburgh from New York City
to open his own studio. The pottery studio business model can vary, but often
includes some combination of a potter-owner with their own business and
clients; a membership system whereby local potters can rent space in the
studio for their own business, art or personal creations; and classes for the
public to learn pottery. An owner can use any one or a combination of these
revenue streams to subsidize the other(s). Joseph loves throwing and has his
own clients, but also happens to enjoy the community of having other potters
become members at his studio and has a passion for teaching. His attitude
toward craft and learning is worth quoting at length:

> This is very much a process-driven craft. It's about the process as much as it is about
> the product you get out of it. I didn't become a potter because I am obsessed with
> mugs, or bowls. I didn't start because I was just like, 'I gotta make some plates,
> man. I just love plates!' The world doesn't need more plates, you know? I don't
> know if the world needs more pots. Like, I really don't. I have a deep appreciation
> for that stuff now that I make it, but that wasn't the driving force. I fell in love with
> the process of making and that appreciation for those things that I make came later
> on. I don't have a degree in design or art or anything. I learned design through
> making things, and what works, what doesn't work, what looks good, what doesn't
> look good, why. A lot people do it the other way. I've taught a lot of designers,
> they've come with all these ideas already drawn out in their head. They started with
> a love for products—they love things, they love objects, and now they want to make
> objects. Whereas me, I was always indifferent toward objects and learned to love
> objects because I love making things.
>
> For me personally, the process of learning, the whole journey of learning this
> process, this craft did so much for me, like on a personal level, just as far as confi-
> dence and creativity, now I love connecting with people and helping draw that out
> of other people. It gives them a sense of satisfaction, it gives you a sense of satisfac-
> tion. I think it's important what we do and what we make. And of course, I always
> think something handmade is more beautiful than something mass produced. This

day and age, learning *how* to do this and how to make things are more important than *what* we're making, especially as we get more drawn into screens and more and more of life is automated and we don't have to get our hands dirty anymore if we don't want to. Putting aside time to put away your phone, not look at screens, sit down and do something real, intangible and messy. I think it's important, and I think that's the future, you know, I think that's what makes this so sustainable is that I don't think that need or desire from people goes away. I think people always have and always will need that sort of outlet.

There is much to unpack here. Joseph bases his teaching philosophy on his own journey into pottery. His love emerged from the making, not the having. Or, the product, the end result, was only significant insofar as it came at the end of a craft process (which, as he claims, is superior to a process of mass production or automation). By teaching this process to consumers, Joseph aims to educate them on the meanings of craft production, including the production of value in objects that extends beyond their utility. He continues:

It's not just the dishes you're eating out of or baking out of. It's the tiles on the wall. You go into the bathroom, that whole room's made out of clay. And that's a process that's been built up for thousands and thousands and thousands of years. And so I think people, when they come out of a course like this, [they] see the world a little differently. Or walk around and you notice all the little things, you know. You notice that tile on that subway wall or you notice that mug at the diner, and you start picking it apart and you just start noticing things.

Joseph here is stating his teaching's main intent. He wants people to make pots and mugs, and he wants them to learn the basic pottery techniques. But he mostly wants to foster a connection for people between themselves and the human-made material world. He wants them to have an understanding of production that reveals the value behind everyday objects. 'The world doesn't need more pots' is an odd statement from someone who makes pots and teaches others how to make pots for a living. But it makes sense when seen as part of a larger social enterprise around craft. To return to the basic definitions of craft (Sennett, 2008), righteous production serves as a legitimizing mechanism for doing work well for its own sake.

These examples of a discourse of anti-consumption have focused on workers' attitudes and worker–consumer interactions at the point of sale. Not many, but some craft businesses express this discourse more formally, such as through marketing materials. A whole animal butcher shop in Brooklyn, for instance, has a sign on the roof of its building (visible from an elevated highway) that reads: 'Eat Less Meat.' Its aim, as Stuart, the head butcher, explains, is to 'Start a dialogue with customers. We have people come in who ask what we mean. It's probably not obvious.' For the most part, craft workers reserve the distribution of this discourse for interpersonal interactions.

CONCLUSION

This chapter has aimed to explain the paradox of how craft workers who venerate and sell what they make can simultaneously hold and promote an anti-consumerist stance to consumers. The reason is because of how they interpret consuming less: as an active way to support the qualities and processes inherent to craft production. They enact this distinct anti-consumption discourse through promoting righteous consumption and righteous production directly to consumers. The craft version of anti-consumption, then (and also paradoxically), supports and even fetishizes consumption by elevating the status of craft objects even further than they already are. Through this distinct anti-consumption discourse, craft workers use consumer capitalism's most basic tenets to both criticize it and position their products within its cultural stratification system.

The findings and arguments in this chapter offer some possible avenues for further research. First, this research has mentioned but only briefly touched on the more formal forms of marketing craft businesses deploy for their brands. Scholars of craft ought to focus more attention on these strategies to determine if and how these anti-consumption discourses get dispersed beyond in-person interactions. Second, I have only focused on the role anti-consumption discourses play in the legitimation of craft products and craft work from the perspective of producers. Craft scholars should also analyze how these messages get received by and shape consumers and their tastes and behaviors. Finally, a key limitation of this research is its focus on people and places in New York City and the metropolitan area, or an extreme case of a spatial and market context. Future research must explore how anti-consumption discourses among craft workers and businesses interact with contextual effects of other municipalities, regions, and markets of varying sizes and configurations.

NOTES

1.   All names of participants are pseudonyms.
2.   I should note that this perspective was popular in the craft cocktail world of New York City and much of the United States at the time of my research, but it has since shifted. Today, vodka has a more prominent role in craft cocktail bars than it used to.

REFERENCES

Beaman, J. (2017). *Citizen Outsider: Children of North African Immigrants in France.* Berkeley: University of California Press.
Binkley, S. (2008). Liquid consumption. *Cultural Studies*, *22*(5), 599–623.

Borer, M.I. (2019). *Vegas Brews: Craft Beer and the Birth of a Local Scene*. New York: New York University Press.

Bourdieu, P. (1993). *The Field of Cultural Production: Essays on Art and Literature*. New York: Columbia University Press.

Chapman, N.B. and Brunsma, D.L. (2020). *Beer and Racism: How Beer Became White, Why It Matters, and the Movements to Change It*. Bristol: Bristol University Press.

Chayka, K. (2020). *The Longing for Less: Living with Minimalism*. New York: Bloomsbury.

Cherrier, H. (2009). Anti-consumption discourses and consumer-resistant identities. *Journal of Business Research, 62*(2), 181–90.

Crawford, M.B. (2009). *Shop Class as Soulcraft: An Inquiry into the Value of Work*. New York: Penguin.

Fine, G. (1992). The culture of production: aesthetic choices and constraints in culinary work. *American Journal of Sociology, 97*(5), 1268–94.

Gibson, C. (2016). Material inheritances: how place, materiality, and labor process underpin the path-dependent evolution of contemporary craft production. *Economic Geography, 92*(1), 61–86.

Henderson, W. (2012). *John Ruskin's Political Economy*. London: Routledge.

Hollenbeck, C.R. and Zinkhan, G.M. (2010). Anti-brand communities, negotiation of brand meaning, and the learning process: the case of Wal-Mart. *Consumption Markets & Culture, 13*(3), 325–45.

Holt, D.B. (1998). Does cultural capital structure American consumption? Journal of Consumer Research, 25(1), 1–25.

Holt, D.B. (2002). Why do brands cause trouble? A dialectical theory of consumer culture and branding. Journal of Consumer Culture, 29(1), 70–90.

Hubbard, P. (2019). Enthusiasm, craft and authenticity on the high street: micropubs as 'community fixers'. *Social & Cultural Geography, 20*(6), 763–84.

Jakob, D. (2012). Crafting your way out of the recession? New craft entrepreneurs and the global economic downturn. *Cambridge Journal of Regions, Economy and Society, 6*(1), 3–21.

Jerolmack, C. and Khan, S. (2014). Talk is cheap: ethnography and the attitudinal fallacy. *Sociological Methods & Research, 43*(2), 178–209.

Johnston, J. and Baumann, S. (2010). *Foodies: Democracy and Distinction in the Gourmet Foodscape*. New York: Routledge.

Kapp, P.H. (2016). The artisan economy and post-industrial regeneration in the US. *Journal of Urban Design, 22*(4), 477–93.

Khan, S.R. (2010). *Privilege: The Making of an Adolescent Elite at St. Paul's School*. Princeton, NJ: Princeton University Press.

Klein, N. (1999). *No Logo: Taking Aim at the Brand Bullies.* London: Flamingo.

Kozinets, R.V., Handelman, J.M. and Lee, M.S.W. (2010). Don't read this; or, who cares what the hell anti-consumption is anyways? *Consumption, Markets & Culture, 13*(3), 225–33.

Krugh, M. (2014). Joy in labour: the politicization of craft from the Arts and Crafts Movement to Etsy. *Canadian Review of American Studies, 44*(2), 281–301.

Lareau, A. (2003). *Unequal Childhoods: Class, Race, and Family Life.* Berkeley: University of California Press.

Ocejo, R.E. (2017). *Masters of Craft: Old Jobs in the New Urban Economy*. Princeton, NJ: Princeton University Press.

Ocejo, R.E. (2019a). The creative class gets political: gentrifier politics in small city America. *Journal of Urban Affairs, 41*(8), 1167–82.

Ocejo, R.E. (2019b). From apple to orange: narratives of small city migration and settlement among the urban middle class. *Sociological Perspectives*, *62*(3), 402–45.

Ocejo, R.E. (2020). The precarious project and the wasted opportunity: the social and cultural dynamics of conflict over urban development. *Urban Affairs Review*. http://doi.org/10.1177/1078087420908943.

Peterson, R.A. and Kern, R.M. (1996). Changing highbrow taste: from snob to omnivore. *American Sociological Review*, *61*(5), 900–907.

Peterson, R.A. and Simkus, A. (1992). How musical taste groups mark occupational status groups. In M. Lamont and M. Fournier (eds.), *Cultivating Differences: Symbolic Boundaries and the Making of Inequality*. Chicago, IL: University of Chicago Press.

Schor, J. (1998). The Overspent American: Why We Want What We Don't Need. New York: Harper Perennial.

Sennett, R. (2008). *The Craftsman*. New Haven, CT: Yale University Press.

Thorlindsson, T., Halldorsson, V. and Sigfusdottir, I.D. (2018). The sociological theory of craftsmanship: an empirical test in sport and education. *Sociological Research Online*, *23*(1), 114–35.

Thrift, N. (1997). The rise of soft capitalism. *Journal for Cultural Research*, *1*(1), 29–57.

Thurnell-Read, T. (2019). A thirst for the authentic: craft drinks producers and the narration of authenticity. *British Journal of Sociology*, *70*(4), 1448–68.

West, C. and Zimmerman, D. (1987). Doing gender. *Gender & Society*, *1*(2), 125–51.

Zalewska, J. and Cobel-Tokarska, M. (2016). Rationalization of pleasure and emotions: the analysis of the blogs of Polish millennials. *Polish Sociological Review*, *196*, 495–512.

Zavestoski, S. (2002). The social–psychological bases of anticonsumption attitudes. *Psychology & Marketing*, *19*(2), 149–65.

12. The resurgence of craft retailing: marketing and branding strategies in the food and beverage sector

Alessandro Gerosa

INTRODUCTION

In recent times, artisanal production has been experiencing renewed fortune (Bell & Vachhani, 2020; Naudin & Patel, 2020; Ocejo, 2017; Thurnell-Read, 2019), making neo-craft industries (Land, 2018) an economic sector capable of earning its place and legitimacy in the contemporary economy. The reasons for the success of neo-craft sectors seem to be much more related to consumption trends than with technological developments in production or novel competitive advantages. Indeed, artisanal products seem to be significantly fitted to meet the taste of culturally omnivorous, cosmopolitan middle-class consumers (Johnston & Baumann, 2015). Craft production certainly benefits from current technological developments both in the production of the goods and in their commercialisation – consider, for example, the maker movement and the Etsy platform[1] – but is still rooted for the most part in manual work and face-to-face retailing. To summarise, craft is still a labour-intensive and capital-poor economic sector, part of the 'industrious economy' that is rising at a global level with different forms and intensities (Arvidsson, 2019).

Notably, this resurgence of craft consumption is attributing renewed social and academic relevance to a professional figure, the small and independent retailer, which industrialism seemed to relegate to a state of unresolvable obsolescence. Industrial production, and more precisely the Fordist system of economic organisation based on the pairing of 'mass production for mass consumption', stripped small retailers of their previous role as acknowledged and knowledgeable actors, capable of directing the consumption patterns of customers. Furthermore, it left them as uninfluential intermediaries between mass production factories and mass consumers (Hilton, 1998). Moreover, it favoured the retailing structure of the supermarket first, and the shopping centre after (Humphery, 1998), leaving small and independent shops to the margins of the twentieth-century retailing scenario.

Today, the demise of the Fordist economy also entailed the crisis of the connected retail structures. The digital platform economy and e-commerce brought the supermarkets and shopping centres into what is now widely known as the 'Retail Apocalypse', a phenomenon that is likely to produce a permanent restructuring of the retail sector with a drastic reduction of physical retailers (Helm et al., 2020). In this context, neo-craft retailing is imposing itself as one of the few viable, successful strategies to pursue for small and independent shopkeepers.

This chapter aims to shed light on the apparently unexpected resurgence of craft retailing, based on the literature on the topic and the results of ethnographic research of food truck operators and hipster bar owners in Milan. After a brief methodological section, first contemporary small and independent craft retailing will be historically contextualised, arguing that its marginality during the twentieth century should be read as a parenthesis induced by Fordism rather than a permanent disappearance. Craft retailing should be framed as an innovative resurgence rather than a novel trend. The chapter goes on to argue why craft retailing appears an emerging paradigm in retailing, in particular for small and independent shopkeepers, in post-Fordist society. Finally, the fundamental marketing and branding strategies used in this sector will be schematised, based on the results of ethnographic research.

METHODS

The results derive from ethnographic research composed of participant observation and 40 in-depth semi-structured interviews with 'gourmet food trucks' and 'hipster bar' owners, located in the city of Milan and collected between 2017 and 2018 by the author of the chapter. The participants were sampled based on distinctive features that, in our opinion, characterise neo-craft retailing shops: the authenticity and distinctiveness of the product, the authenticity and distinctiveness of the atmosphere, and the display of a passionate attachment to the job.

The interviewees' sampling follows a non-probabilistic 'purposive homogeneous sample' strategy (Etikan et al., 2016). During the participant observation of street food festivals, the author identified food truck operators belonging to the gourmet food truck scene – based on the truck features – and other participants were selected by reviewing secondary materials such as press articles. The author first identified two neighbourhoods in Milan for the hipster bars, recently characterised by a steady growth of new shops serving young customers, even if with some differences between them. Following a period of participant observation in the two areas, a set of hipster bars relevant for the research was identified, and the author interviewed their owners or managers. The final corpus of interviews comprises 40 formal, in-depth, semi-structured interviews, 20 with food truck owners and 20 with hipster bar owners. Of the 20 food trucks, most prepare food from Italian regional cuisine, while some offer ethnic cuisine and two craft beers. The 20 hipster bars are a mix of shops specialising in serving food, beers, wine or cocktails, many also with a hybrid identity that mixes the delivery of food and beverages with other functions (to sell clothes, repair bicycles, act as a social and cultural hub, etc.).

Almost all the interviews lasted between 45 and 75 minutes and were conducted with one or more founders, with only one exception constituted by an employee, chosen because the business owner did not work directly in the shop. In addition to interviews, the researcher did extensive participant observation at the bars – attending during regular hours and special social events – and during street food festivals.

All the interviews were transcribed and the results coded by the author, adopting an open thematic coding approach (Gibbs, 2018) through the use of the qualitative software RQDA.

THE CRAFT STRIKES BACK: EXPLAINING AN UNEXPECTED RESURGENCE

In *The Craftsman*, Sennett (2008, p. 108) argued that, 'by the mid-nineteenth century, as the modern economic system crystallised, the enlightened hope dimmed that artisans could find an honoured place in the industrial order.' In the first analysis of the socio-economic development of capitalism in Europe, Werner Sombart (1928) significantly distinguished in the European economic history from the Middle Ages onwards, two economic paradigms: the 'craft economy' and the 'industrial economy'. The first was characteristic of the Middle Ages, and the second of the contemporary age, while the modern age represented a long period of transition between the two paradigms, in which the majority of artisanal producers – in manufacturing and beyond – started to adopt industrial approaches and machinery.

That industrialisation led craft production to inevitable obsolescence is a standard assumption in analyses of contemporary economy and society. However, if this oppositional depiction can be useful to summarily schematise the shift in the manufacturing of goods between the modern and contemporary age, it appears inaccurate on a more fine-grained level of analysis. In particular, the historical reconstructions of the conditions of artisans and independent retailers during the ninetieth century, that shared a similar fate, allow the adoption of an important distinction. Indeed, Crossick and Haupt (2013) in their history of the petite bourgeoisie in Europe between late eighteenth century and the First World War, state that the decline of small-scale retailing and craft is not intrinsic to either industrialisation or capitalistic production. Based on archival and statistical data, they show that during the early industrialisation of Europe in the nineteenth century in most countries small artisanal, and retailing businesses co-existed and were even stimulated by industrialisation, through three different kinds of relationship: they integrated with industries; they benefitted from the technological development led by industrialisation; and they positioned themselves in the market niches between the interstices of industrial production, interlocking with it. Rather than industrialisation or capitalism per se, it is the industrial mode of production based on industrial concentration and standardised mass production and consumption that caused the decline of small shopkeepers. This process started to emerge during the second industrial revolution during the second half of the nineteenth century (Mokyr, 1998) and became paradigmatic of Western economies under the denomination of Fordism for a large part of the twentieth century.

Indeed, for small retailers and artisans, the period between 1850 and 1914 was characterised by a struggle for survival, with them already investing in strategies entailing diversification, rituals to provide unique experiences to customers and even home delivery (Winstanley, 1983). In the same period, as standardised production became the norm in a growing set of industries, small retailers and artisans suffered a loss of independence (Crossick & Haupt, 2016).

Mass, standardised production not only brought shopkeepers and artisans to their knees at the economic level and undermined their social prestige but even impoverished their working prerogatives and practices. This fact remained almost wholly overlooked in academic literature but has great relevance in light of the recent trends. The only exception to this oversight is fundamental research over tobacco retailers from the nineteenth to the twentieth centuries by Hilton (1998). Based on archival material, he describes in detail the vital cultural role that the (male) independent shopkeeper, who regarded himself also as a craftsman, played in the performance of his job in the nineteenth century:

> For as well as performing the purely economic act of engaging in commodity exchange with his customers, he was also in a position to direct the precise nature of these economic transactions. His specialist knowledge of twists, flakes, pigtails, rolls and cakes guided the choice of the smoker, who could taste, feel and test the products on offer, with the reputation of the artisan trader forming part of the guarantee of the quality of the article to be purchased. (Hilton, 1998, p. 115)

Instead, in opposition, the tobacco trade in 1930 was dominated by mass-produced products. By that period, the shopkeeper 'merely handed over to hundreds of faceless customers whose purchasing decisions had been decided in advance of entering the retail establishment: the guarantee of quality now came from the product, not the assurance of the retailer' (Hilton, 1998, p. 116).

These are ideal-typical representations, but well represent the de-skilling process that took place. Shopkeepers as a category were able to maintain their economic function, benefitting from the growth in demand caused by mass production, but at the cost of losing their cultural role as intermediaries that they had held, and their identity as craftsmen other than shopkeepers. Mass-produced products came with their own brands and advertisements, leaving the shopkeeper with a marginal role in the process of influencing customer taste and choices. This process paralleled that experienced (and much more covered by the literature) by labourers in the same period (Braverman, 1998).

What has been illustrated to this point has two fundamental implications. The first is that a craft economy can perfectly co-exist with an industrial economy, and even be reinforced by it. The crisis craft suffered during the second half of the nineteenth century, and demise during most of the twentieth century, means its obsolescence only if economic history is read with a simplified positivistic bias, one assuming that every new paradigmatic economic system overrides the previous one, with radically innovative features that make past versions obsolete. Instead, if we consider that subsequent economic configurations may recover features and mechanisms from the past, modified and influenced from the different context, it becomes possible to explain an apparent paradoxical trend inversion. Read in these terms, the industrial and the artisanal can constitute two interdependent realms of production and consumption (Hirsch & Tene, 2013). The second implication is that the figure of the 'master of craft' (Ocejo, 2017) – a craft shopkeeper who performs both cultural and economic labour, possessing a high reputation for them – rather than being a novel figure generated by the new hipster economy – has much in common with the pre-Fordist shopkeeper that often held the roles of the artisan and the retailer together. The tobacco retailer described by Hilton and the mixologists or craft brewers described by contemporary literature, are individuals embedded in very different times. However, they perform a very similar role of taste dealers (Gerosa, 2021), orienting the choices of the customers on the basis of their mastery and translating aesthetic regimes in the handicraft goods.

THE RETAIL APOCALYPSE AND THE PARADIGM OF NEO-CRAFT RETAILING

In 1964, Doody and Davidson authored an article in the *Harvard Business Review* in which they argued that 'despite many prevailing prophecies of doom, there is underway growing strength in small retailing' (p. 69). The claim was original, and opposed to the general opinion of the time. In the 1960s,

Fordism was still the dominant paradigm, and supermarkets together with shopping centres were the symbol of mass consumption of industrial products. However, the two authors were among the first to note that something was changing in the patterns of consumption of customers, something that small and independent retailers could be well placed to exploit. In particular, Doody and Davidson discerned three growing opportunities for small retailers: the quasi-integration between shops, the problems of large-scale retailing, and the changing nature of consumer markets. The last two arguments appear of particular interest for our aims. Supermarkets and shopping centres started to experience issues because of their extensive conformity, the mass standard-isation of the goods for sale, and diminishing returns. At the same time, the consumer taste started to change, demanding more diverse products and a frag-mented market. These two arguments, the authors observe, bring an end of the fundamental assumption of Fordist retailing, namely to deliver the highest possible number of physical products per dollar spent, in favour of a vision characterised by market segmentation and product differentiation. Small and independent retailers could benefit from these phenomena through speciality shops, with a core emphasis on uniqueness in the store design and appearance, and store personality.

The foresight of this analysis is remarkable: very similar features dominate the contemporary depictions of small retailing strengths (D'Andrea et al., 2006; Megicks & Warnaby, 2008). However, even if capitalism in the follow-ing decades effectively transformed itself, abandoning the production of stand-ardised goods to satisfy the thirst for the authentic (Boltanski & Chiapello, 2007), small and independent retailing mainly remained in a position of marginality. A vast array of studies continued to argue the death of the high street and the chronic state of crisis of small retailing (Bromley & Thomas, 1995; Hughes & Jackson, 2015; Kacker, 1986), also confirmed by a diffused nostalgia of shopkeepers towards an idealised better past (Wells & Watson, 2005). Small and independent shops continue to be considered fundamental for the economic vitality of neighbourhoods and places, but this relevance is at odds with their difficulties in remaining competitive in the market (Clarke & Banga, 2010). Local institutions praise them and declare the will to sustain them for their supposed benefits, but generally fail to support them concretely (Smith & Sparks, 2001).

Today, supermarkets and shopping centres are indeed in a state of deep crisis, a crisis that has been labelled as a 'retail apocalypse'. However, the origins of this apocalypse are neither independent shops, nor the shift towards omnivorous taste. Instead, it has been technological innovation and the digi-talisation of retail that has brought brick-and-mortar retail stores to the point of bankruptcy (Bhattarai, 2019), together with growing market concentration, income inequalities and the service economy (Goolsbee, 2020). The struggle for survival for physical stores depends on their ability to innovate. The contemporary drivers of retailing innovation mostly pertain to technological developments and digital trends (Grewal et al., 2017), only available to supermarket chains and shopping centres. Even an extensive research about small retailing innovation (Quinn et al., 2013) had to conclude that very few examples existed in the literature, relying upon theoretical developments to discern possible trends. Significantly, it argued that the nature of small retailer innovation would be incremental, focusing on 'customer service, product assortments, product range expansion, diversification, brand image'.

It appears straightforward that in the age of the 'retail apocalypse', for small shops to engage in price competition in the market would be even less viable than before, due to the competitive advantages of e-commerce (Burt & Sparks, 2003; Wrigley & Currah, 2006). Online retailing also allows for the offering of an incredible range of diverse products, in many variants, and by different producers (Bakos, 2001). Product diversification in itself also does not appear as a field in which small shops can achieve competitive advantage. However, small shops seem to be particularly fitted to exploit the trends in consumers' taste and behaviour, predicted by Doody and Davidson in the 1960s and described in detail by more recent analyses, in food retailing and other sectors (Boltanski & Chiapello, 2007; DeSoucey, 2010; Ocejo, 2017; Peterson & Kern, 1996; Smith Maguire, 2018; Thurnell-Read, 2019; Zukin, 2008), based on the principles of providing an authentic experience to the customer, through unique, highly differentiated products, and atmospheres of high quality.

What emerges is a second paradigm of 'neo-craft retailing', alongside the most prominent and discussed one of e-commerce and omnichannel retailing (Piotrowicz & Cuthbertson, 2014). Neo-craft retailing seems suited to become a predominant formula for brick-and-mortar shops because artisanal products can satisfy the requirements of authenticity and uniqueness, in symbolic and material opposition to the industrial mode of production. Furthermore, as craft production remains overwhelmingly a matter of manual labour, with modest seed capital needed to start the business and a generally cheap production process, it is particularly suitable for individuals without high-level education and proficiency and with limited economic resources, aiming to start small, independent shops.

What links together these two models is the focus on the customer experience model for retailing (Grewal et al., 2009; Puccinelli et al., 2009; Sachdeva & Goel, 2015), the principle that retailing has much more to do with the provision of an experience uniquely tailored to the customer than of a product.

AN OVERVIEW OF MARKETING AND BRANDING STRATEGIES OF NEO-CRAFT RETAILERS IN FOOD AND BEVERAGE SECTORS

The Authenticity and Distinctiveness of the Product

Unsurprisingly, marketing strategies in neo-craft retailing revolve around the goods sold to customers. Quite surprisingly, though, products in craft retailing are not necessarily handcrafted with different techniques than the ones used by more classical brick-and-mortar shops of the same sector. In other words, what distinguishes neo-craft retailing is not a difference in manual proficiency but a difference in cultural and symbolic mastery. What makes a food truck operator an 'artisan of food' is not a superior manual ability in the preparation of the hamburger, but rather the mastery in the conferment of an authentic taste and aesthetics to the product, in ways that can be recognised by the customers. In this sense, the assemblage of the final food or drink is in itself both manual work and the appliance of a marketing strategy, with the aim of branding it as authentic (Beverland, 2005).

The artisan in this act aims to craft a product that is perceived both as authentic, and as distinctive from the mass of competitors. A vast literature describes the relevance of the concept of authenticity for contemporary consumption patterns (Beverland & Farrelly, 2010; Grayson & Martinec, 2004; Peterson, 2005; Zukin, 2008), albeit its evocative potential seems to be paired with an intrinsic ambiguity in the meanings it assumes. Here, the chapter assumes the most general and commonly accepted interpretation of authenticity as 'staying true to oneself' (Trilling, 1972). Distinctiveness is a feature that instead derives from the trends of product differentiation and market segmentation (Dickson & Ginter, 1987; Smith, 1956) that characterised retailing in recenet decades. It is in some senses connected to the concept of authenticity, but rather than being true to oneself, it indicates the necessity to distinguish oneself from the competitors and stand out among the crowd. Both concepts are best understood if considered in opposition to the Fordist equivalent value: the 'authentic' is opposed to the 'industrial', the 'distinctive' is opposed to the 'standardised'. Notably, as we are discussing values attributed to products, what matters here is perception, the experience lived by the customers and the artisan (Beverland & Farrelly, 2010), not the actual mode of production. A simple proof of this last corollary is the vast tendency of food and beverage industries to adapt to this paradigm, crowding supermarket shelves with products that are industrially produced but are framed as 'artisanal'.

The most typical way to brand a product as 'authentic' in the neo-craft food retailing sector is to rely on the notions of typicality and genuineness of the link between the product and a tradition. Most commonly, these values derive from the raw ingredient crafted together in the final dish by the artisan. The authenticity infuses the entire food piece from the single components. However, it is not enough that the single ingredients are 'typical' of some-place. What is critical, to present the final food piece as authentic, is the coher-ence of the *ensemble* to the narrative and the mission displayed by the artisan. However, the coherence of the ensemble must be calibrated with the inclusion of a distinctive set of ingredients to display the food piece as unique from all the others. This calibration can be understood by the following excerpt, taken from an interview with a vegan neo-craft retailer that proposes to recover the rural food tradition of a specific region:

> We prepare the sandwich with carrot cream and grapefruit peel, with chickpea 'panella' and hemp, that is, with ingredients that are not obvious, but are homemade if you think about them. Panella is panella, a traditional Palermitan dish; carrots are carrots; hemp is hemp. I do not like to use algae or things ... my cooking is that of grandma pinuccia. (Food Trucker A)

The mix of ingredients is calibrated for coherence and distinctiveness, being unexpected ('not obvious') but also coherent to the overall narrative of being homemade and represent the rural tradition of the archetypal Italian grandma. Algae are instead used as an exemplification of a potential source of incoher-ence, rupturing the efficacy of the marketing strategy. It is an ingredient com-monly used in vegan cuisine and is both typical of a particular food tradition and distinctive, but it would be out of place in the overall narrative.

This coherence has not to be necessarily built based on a typical local geographic provenance. Different culinary traditions can be innovatively combined to reach distinctiveness and still maintain narrative coherence. This is the case, for example of these neo-craft artisan retailers:

> The tradition is Apulian, but the breath is international. We also served gazpacho for example; it is a dish that tells a story, it is made with tomatoes anyway, for us it reflects this ... it had the characteristics to be considered in line with our offer. We would hardly serve sushi type ... which is a traditional dish anyway. (Food Trucker B)

He grafted an 'international breath' on the Apulian traditional cuisine in order to gain distinctiveness on the market, but it did so with a dish, gazpacho, that 'told a story' in line with Apulian tradition. At the opposite, sushi is cited as an example of a traditional dish that would not be coherent with their narrative. The artisan retailer embodies the marketing strategy in the food through the crafting act. The ingredients become the symbolic vectors of the foundational values of the own identity, through which the artisan promotes itself as a legitimate member of the neo-craft industries with an ethical mission.

In neo-craft retailing involving drinks rather than food, some variation exists due to the different characteristics of the products, but the fundamental mechanism at the base of the marketing strategy remains the same. Drinks cannot rely on raw ingredients in the same way food does. Furthermore, the crafting act performed by the retailer is more limited or at least differs in time. The craft of beer or wine happens before, often by another person. Even in the case of cocktails, where an assemblage exists, it is more limited. The artisanal nature of the retailer expresses itself in the masterfulness of the knowledge of the drinks, in the possession and fulfilment of a mission to promote a specific kind of taste or variety of a drink. This brings the appliance of the same fundamental marketing principles to display the products as artisanal, to rely on the two principles of authenticity and distinctiveness of the products to frame them as opposed to industrial and standardised goods, and to accurately choose an offer that is coherent to a familiar narrative proposed by the neo-craft retailer. As for food neo-craft retailers, they have, too, to balance the coherence to their own philosophy with the distinctiveness of the products, like in the following case: 'we are of Anglo-Saxon inspiration, then we have chosen to compromise […] we are focusing a lot on product diversification, and quality […]' (craft beer pub owner).

In this case the philosophy of the owner is the one to promote Anglo-Saxon craft beer scene to the public, but they also recognise the need to compromise with other beer traditions to reach diversification and quality. However, to balance authenticity and distinctiveness does not mean they are opposed concepts; rather, that they are inextricably connected. Following Walter Benjamin's conceptualisation of aura, authenticity and uniqueness (Benjamin, 1969 [1936]) together with Charles Sanders Pierce's indexicality and iconicity as applied to authenticity by Grayson and Martinec (2004), the aura of authenticity of a crafted product derives from its uniqueness and fades if the product is reproduced. However, crafted products base their authentic value on iconic authenticity, that is, they are made to resemble a (supposedly) original recipe, tradition or typical food through an array of strategies such as placement, inference, reduction or projection (Beverland & Farrelly, 2010). As such, each craft is an 'authentic reproduction' under constant risk of losing its uniqueness, and therefore its authentic aura in the eyes of the customers. Distinctiveness becomes the marketing antidote to this risk, strengthening the claim of uniqueness of the product.

The Authenticity and Distinctiveness of Atmosphere

As mentioned in the previous section, it appears predictable that the marketing strategies of neo-craft retailers significantly revolve around the craft products sold to customers. However, products are not the only strategic devices that concur to the framing of the business and the orientation of consumers' taste: atmosphere also plays a significant role (Kotler, 1973). Indeed, the efforts of neo-craft retailers are also directed toward the realisation of an authentic and distinctive atmosphere in the shop or the truck, to be obtained through a coherent combination of style, design and furniture. The main goal is to create a unique environment that mirrors and transmits the 'true self' and the passion of the owner, reinforcing the claim of the retailer to be a cultural and symbolic actor rather than a mere manual worker and, consequently, an artisan. This process requires actively planning and manipulating the environment's atmosphere to stage a specific experience (Bille et al., 2015).

The environment's role, be it the shop or the food truck, is inseparable from the one of the products. Both must appear coherent for the neo-craft retailer to appear as authentic. As such, for example, a bartender presenting as a mixologist committed to rediscovering traditional American cocktails from the prohibitionist era, coherently designed his cocktail bar, trying to re-build that atmosphere. Food trucks, too, even if they can only be seen and not lived by the inside, are designed uniquely to transmit in some way the essence of the owner and the corresponding mission. A food truck operator selling craft beer spoke about the style of their food bike: 'we try to follow our brand, a little modern but tied to the traditions of beer: we produce and sell classic Belgian style and classic German style beers. Even the wooden counter wants to recall a classic pub' (Food Trucker C).

This example is illustrative of two general tendencies. The first is the link between the design and appearance of the truck or the bar/pub/shop and the branding of the neo-craft business. The second is the trend towards a combination of traditional elements that want to recall old, 'authentic' places of the pre-industrial era visually and symbolically, and modern and contemporary elements that project the place and the brand of the business towards the future, distancing it from that same traditional counterpart. These businesses are collectively promoting a visual branding with shared, fixed features which aim to answer to the new and growing cultural demands advanced by customers, establishing a new cultural orthodoxy (Holt & Cameron, 2010). This second oscillation between the recall of old places and a modernist design is fundamental to a better understanding of the nature of neo-craft retailing and the two pillars of authenticity and uniqueness. Chris Land called this feature of neo-craft industries a movement 'back to the future' (Land, 2018): neo-craft retailing, too, is a contemporary phenomenon, a resurgence, that nevertheless marketises and brands itself by referring to the pre-industrial past, leaning on a 'progressive nostalgia' (Gandini, 2020).

CONCLUSIONS

In this chapter, the fundamental features of craft retailing's resurgence – an economic sector that seemed irremediably obsolete – has been illustrated. First, the chapter explained which historical, cultural and economic processes allowed an inversion of the trend in this sense. On the side of artisanal production, it argued that the claim of incompatibility between industrial and craft production is false, and that incompatibility regarded perhaps a specific industrial mode of production, that is, Fordism. It also argued that in the post-Fordist economy, craft not only seems suited to satisfy the consumers' demand for authenticity but also can well combine with the business form of the small and independent retailer – another figure that Fordism relegated to economic and cultural marginality – to give birth to a new retail paradigm. The fundamental marketing and branding strategies used by retailers of this new field of neo-craft retailing in the food and beverage sector were summarised. The analysis focused on using craft products and the atmosphere of the place to frame themselves as artisans and their offer as authentic and distinctive from every other competitor, positioning themselves in open opposition to industrial and standardised products. In sum, the new paradigm of neo-craft retailing appears as one of the primary outcomes of the surge of authenticity value in the orientation of customers' taste, and one of the principal channels through which brick-and-mortar stores, in particular the independent ones, can develop and strengthen.

The implications for small business owners in the retail sector are relevant. Current trends demonstrate that small and independent brick-and-mortar shops are more suited to efficiently capture and exploit the current trends in consumption patterns and taste compared to shopping malls. In order to do so, however, they have to manage to successfully brand themselves as authentic and distinctive in the eyes of the customers they target. The entrepreneur needs to craft a business concept – and a visual branding to accompany it – contemporarily peculiar and well-inscribed into the aesthetic and symbolic canons of the neo-craft sector. Furthermore, they have to balance these two aspects with the planning of a business model capable of ensuring economic viability: in other words, they have to identify a niche sufficiently original to allow distinctiveness but sufficiently popular to attract enough clientele. Another fundamental challenge entrepreneurs in the neo-craft economy must face is the price setting of their commodities. Small businesses positioning themselves in the neo-craft sector usually serve a middle-class clientele that wants crafted products made with high-quality raw materials but at an accessible price. In other words, they look for gourmet products clearly distinct from industrial, mass-produced goods but without the prices associated with highbrow, posh locations. If the neo-craft entrepreneur sets too low a price, the promise of an authentic and distinctive taste will lose credibility due to suspicion towards the quality of the raw materials. If the prices are too high, the authentic claim will lose credibility for drifting too far from the craft tradition. A last relevant challenge for neo-craft retailers lies in the relationship with their neighbourhood: as we have observed in the chapter, it is fundamental that the brick-and-mortar retail businesses also build an identity coherent with the one of the neighbourhood and establish roots in the economic, cultural and even social surrounding area.

Naturally, the current study has also many limitations that, hopefully, future research will overcome. The historical analysis of retailing in the transition between a Fordist and a post-Fordist model of production and consumption has only been sketched, and can be developed into a much more complex and insightful account. Also, the relationship between authenticity and distinctiveness in neo-craft production needs further research to be adequately untangled. Finally, the empirical section is based on an analysis of the neo-craft retailing of food and drinks, a relevant but limited category of brick-and-mortar retail shops, in a specific city (Milan). Thus, further research in other sectors and contexts could enlighten new phenomena and add novel empirical insights.

NOTE

1.　Etsy is an e-commerce platform where often small and independent craftspeople exhibit and sell their creations to customers.

REFERENCES

Arvidsson, A. (2019). *Changemakers: The Industrious Future of the Digital Economy.* Polity Press.

Bakos, Y. (2001). The emerging landscape for retail e-commerce. *Journal of Economic Perspectives, 15*(1), 69–80. https://doi.org/10.1257/jep.15.1.69.

Bell, E., & Vachhani, S. J. (2020). Relational encounters and vital materiality in the practice of craft work. *Organisation Studies, 41*(5), 681–701. https://doi.org/10.1177/0170840619866482.

Benjamin, W. (1969 [1936]). The work of art in the age of mechanical reproduction. In H. Harendt (ed.), *Illuminations* (pp. 217–51). Schocken.

Beverland, M. B. (2005). Crafting brand authenticity: the case of luxury wines. *Journal of Management Studies, 42*(5), 1003–29.

Beverland, M. B., & Farrelly, F. J. (2010). The quest for authenticity in consumption: consumers' purposive choice of authentic cues to shape experienced outcomes. *Journal of Consumer Research, 36*(5), 838–56. https://doi.org/10.1086/615047.

Bhattarai, A. (2019). 'Retail apocalypse' now: analysts say 75,000 more U.S. stores could be doomed. *Washington Post*. https://www.washingtonpost.com/business/2019/04/10/retail-apocalypse-now-analysts-say-more-us-stores-could-be-doomed/.

Bille, M., Bjerregaard, P., & Sørensen, T. F. (2015). Staging atmospheres: materiality, culture, and the texture of the in-between. *Emotion, Space and Society*, *15*, 31–8. https://doi.org/10.1016/j.emospa.2014.11.002.

Boltanski, L., & Chiapello, È. (2007). *The New Spirit of Capitalism*. Verso.

Braverman, H. (1998). *Labor and Monopoly Capital: The Degradation of Work in the Twentieth Century*. Monthly Review Press.

Bromley, R. D. F., & Thomas, C. T. (1995). Small town shopping decline: dependence and inconvenience for the disadvanged. *The International Review of Retail, Distribution and Consumer Research*, *5*(4), 433–56. https://doi.org/10.1080/09593969500000025.

Burt, S., & Sparks, L. (2003). E-commerce and the retail process: a review. *Journal of Retailing and Consumer Services*, *10*(5), 275–86. https://doi.org/10.1016/S0969-6989(02)00062-0.

Clarke, I., & Banga, S. (2010). The economic and social role of small stores: a review of UK evidence. *The International Review of Retail, Distribution and Consumer Research*, *20*(2), 187–215. https://doi.org/10.1080/09593961003701783.

Crossick, G., & Haupt, H.-G. (2013). *The Petite Bourgeoisie in Europe 1780–1914: Enterprise, Family and Independence*. Routledge.

Crossick, G., & Haupt, H.-G. (2016). *Shopkeepers and Master Artisans in Nineteenth-Century Europe*. Routledge.

D'Andrea, G., Lopez-Aleman, B., & Stengel, A. (2006). Why small retailers endure in Latin America. *International Journal of Retail & Distribution Management*, *34*(9), 661–73. https://doi.org/10.1108/09590550610683184.

DeSoucey, M. (2010). Gastronationalism: food traditions and authenticity politics in the European Union. *American Sociological Review*, *75*(3), 432–55. https://doi.org/10.1177/0003122410372226.

Dickson, P. R., & Ginter, J. L. (1987). Market segmentation, product differentiation, and marketing strategy. *Journal of Marketing*, *51*(2), 1–10. https://doi.org/10.1177/002224298705100201.

Doody, A. F., & Davidson, W. R. (1964). Growing strength in small retailing. *Harvard Business Review*, July–August, 15.

Etikan, I., Musa, S. A., & Alkassim, R. S. (2016). Comparison of convenience sampling and purposive sampling. *American Journal of Theoretical and Applied Statistics*, *5*(1), 1–4.

Gandini, A. (2020). *Zeitgeist Nostalgia: On Populism, Work and the Good Life*. Zero Books.

Gerosa, A. (2021). Cosmopolitans of regionalism: dealers of omnivorous taste under Italian food truck economic imaginary. *Consumption Markets & Culture*, *24*(1), 30–53. https://doi.org/10.1080/10253866.2020.1731483.

Gibbs, G. R. (2018). *Analyzing Qualitative Data* (2nd edition). Sage.

Goolsbee, A. (2020). Never mind the internet: here's what's killing malls. *The New York Times*. https://www.nytimes.com/2020/02/13/business/not-internet-really-killing-malls.html.

Grayson, K., & Martinec, R. (2004). Consumer perceptions of iconicity and indexicality and their influence on assessments of authentic market offerings. *Journal of Consumer Research*, *31*(2), 296–312. https://doi.org/10.1016/s0098-7913(78)80071-9.

Grewal, D., Levy, M., & Kumar, V. (2009). Customer experience management in retailing: an organising framework. *Journal of Retailing, 85*(1), 1–14. https://doi .org/10.1016/j.jretai.2009.01.001.

Grewal, D., Roggeveen, A. L., & Nordfält, J. (2017). The future of retailing. *Journal of Retailing, 93*(1), 1–6. https://doi.org/10.1016/j.jretai.2016.12.008.

Helm, S., Kim, S. H., & Van Riper, S. (2020). Navigating the 'retail apocalypse': a framework of consumer evaluations of the new retail landscape. *Journal of Retailing and Consumer Services, 54.* https://doi.org/10.1016/j.jretconser.2018.09 .015.

Hilton, M. (1998). Retailing history as economic and cultural history: strategies of survival by specialist tobacconists in the mass market. *Business History, 40*(4), 115–37. https://doi.org/10.1080/00076799800000341.

Hirsch, D., & Tene, O. (2013). Hummus: the making of an Israeli culinary cult. *Journal of Consumer Culture, 13*(1), 25–45. https://doi.org/10.1177/1469540512474529.

Holt, D., & Cameron, D. (2010). *Cultural Strategy: Using Innovative Ideologies to Build Breakthrough Brands.* Oxford University Press.

Hughes, C., & Jackson, C. (2015). Death of the high street: identification, prevention, reinvention. *Regional Studies, Regional Science, 2*(1), 237–56. https://doi.org/10 .1080/21681376.2015.1016098.

Humphery, K. (1998). *Shelf Life: Supermarkets and the Changing Cultures of Consumption.* Cambridge University Press.

Johnston, J., & Baumann, S. (2015). *Foodies* (2nd edition). Routledge.

Kacker, M. P. (1986). The metamorphosis of European retailing. *European Journal of Marketing, 20*(8), 15–22. https://doi.org/10.1108/EUM0000000004659.

Kotler, P. (1973). Atmospherics as a marketing tool. *Journal of Retailing, 49*(4), 48–64.

Land, C. (2018). Back to the future: re-imagining work through craft. Futures of Work. https://futuresofwork.co.uk/2018/11/19/back-to-the-future-re-imagining-work -through-craft/.

Megicks, P., & Warnaby, G. (2008). Market orientation and performance in small independent retailers in the UK. *The International Review of Retail, Distribution and Consumer Research, 18*(1), 105–19. https://doi.org/10.1080/09593960701778192.

Mokyr, J. (1998). The second Industrial Revolution, 1870–1914. In V. Castronovo (ed.), *Storia dell'economia Mondiale* (p. 18). Laterza.

Naudin, A., & Patel, K. (eds) (2020). *Craft Entrepreneurship.* Rowman & Littlefield. https://rowman.com/ISBN/9781786613745/Craft-Entrepreneurship.

Ocejo, R. E. (2017). *Masters of Craft: Old Jobs in the New Urban Economy.* Princeton University Press.

Peterson, R. A. (2005). In search of authenticity. *Journal of Management Studies, 42*(5), 1083–98.

Peterson, R. A., & Kern, R. M. (1996). Changing highbrow taste: from snob to omnivore. *American Sociological Review, 61*(5), 900–907. https://doi.org/10.2307/ 2096460.

Piotrowicz, W., & Cuthbertson, R. (2014). Introduction to the Special Issue Information Technology in Retail: toward omnichannel retailing. *International Journal of Electronic Commerce, 18*(4), 5–16. https://doi.org/10.2753/JEC1086-4415180400.

Puccinelli, N. M., Goodstein, R. C., Grewal, D., Price, R., Raghubir, P., & Stewart, D. (2009). Customer experience management in retailing: understanding the buying process. *Journal of Retailing, 85*(1), 15–30. https://doi.org/10.1016/j.jretai.2008.11 .003.

Quinn, B., McKitterick, L., McAdam, R., & Brennan, M. (2013). Innovation in small-scale retailing: a future research agenda. *The International Journal of Entrepreneurship and Innovation*, *14*(2), 81–93. https://doi.org/10.5367/ijei.2013 .0111.

Sachdeva, I., & Goel, S. (2015). Retail store environment and customer experience: a paradigm. *Journal of Fashion Marketing and Management*, *19*(3), 290–98. https:// doi.org/10.1108/JFMM-03-2015-0021.

Sennett, R. (2008). *The Craftsman*. Yale University Press.

Smith, A., & Sparks, L. (2001). Planning for small-scale retailing: evidence from Scotland. *Planning Theory & Practice*, *2*(3), 277–92. https://doi.org/10.1080/ 14649350120096820.

Smith, W. R. (1956). Product differentiation and market segmentation as alternative marketing strategies. *Journal of Marketing*, *21*(1), 3–8. https://doi.org/10.1177/ 002224295602100102.

Smith Maguire, J. (2018). The taste for the particular: a logic of discernment in an age of omnivorousness. *Journal of Consumer Culture*, *18*(1), 3–20. https://doi.org/10 .1177/1469540516634416.

Sombart, W. (1928). *Der moderne Kapitalismus: Historisch-systematische Darstellung des gesamteuropäischen Wirtschaftslebens von seinen Anfängen bis zur Gegenwart*. Duncker & Humblot.

Thurnell-Read, T. (2019). A thirst for the authentic: craft drinks producers and the narration of authenticity. *The British Journal of Sociology*, *70*(4), 1448–68. https:// doi.org/10.1111/1468-4446.12634.

Trilling, L. (1972). *Sincerity and Authenticity*. Harvard University Press.

Wells, K., & Watson, S. (2005). A politics of resentment: shopkeepers in a London neighbourhood. *Ethnic and Racial Studies*, *28*(2), 261–77. https://doi.org/10.1080/ 01419870420000315843.

Winstanley, M. J. (1983). *The Shopkeeper's World, 1830–1914*. Manchester University Press.

Wrigley, N., & Currah, A. (2006). Globalising retail and the 'new e-conomy': the organisational challenge of e-commerce for the retail TNCs. *Geoforum*, *37*(3), 340–51. https://doi.org/10.1016/j.geoforum.2005.06.003.

Zukin, S. (2008). Consuming authenticity. *Cultural Studies*, *22*(5), 724–48. https://doi .org/10.1080/09502380802245985.

13. Innovating through craft: from happenstance to strategic culture

Ginevra Addis

INTRODUCTION

This chapter analyzes the conflicted transition from the works labeled under the name *arte popolare* to the innovative artistic products of the Pop Art trend (Italy vs. USA), which took place in the 1960s and inspired the strategic marketing culture that underlies Pop Art enterprises (museums, foundations, archives; e.g., The Andy Warhol Museum). Such a transition dislodged the value of crafts, both as objects and icons, and instead positioned the cultural marketing strategy as the driving force behind the artist's success. Studies on *arte popolare* had begun in 1891–92 and stopped during World War II because part of its heritage had been destroyed (e.g., the bombing of Villa d'Este in Tivoli that hosted some of the objects from the Museo Nazionale delle Arti e Tradizioni Popolari). They re-started after the war, with the most representative episode being the placement of the Museo Nazionale delle Arti e Tradizioni popolari in Rome, 1953 (Alario & Mirizzi, 1986, p. 40; Massari 2007; Centroni, 2011). In *Arte popolare italiana* (Toschi, 1960, pp. 13–35), Paolo Toschi thoroughly documented the meaning of the name *arte popolare* and how it was perceived at the beginning of the 1960s: critics and scholars generally used *arte rustica* and *arte paesana* to emphasize the importance of craftsmanship, a uniform and monotonous aesthetic process that proposed the same representations of traditions, while *volgo* was used to highlight the focus on citizens (Danilowicz, 1941; Brezzo, 1938).

Arte popolare stands out for its ingenuousness, its simplicity, and its unstudied quality—in contrast to the *grande arte* born from deeper thoughts and more professional art techniques. However, to the eyes of history, *arte popolare* and *grande arte* now stand equal in value and stature (Toschi, 1960, pp. 13–14). Finally, *arte popolare* represents the heritage of people; the word *popolare*, stemming from *popolo*, encompasses the idea of community.[1] On this topic, several recent studies have investigated the works produced under the label *arte popolare* and how they contributed to the creation of the Made in Italy brand. Such studies underscore the strong importance that craftsmanship has assumed in the Italian national identity (e.g., Pellegrini, 2017).[2] This debate over Italian identity began with the *Esposizione Universale* of 1911—a huge ethnographic and regional exhibition of art and culture located in Rome. That exhibition, especially the section related to popular iconography, underscored that a large amount of crafts are still unknown to the public. A portion of those crafts constituted the nucleus of the collection of the Museo Nazionale delle Arti e delle Tradizioni Popolari in Rome. That exhibit triggered debates about the Italian tradition, and particularly the contribution of craftsmanship itself to Italian identity. Those debates culminated in the Congresso Nazionale delle Tradizioni Popolari, which first took place in Florence in 1929 and again in Udine in 1931. Both conferences directed researchers and committees focused on popular art and traditions to maintain the folkloristic heritage of crafts as an essential part of the Italian national identity. Among craft scholars, the main point of debate arising from these conferences was the risk of modernizing craft and losing its local features, replaced instead with a pan-Italian art focused on creating new ornamental motifs derived from different objects belonging to the Italian tradition (Bertarelli, 1938, pp. 53–6; Danilowicz, 1941).

Expectedly with the onset of American Pop Art at the 1964 Venice Biennale, the concept of *arte popolare* clashed with the idea of American Popular Art, on both a terminological and iconographical level (Atkinson, 1965). Despite warnings about the risk of craft modernization in the 1920s, 1930s and 1940s, the decades following the 1964 Venice Biennale saw those concerns come to life: certain Italian artists, working under the Pop label, chose to utilize those traditions in new ways. While some Pop Italian artists initially appropriated artisanal products and their physical properties into their artworks (e.g., Tano Festa's *Persiana*, 1962; Enrico Baj's *Il riposo del decorato*, 1963), they soon abandoned this practice to embrace the American Pop style, while still considering their work as part of the Italian tradition under the label of *arte popolare*. The artisanal products were de facto replaced by consumer ones, with graphic and advertising images substituting for the objects originally included in Pop Italian artworks. Granted, this transition proved to be a major success in terms of artwork sales and exhibits. The business model behind the successful turn of Italian Pop Art seemed totally new and detached from the Italian craft tradition, but it was not: Italian Pop Artists embraced the sense of monotony and motif repetition that characterized American Pop Art precisely because the Italian crafts tradition was already undergoing change. Indeed, the loss of its localism had seeded the terrain for the fertile reception of American Pop Art. However, that success did not endure: the substitution of crafts did not elevate Italian Pop Artists' names into important cultural enterprises (e.g., museums that employ consumer and marketing strategies), in contrast to the reception of their American Pop colleagues (e.g., The Andy Warhol Museum and Foundation).[3]

In light of this situation, this chapter will first investigate the meaning of *arte popolare* in Italy in the 1950s and 1960s, outlining the similarities that *arte popolare* had with the craftsmanship process. The chapter will specifically look at Italy's historical context and the points of contact that such a process had with the USA. Second, the chapter will compare the cultural enterprises that originated from the Pop experience in both the USA and Italy, with a particular focus on successful artists' branding strategy in relation to the art dealers that kept the Pop market afloat in both countries. Through its methodological approach, this chapter will try to deeply understand how the transition occurred at first haphazardly and then strategically, and also what innovations arose from this shift.

THE MEANING OF *ARTE POPOLARE* IN ITALY IN THE 1950s AND 1960s

Since the late twentieth century, Italian philologists have documented the meaning of *popolare* as anything that is made by common people, for common people; however, recent decades have sought to produce a more focused definition. In the 1930s, *popolare* identified something related to people, but with the connotation of untaught ingenuousness, reflecting the condition of regular people in simple terms. This meaning persisted through the 1940s and 1950s, when it referred to something that had qualities that were appropriate for and in vogue among common people. In the 1960s, scholars adopted the concept of an uninterrupted tradition and its importance to further clarify the meaning of *popolare*. Ironically, that decade also contained the conflicting passage from Italian *arte popolare* to American *Pop Art*. Since at least the beginning of the twenty-first century, *arte popolare* connoted a historical tradition of folkloristic craft production; however, in the 1960s, Italian Pop Artists shifted their art to match the US Pop current. On both an iconographic and a philological level, it seems that Pop Italian artists appropriated this trend to preserve the features of Italian localism, which drew on the elevated and traditional images of high Italian culture. At the same time, the name *arte popolare* would signify an equivalence with American Pop Art in terms of the uniform and monotonous craft process (see, for instance, Warhol's serigraphies, Indiana's sculptures, Dine's representation of objects and Oldenburg's giant sculptures).[4]

In the twentieth and twenty-first centuries, Italian historians used the term *arte popolare* to document the object of Italian traditions and costumes, most of them sold in artisanal local markets, artisanal shutters, and art galleries, and eventually collected in museums and private collections. However, it seems that dictionaries treat the name *arte popolare* as arising in the 1940s, reflecting a compliance with broad public tastes and mentality (Zingarelli, 1941, p. 1171; Migliorini, 1963, pp. 1043–4; Devoto, 1967, p. 575; Cusatelli, 1971, p. 1295). The fact that Italian language experts in the 1970s feel the need to underline such a meaning is indicative of the new circumstances that the previous decades (the 1950s and the 1960s in particular) produced on a historical, socio-economic and artistic level. When analyzing the situation that arose in Italy during the 1960s, certain conditions can be specified: (1) the revitalization of the American dream; (2) the society of consumerism; and (3) the advent of Pop Art.

The so-called American dream had its European antecedents in the eighteenth century—a seeming consequence of the American Revolution that corresponded with the European Age of Enlightenment. Over the centuries, the American dream has undergone periods of renewal based on historical events that touched nations. Italy gained a new interest in the USA amidst the rise and collapse of fascism, particularly in the post-World War II years, given that the USA not only substantially helped Italy with the Marshall Plan (which provided economic aid), but also culturally involved Italian people in the American model (Palmer, 2014, p. 179). The Italian orientation to the USA was bolstered by the economic boom of the 1950s, which imported a way of life from America (e.g., Coca Cola, blue jeans) and made Italy into a consumerist society. These two elements prompted Italy to welcome the new type of art that the USA was promoting, meaning their own type of *arte popolare*, named Pop Art, which gleaned its distinctive imagery largely from the mass-produced cultural objects, comics and advertisements that were common in the USA at that time. Such a promotion served a cultural-diplomatic purpose at the onset of the Cold War. Recent studies of the CIA's records reveal how under Eisenhower's presidency, particularly in 1953, the National Security Council (NSC) was put in charge of promoting the cultural image of the USA abroad. The core members of the NSC were the secretaries of Defense and State, the CIA, and Nelson Rockefeller, who served as President Representative and Chair of the board due to his strong financial and administrative role in New York's Museum of Modern Art. During Eisenhower's presidency, the NSC chose to promote the trend of Abstract Expressionism, a free and tolerant aesthetic model, in contrast to the Russian Socialist Realism, a realist style that mirrored communist values. During the Kennedy presidency (from 1961), the NSC promoted the Neo-Dada trend that encompassed Jasper Johns and Robert Rauschenberg, the latter of whom is today known as the father of Pop Art. Shortly thereafter, Pop Art was officially imported from the USA at the 1964 Venice Biennale, where Solomon Guggenheim directed the US pavilion and presented Robert Rauschenberg alongside several American Pop artists such as Andy Warhol, Roy Lichtenstein, Jim Dine, Robert Indiana and Claes Oldenburg. Among them, Rauschenberg was the artist awarded with the *Leone d'oro*, through which the Venice Biennale's judges recognized him as the best foreign artist. This had the effect of directing Italian artists' and art critics' attention to the US Pop Art movement and its related market.[5]

Italian art critics eventually recognized Rauschenberg as the father of Pop Art, even though his art did not properly reflect the Pop style that American artists later developed. His art was instead classified as belonging to the Neo-Dada current, which encompassed different types of popular objects in the so-called *combine paintings*: objects that belonged to the American popular tradition, but that later protagonists of American Pop Art would replace with graphic images and advertisements re-elaborated with brilliant colors that stemmed from TV and posters. In the wake of Venice Biennale 1964, Italian artists began to adopt the American translation of *arte popolare*, swapping their artisanal crafts for the American graphic representations (Kozloff, 1962; Swenson, 1962, 1964a, 1964b). The appearance of Neo-Dada in the USA and Nouveau Réalisme in France seemed to encourage this transition. In the Italian tradition of the twelfth and thirteenth centuries, artists primarily chose to represent sacred images; this interest in religious images continued through the Renaissance and then was abandoned for several centuries. By the beginning of the twenty-first century, artists' daily objects mostly encompassed those in the still life series, until the Avant-garde era prompted a change in viewing objects that then altered how the objects were represented.

This change in how objects were chosen and scrutinized persisted in Dadaism (with its emphasis on irony) and Surrealism (with its focus on the subconscious, as reflected in collages of images, words and thoughts). With Neo-Dada and Nouveau Réalisme, artists shifted their focus once again: namely, to realizing a new type of image that could establish a new perceptual relationship between shapes and common objects. The artwork itself tended to become a concrete witness of the artist's production process. In this vein, the physical presence of the object becomes less important than the conceptual process enacted upon it. The fact that protagonists of the Pop style substituted concrete objects with their related images, or with other images that emphasized a new idea of art, is a natural development of the process rather than a strong break with tradition.

Enrico Baj, an artist who the modern literature sees as one of the antecedents of the Italian Pop Art trend, included textiles (e.g., jackets) and wood decorations (e.g., cabinets) in his works in the 1950s. After meeting with the US Pop Art and UK Pop culture in his multiple travels to London and the USA, he started to paint a series called *Ultracorpi*, which embedded images of body-builders in a style belonging to the US Pop Art tradition (Battisti, 1964; Celant, 2009, p. 180; Sanna, 2018; Sanguineti, 1957; Paz, 2008; Sauvage, 1952; Cisventi, 1965). Likewise, Tano Festa—an artist from Rome who worked with wood and produced several window blinds that were presented in the USA at the Sidney Janis Gallery's exhibit in 1962, NYC—abandoned the materiality of objects in the 1960s, instead depicting images from the Italian modern art tradition (e.g., from the Sistine Chapel) in the American Pop style (e.g., *La creazione dell'uomo*, 1964) (Gallo, 1990; Francesconi, 2018; Guastalla & Guastalla, 2013, 2016; Vivaldi, 1961; De Marchis, 1963, 1967; Janis 1962). Franco Angeli, another artist based in Rome, began his career by working with *velatino*, a special textile used for mannequins and lamp light diffusion, but after 1964, he painted numerous images of American dollars using the wide range of colors from American Pop (e.g., the Half Dollar series) (Fagiolo dell'Arco, 1966; Barbero, 2017; Guastalla & Guastalla, 2013, 2016; Gallo, 1990; Francesconi, 2018).

These artists' transitions seemed to mirror Italy's own artistic transformation in the wake of societal, cultural and economic change. While there were upsides to the development, the transformation nonetheless entailed a conflict among Italian artists. In their apparent embrace of American art and the American way of life, such artists were not only casting aside elements of the Italian tradition (abandoning the craft emphasis of Italian *arte popolare* in favor of graphic and advertising images), but were adopting a style that belonged to a foreign culture's traditions (Guadagnini, 2005, p. 31; Mecacci, 2011, p. 62; Bossaglia & Zatti, 1983; Salvi et al., 1987, p. 117). While this change seemed to happen softly for the majority of artists, it soon triggered intense conflicts, especially among Italian art gallerists and art critics—the former interested in affirming the Italian art market and the latter seeking to maintain the Italian avant-gardist tradition.[6] This clashing evolution appears to have influenced not only the Italian artists who found success in the related art market system, but also certain cultural enterprises (e.g., museums, foundations and archives) that were more fruitful for American Pop artists. Italian Pop artists' approach—of treating crafts not as concrete objects that artists include in their artworks, but rather as sources of iconographic inspiration—was likely another driving element in the market dynamics. The transfer of interest from the object itself to the artistic process triggered by said object allowed the artworks to be adaptable to market demands, which appealed to art dealers. The uniformity that crafts went through in the first half of the twenty-first century reached its peak in this period, where objects became deprived of their distinctive features and content. Instead, they became the sources of new images in which their materiality was not only unnecessary, but adaptable to the artist's aim. The case of Festa is emblematic in this sense: after 1964, his works did not use blinds as the main subject, but as a canvas or supporting material. Likewise, the greatest demand for his paintings came from the Pop Art market system, and especially from the New York dealer Leo Castelli—a bridge figure between the USA and Italy (Lublin, 1993; Cohen-Solal, 2010, pp. 233–8).

FROM CRAFT TO MARKETING AMONG AMERICAN AND ITALIAN POPULAR CULTURAL ENTERPRISES: MUSEUMS, FOUNDATIONS AND ARCHIVES

The Pop Art market mainly revolved around the network developed by Castelli and his former wife Ileana Shapiro (Sundell, 2002; Gandini and Bonito Oliva, 2008; Hunter et al., 1991). After the two split, Shapiro worked with her new husband Michael Sonnabend to open a gallery in Paris that promoted several Italian (e.g., Mario Schifano, Michelangelo Pistoletto) and American Pop artists (Sperone et al., 1965). Both Castelli and Schapiro were surely important for those artists' success; however, the real success of these cultural institutions was not simply their prominence as art gallerists, nor the value of the artworks themselves, but the marketing strategies that their artists developed and embodied. Crafts themselves were pointless unless they contributed to the artist's brand, which was integral to the cultural marketing strategy itself (e.g., Warhol and Rauschenberg within the Pop Art current and Barbara Kruger and Cindy Sherman out of the Pop sphere). In the last decade, several consumer behaviorists have focused on such strategies and identified artists who were brand icons while alive. This research, which has been in place since the end of the 1990s, has prompted an important reconsideration of branding processes and brand meaning by shifting attention from brand producers to consumers and their responses (Schroeder, 2005, p. 1291). Through their relationship to advertising, brands and mass media, consumers seem to create "their self-image, within and in collaboration with, brand culture" (Schroeder, 2005, p. 1291). In other words, researchers have established that neither managers nor consumers completely control the branding process. Consumer behaviorists have taken an interest in this interaction between brands and culture and discussed it from many perspectives (e.g., McCracken, 1986; Guzmàn & Paswan, 2009, p. 72). For example, Hatch and Rubin described brands as "symbols in popular culture with their meanings contingent on particular cultural contexts" (cited in Guzmàn & Paswan, 2009, p. 72).

In examining Pop artists from this angle, the most useful point of comparison is American artist Andy Warhol, whose art and personality loom large in the cultural consciousness. In the 1960s, he became a symbol of popular culture due to his intuition as a brand manager to convert himself into a recognizable product (Schroeder, 2005). "Warhol provides a stunning example of artist as brand – he was extremely articulate about his ambition to become famous – and his work reflectively comments on brands and consumer culture. Warhol's contributions to branding are many, and he remains a hot brand almost 20 years after his untimely death" (Schroeder, 2005, p. 1292). Schroeder's analysis first reveals how Warhol marketed himself as a brand name and a successful artist, managing his own brand in a way similar to non-Pop American artists (e.g., Barbara Kruger and Cindy Sherman) (Schroeder, 2005, pp. 1296–8). Warhol indeed appears to have studied the market system and marketing strategies (Schroeder, 1997), choosing to paint important celebrities, producing a series of famous brands sold in the world market, and making people aware of everything he was doing through his published diaries and books such as *The Philosophy of Andy Warhol* (1975). Surely the most popular quote of Warhol about Coca-Cola, an iconic brand that granted common people an opportunity to drink the same product as presidents and divas, is one of his primary reflections on consumerism: "What's great about this country is that America started the tradition where the richest consumers buy essentially the same thing as the poorest. [...] You can be watching TV and see Coca-Cola, and you know that the President drinks Coke, and no amount of money can get you a better Coke than the one the bum on the corner is drinking" (Warhol, 1975, p. 100). He made a similar observation on the mass production of blue jeans: "I wish I could invent something to be remembered by something mass" (Warhol, 1975, p. 13). In relation to the idea of art as a business, he opined: "Business art is the step that comes after Art. I started as a commercial artist, and I want to finish as a business artist. [...] I wanted to be an Art Businessman or a Business Artist. Being good in business is the most fascinating kind of art [...]" (Warhol, 1975, p. 92).

Second, Schroeder's analysis prompts one to ask: "How long did this icon survive? Are there are any art institutions that can benefit from the same survival?" In trying to answer this question, it is helpful to assess the relationship between Warhol's brand icon and the two institutions born from his vision: The Andy Warhol Foundation for the Visual Arts and The Andy Warhol Museum, both of which are based in Pittsburgh, Pennsylvania.

Andy Warhol's Branding Strategy

Schroeder's research offers a starting point to answering the above question. According to the author, art creates wealth for artists, dealers, collectors and investors, as well as via tourism and cultural development, given that:

> The branded world intersects with the art world in numerous ways – art museum shops play increasingly important roles in revenue streams and consumer/viewer experience, branded organizations sponsor art exhibitions, art auction houses such as Christie's and Sotheby's have developed strong brands, and branding strategy informs the contemporary milieu of superstar artists and collectors. (Schroeder, 2005, p. 1293)

Under such a perspective, it is useful to consider two successful examples of institutions built up around the figure of Andy Warhol: The Andy Warhol

Foundation for the Visual Arts and The Andy Warhol Museum. The two rely on different business models and strategies: While the former benefits from Warhol's personal style of marrying controversial ideas of art, the latter benefits from the brand icon that Warhol built up himself.

The Andy Warhol Foundation emphasizes Warhol's spirit in its founding statute, which speaks of its efforts to "ensure that Warhol's inventive, open-minded spirit will have a profound impact on the visual arts for generations to come" (The Andy Warhol Foundation for the Visual Arts, n.d.a). Perhaps appropriately, the Foundation's launch coincided with some of the fiercest battles of the culture wars; and like Warhol himself, the Foundation has spent decades supporting the *First Amendment rights of artists and their organizations*. This mission, bound to Warhol's expressed desire for the advancement of the Visual Arts, led the Foundation to fund artworks and exhibitions with potentially controversial content (e.g., of a sexual, political or religious nature) through its regular program grants. The Foundation supported four noteworthy exhibits that triggered cries of immorality from critics or officials (The Andy Warhol Foundation for the Visual Arts n.d.b). First was the retrospective *Fever*, where *The Art of David Wojnarowicz* at the New Museum (NYC, 1999) showed works with sexual and violent content that directly addressed the topic of AIDS (Cameron & Scholder, 1999). Second was the exhibit at the Brooklyn Museum of Art (NYC, 1999): then-Mayor of New York City, Rudolph Giuliani, was outraged by British artist Chris Offili's painting of the Virgin Mary decorated with elephant dung; he threatened to cut off all city funding to the museum if it did not remove the picture from the exhibition (Horsley, n.d.; Goodnough, 1999).[7]

While the Foundation focuses on realizing Warhol's belief in artistic expression, The Andy Warhol Museum's marketing strategy focuses on the promotion of a variety of exhibitions that valorize Warhol's artworks and sell merchandise associated with Warhol's figure, artworks and mottos. Surely the museum's collection is its most important treasure; thus, the museum's ability to valorize and sell said collection remains a major factor behind its success. However, the fact that the Warhol Museum benefits from Warhol's icons is evident even in the exhibitions, which are presented year-round and sometimes feature never-before-seen Warhol artworks from the collection. The Museum is keen to underline these pieces as being as unique and intellectually stimulating as the icon of Warhol himself.[8] Another initiative that benefits from Warhol's creative icon is the Museum's donation drives, where it asks clients for any support in "maintaining a forum where diverse audiences can be inspired by the creative interaction with Andy Warhol's life and art" (The Andy Warhol Museum, n.d.b). To this end, the Museum adopted a "Give what you can" format to let people donate their preferred amount (e.g., $25, $50, $100, $200). An additional initiative that benefits from Warhol's creative icon is the launch of the Museum's first affinity group, The Portrait Society, which is intended to create a more in-depth relationship between The Warhol Museum and the viewer, aligning the latter's passion with the former's mission of publicly and creatively interacting with Andy Warhol's life and art.[9] The Andy Warhol Museum's for-profit activities that benefit from Warhol's icon mostly revolve around the shop. The Museum not only contains a physical shop inside, but has also opened an online store as part of an e-commerce strategy. Both shops sell products that use Warhol's iconography and painted images, including calendars, CDs & DVDs, chocolate, home décor, posters, magnets, puzzles and iPhone cases. Regarding tickets, the Museum offers entrance tickets ranging from $8 to $18, guided tours for up to 20 people for $50, and workshops for up to 30 people for $400.

Relative to other American Pop artists, it seems that only Rauschenberg had a similar marketing promotion through his foundation. Meanwhile, it seems that Italian Pop artists did not achieve a similar branding phenomenon, nor did they find lasting cultural institutions (with the exception of Pino Pascali, although that one cannot be explained by a strong cultural marketing model[10]). The main reason seems to be that the heritage of Italian Pop artists is conserved in archives, many of which are private and have not adopted a marketing methodology. Some of them are part of museums—such as the one of Enrico Baj, part of MART (Museo di Arte Moderna e Contemporanea di Trento e Rovereto)—but the museum does not focus its marketing strategy or merchandising around the artist, while its website focuses on multiple exhibits of several artists. Even Mario Schifano—a strong personality among Italian Pop artists who had several analogies with Warhol—did not achieve a parallel fortune in terms of cultural enterprise (Galdaston, 2001; Bonito Oliva, 1995, 2008, 2017; Guadagnini, 2018; Guastalla & Guastalla, 2013, 2016; Gallo, 1990; Marconi, 2005, 2006). Granted, his estate saw a long legal battle that split its heritage between his wife (who manages the archive) and his assistants (who manage his foundation). Moreover, because of legal agreements, the foundation is restricted to using Mario's initials (MS) and cannot leverage his full name to build its brand.

There are only two museums that preserve a collective heritage of Italian Pop artists, although they lack any developed marketing strategy: the first is GNAM (Galleria Nazionale d'Arte Moderna), based in Rome. In the 1960s and 1970s, its director, Palma Bucarelli, bought several Italian Pop artworks and created a bio-iconographic archive that conserves relevant documents (e.g., newspaper articles) (Mazzella, 2018; Cicalini, 2016; Margozzi, 2009). The second is GAM (Galleria d'Arte Moderna), based in Turin. In the 1960s, the museum received the collection of the former Museo Sperimentale d'Arte Contemporanea in Genoa, thanks to the efforts of the Italian art critic Eugenio Battisti (Bandini & Serra, 1985, pp. 11–12, 22–3; Mallé, 1970).

The interests of these museums and foundations in promoting such artists clearly prompts us to look closely at the relationship between Pop Art and marketing and uncover a deeper understanding about marketing in the context of arts and crafts. In this vein, several marketing scholars have noted that despite the vague dissimilarity between arts and crafts, both of them benefit from the marketing principles thanks to their shared features. For instance, "they both produce basically hand-made products, most times culturally rooted, whose characteristic quality or inherent character has principally an aesthetic appeal which is judged mostly by the eye" (Archi & Umoh, 2019, p. 236). While marketing channels used by artisans could differ from those use by artists, "the basics of the business cycle remain equally applicable to marketing original artworks, even though the artist's reputation somehow has a greater impact on the demand for his or her works and therefore, on the price of the artwork" (Archi & Umoh, 2019, p. 236). While each has its own market (e.g., artists sell art in galleries, museums and art fairs, while artisans sell crafts in exhibitions, street markets and tourists venues) they both seem to have an "interdependent relationship including their linkages with the industrial design and formal factory-oriented mass production sectors" (Archi & Umoh, 2019, p. 236). In light of these analyses, one can argue that the orientation to the mass production sector underpinned the cultural marketing strategies that allowed craft products to become successful Pop artworks. Granted, the marketing strategies seemed to be more successful for those American artists who had a stronger reputation in the art market system when they were still living.[11] Nevertheless, for Italian artists, applying a more robust cultural marketing strategic model could benefit their foundations, museums and archives.

CONCLUSION

This chapter first concludes that the strategic culture of Pop Art successfully worked when translated into a mass marketing strategy. In Italy, consumerist images usurped traditional crafts, forcing the latter to become a mainstay of collections rather than a pillar of marketing strategies.

Second, the chapter synthesizes research on the branding strategies of Pop artists, who largely followed the example of Andy Warhol. This is likely because Warhol had been avant-gardist in understanding both the art market dynamics and the marketing strategies of the 1950s and 1960s. Additionally, his beliefs, artworks and personal iconography created a strong heritage that endures through his titular institutions.

Finally, future research on other art trends—such as Minimalism—should use the same methodology adopted in this research (i.e., affirming the relationship between the art trend and marketing systems). Historically, the Pop Art phenomenon was born in the UK, migrated to the USA, and was then imported into Italy.

NOTES

1. The comparison between high and low culture has been an object of studies in both Europe and the USA, especially after the exhibition *High and Low: Modern Art and Popular Culture*, MoMA, NYC, October 1990–91, organized by Kirk Varnedoe.

2. This tension was equally present at the *Voglia di Collezionismo* exhibit held at Palazzo Venezia and Gallerie Sacconi in the Vittoriano complex in Rome, from December 2017 to March 2018. The exhibit presented a wide collection assembled by the US couple George Washington Wurts and Henriette Tower, donated to Palazzo Venezia. The collection features multiple examples of artisanal production from the nineteenth and the twentieth centuries.

3. The multiple connections between the USA and Italy—reflected, for instance, in the Italian and American Pop artists' travels and residencies in the USA, as well as shared network of gallerists, editors and curators—are deeply documented in the author's PhD thesis *The re-identification of Pop Art: its reception from an Italian perspective*, discussed at IMT School for Advanced Studies, Lucca (IT), published with European Press Academic Publishing. The thesis sought to revisit Italy's import of the Pop phenomenon in the 1960s, historically contextualizing its advent at the critical, iconographical, and institutional level. In particular, Chapter 1 widely discusses the relation of the term *popolare* to art, while accounting for the meaning of Pop Art in the USA. Some examples include Tano Festa and Enrico Baj: Festa has been one of the most important Pop Italian artists, while among art historians, Baj's art remains more closely related to the *Arte Nucleare* (Nuclear Art) that he founded with the painter Sergio Dangelo in 1951 when they published their related *manifesto*.

4. For a detailed evolution on the term *popolare* as reported by dictionaries, see the Dictionary Appendix of the author's PhD thesis, conserved at the IMT School for Advanced Studies' library.

5. Although the origin of the American dream appears to be a consequence of the American Revolution, it was not until the nineteenth century—with the advent of capitalism and the Romantic Era—that the 'American dream' gained prominence among Europeans.

6. Among the art critics and art gallerists interested in the American Pop art current, the two piloting figures were the Roman gallerist Plinio De Martiis (Galleria La Tartaruga) and the French art critic Pierre Restany (De Martiis, 1951–3, 1952, 1999; Restany, 1959, 1973).

7. The $7 million amounted to a third of the museum's budget; its withdrawal would have caused the entire institution to shut down. The foundation immediately responded to the crisis by supporting the museum's lawsuit against the city, which was ultimately victorious. Other exhibits included *Harmful: The Art of American Censorship*, at Georgia State University (a publicly funded institution in the South) (Horsley, n.d.; Byrd & Richmond, 2006). The exhibit—featuring Andreas Serrano's *Piss Christ* and pieces by Karen Finley and Robert Mapplethorpe, among others—sought to provoke a constructive dialogue about art, politics and censorship in America, but instead generated terrible contro-

versy. Fourth was the exhibit *The Eight Square* in 2005, a show about gender politics and marginalized sexuality that took place at the Museum Ludwig in Cologne, Germany, when its state funding was rescinded in the USA due to its controversial content.

8. For instance, the museum often rotates the displayed artworks—which encompass thousands of paintings, drawings, photographs, prints, sculptures, films and videos—thereby providing visitors with an ever-changing experience. The museum also houses the Warhol archives. Meanwhile, the museum's director works with curators to provide a unique, multifaceted experience through an intense exhibition calendar. Secondly, the museum creates other products to sell, such as film and video programming that showcases Andy Warhol's videography, in addition to showing films made by other artists that inform and contextualize Warhol's work, either historically, thematically or graphically. Finally, the museum offers relevant supplemental programs related to the performing arts, as well as educational initiatives such as youth programs, research activities and art lessons. All these products are communicated through the museum's detailed website, social media, and PR and Communication Department. Another example of the museum's marketing strategy is embodied in one of its website initiatives promoted from 2015 to 2017. The museum proposed these questions to the public to facilitate a repository of ideas: "What does it mean to be a museum in the digital age? How can digital and emerging media help a cultural institution successfully meet its mission? Where does a museum begin on its path toward becoming truly optimized for the evolving digital landscape, and why is it important that museums do so?" The Andy Warhol Museum, like many institutions, compared these questions with the museum's first formal digital strategies in order to develop a roadmap for infusing digital activities into its fabric. By developing a structured strategy that encompassed everything from in-gallery interactive projects to the digital literacy of Warhol staff, the museum could pursue its goals and monitor its progress. This strategy led the museum to create an open-source repository of the public's responses, which was made available through a Creative Commons Attribution-Non-Commercial-Share-Alike license (The Andy Warhol Museum, n.d.a).

9. Joining The Portrait Society also connotes other benefits, such as: (1) becoming a member of the Carnegie Museums of Pittsburg, which entitles people to benefits at all four of their museums, namely The Andy Warhol Museum, Carnegie Museum of Art, Carnegie Museum of Natural History, and Carnegie Science Center; (2) unlimited general admission for one year to all four museums, as well as exclusive invitations to exhibition previews, monthly tours, and other special programming; (3) discounts on purchases in all museum stores.

10. Pascali belonged to the second wave of Pop Art from 1966.

11. For more on the relationship between marketing and art and craft, refer to Fariello and Owen (2005). For objects and meaning, see Lieberman and Lieberman (1983); Carosso and Ghezzi (2015); Napolitano and Marino (2016).

REFERENCES

Alario, L. R., Mirizzi, F. (1986). *Regione e cultura popolare: atti del Convegno "Funzioni e finalità dei centri di raccolta e di documentazione della cultura popo-*

lare" (Conference Proceedings, Cassano all'Ionio, CS, IT, January 19–21, 1984). Galatina, Congedo.

Archi, C. F., Umoh, J. J. (2019). Developing art and craft as marketing commodities for contemporary Nigerian economy. *Icheke Journal of the Faculty of Humanities*, 17 (4), 235–41.

Atkinson, T. (1965). *Pop Art and the American tradition* (exhibition catalogue— Milwaukee, Milwaukee Art Center, April 9–May 9, 1965). Milwaukee, Milwaukee Art Center.

Bandini, M., Serra, R. (1985). *Il Museo Sperimentale di Torino. Arte italiana degli anni Sessanta nelle collezioni della Galleria Civica d'Arte Moderna* (exhibition catalogue—Turin, Castello di Rivoli, December 20, 1985–February 10, 1986). Milano: Fabbri editori.

Barbero, L. M. (2017). *Franco Angeli: gli anni '60* (exhibition catalogue—London, Ronchini Gallery, October 4–November 18, 2017). Venezia, Marsilio.

Battisti, E. (1964). Intervista a Baj, *Marcatrè. Notiziario di cultura contemporanea* 2 (5), 212.

Bertarelli, A. (1938). L'iconografia popolare italiana. Sue caratteristiche: come deve essere studiata. *Lares*, 9 (1), 28–32.

Bonito Oliva, A. (1995). *Mario Schifano*. Bologna, Collina.

Bonito Oliva, A. (2008). *Schifano: 1934–1998* (exhibition catalogue—Roma, GNAM, June 11– September 28, 2008). Roma, GNAM.

Bonito Oliva, A. et al. (2017). *Words and Drawings. Frank O'Hara-Mario Schifano*. Roma: Archivio Mario Schifano.

Bossaglia, R., Zatti, S. (1983). *Il Pop Art e l'Italia* (exhibition catalogue—Pavia, Castello Visconteo, June 1–September 30, 1983). Milano, Mazzotta.

Brezzo, I. (1938). I Lavori Femminili Nell'arte Rustica. *Lares*, 9 (1), 53–6.

Byrd, C., Richmond, S. (2006). *Potentially Harmful: The Art of American Censorship*. Georgia State University, Ernest G. Welch School of Art & Design.

Cameron, D., Scholder, A. (1999). *Fever: The Art of David Wojnarowicz* (exhibition catalogue—New York, New Museum of Contemporary Art, January 21–April 11, 1999). New York, Rizzoli.

Carosso, M., Ghezzi, S. (2015). Introduzione. Artigiani fra bottega e artigianato. *Antropologia*, 11 (2), 7–17.

Celant, G. (2009). *Baj: mobili animati* (exhibition catalogue—Milano, Fondazione Marconi, May 26–July 24, 2009). Milan, Skira, Fondazione Marconi.

Centroni, A. (2011). *Villa D'Este a Tivoli. Quattro secoli di storia e restauri*. Roma, Gangemi Editore.

Cicalini, G. (2016). Palma Bucarelli e la Biennale di Venezia (1948–68): acquisizioni, prestiti e interventi critici della direttrice della Galleria Nazionale d'Arte Moderna di Roma (Master's thesis). Venezia, Università Ca'Foscari.

Cisventi, C. (1965). Baj ritorno. *Leader*, 5, 68–71.

Cohen-Solal, A. (2010). *Leo&C. Storia di LeoCastelli*. Truccazzano: Johan & Levi editore.

Cusatelli, G. (1971). *Dizionario Garzanti della lingua italiana*. Milan: Garzanti editore.

Danilowicz, C. D. (1941). Le scuola d'arte applicata e l'arte rustica. *Lares*, 12 (6), 72–5.

De Marchis, G. (1963). *Festa* (Brochure of the exhibit, Rome, Galleria La Tartaruga, May 1963). Rome, Galleria La Tartaruga.

De Marchis, G. (1967). *Festa* (Brochure of the exhibit, Rome, Galleria La Salita, April 1967). Rome, Galleria La Salita.

De Martiis, P. (1951–53). *Roma 11 Aprile: arrivo e disimballaggio delle opere di Pablo Picasso per la mostra che si terrà alla Galleria nazionale d'arte moderna*. Roma, Fotografia associati.

De Martiis, P. (1952). *Cassino 1952: un salone di fortuna*. Roma, Fotografi associati.

De Martiis, P. (1999). *L'arte Pop in Italia: pittura, design e grafica negli anni Sessanta* (exhibition catalogue—Parma, Galleria d'arte Niccoli, December 18, 1999–March 6, 2000). Verona, Grafiche Aurora.

Devoto, G., Oli, G. C. (1967). *Vocabolario illustrato della lingua italiana*. Milan: Casa editrice Felice.

Fagiolo dell'Arco, M. (1966). Angeli, peintre-moraliste. *Marcatrè. Notiziario di cultura contemporanea*, 4 (26–9), 336–7.

Fariello, A. M., Owen, P. (2005). *New Perspectives on Art and Craft*. Lanham, MD: Scarecrow Press.

Francesconi, E. (2018). *Franco Angeli e Tano Festa. Pittori con la macchina da presa*. Milano: postmedia books.

Galdaston, G. (2001). Ileana Sonnabend e Mario Schifano: un epistolario (1962–1963). *Storia dell'arte*, 140 (41), 148–77.

Gallo, F. (1990). *Angeli, Festa, Schifano: destini incrociati* (exhibition catalogue—Paternò, GAM, December 8, 1990–January 31, 1991). Paternò, GAM.

Gandini, M., Bonito Oliva, A. (2008). *Ileana Sonnabend: the queen of art*. Roma: Castelvecchi.

Goodnough, A. (1999). *Giuliani threatens to evict museum over art exhibit*. https://partners.nytimes.com/library/arts/092499brooklyn-museum.html.

Guadagnini, W. (2005). *Pop Art Italia 1958–1968* (exhibition catalogue—Modena, Galleria Civica, Palazzo dei Giardini, Palazzina dei Giradini, April 17–July 3, 2005). Cinisello Balsamo, Silvana editore.

Guadagnini, W. (2018). *Camera Pop: la fotografia nella pop art di Andy Warhol, Schifano & Co.* (exhibition catalogue—Turin, Camera Torino, September 21, 2018–January 13, 2019). Cinisello Balsamo, Silvana.

Guastalla, M., Guastalla, L. (2013). *Area Pop: Franco Angeli, Enrico Baj, Tano Festa, Piero Gilardi, Mark Kostabi, Ugo Nespolo, Mario Schifano, Emilio Tadini, Joe Tilson.* (exhibition catalogue—Livorno, Guastalla Centro Arte, November 30, 2013–January 31, 2014). Livorno, Graphis Arte.

Guastalla, M., Guastalla, L. (2016). *Pop in Italia: Franco Angeli, Enrico Baj, Paolo Baratella, Tano Festa, Piero Gilardi, Concetto Pozzati, Mimmo Rotella, Mario Schifano, Emilio Tadini* (exhibition catalogue—Livorno, Guastalla Centro Arte, November 26, 2016–January 26, 2017). Livorno, Graphis Arte.

Guzmàn, F., Paswan, A. K. (2009). Cultural brands from emerging markets: brand image across host and home countries. *Journal of International Marketing*, 17 (3), 71–86.

Horsley, C. B. (n.d.). *Censorship. The Brooklyn Museum Affair. Pornography, Violence & Art*. http://www.thecityreview.com/censor.html.

Hunter, S., Castelli, L., Sonnabend, I., Sonnabend, M. (1991). *A view from the sixties: selections from the Leo Castelli collection and the Michael and Ileana Sonnabend collection* (exhibition catalogue—East Hampton, Guild Hall Museum, August 10–September 22, 1991). East Hampton, Guild Hall Museum.

Janis, S. (1962). *The New Realists* (exhibition catalogue—New York, Sidney Janis Gallery, November 1–December 1, 1962). New York, Sidney Janis Gallery.

Kozloff, M. (1962). Pop culture, metaphysical disgust and the new vulgarians, *Art International*, 6 (2), 34–6.

Lieberman, L., Lieberman, L. (1983). Second careers in art and craft fairs. *The Gerontologist*, 23 (3), 266–72.

Lublin, M. (1993). American galleries in the twentieth century: from Stieglitz to Castelli. In Vv.Aa (eds.), *American Art in the Twentieth Century: Painting and Sculpture 1913–1933* (pp. 159–60). New York: Te Neues Pub. Co.

Mallé, L. (1970). *I Musei Civici di Torino. Acquisti e doni 1966–1970*. Torino: GAM.

Marconi, G. (2005). *Schifano 1960–1964: dal monocromo alla strada* (exhibition catalogue—Milano, Fondazione Giorgio Marconi, February 9–March 26, 2005). Milano, Skira.

Marconi, G. (2006). *Schifano 1964–1970. Dal paesaggio alla TV* (exhibition catalogue—Milano, Fondazione Giorgio Marconi, February 23–March 30, 2006). Milano, Skira.

Margozzi, M. (2009). *Palma Bucarelli. Il museo come avanguardia* (exhibition catalogue—Roma, GNAM, June 26–November 1, 2009). Milano, Electa.

Massari, S. (2007). *Museo Nazionale delle Arti e delle Tradizioni Popolari*. Roma: Museo Nazionale delle Arti e delle Tradizioni Popolari.

Mazzella, E. (2018). *Palma Bucarelli: cronaca di un incontro*. Napoli: Litografia Vigilante.

McCracken, G. (1986). Culture and consumption: a theoretical account of the structure and movement of the cultural meaning of consumer goods. *Journal of Consumer Research*, 13 (1), 71–84.

Mecacci, A. (2011). *L'estetica del Pop*. Roma: Donzelli.

Migliorini, B. (1963). *Vocabolario della lingua italiana*. Firenze: G.B. Paravia & Co.

Napolitano, M. R., Marino V. (2016). *Cultural Heritage e Made in Italy. Casi ed esperienze di marketing internazionale*. Napoli: Editoriale Scientifica.

Palmer, R. R. (2014). *The Age of the Democratic Revolution: A Political History of Europe and America, 1760–1800*. Princeton, NJ: Princeton University Press.

Paz, O. (2008). *Baj. Dame e generali 1960–1975* (exhibition catalogue—Milan, Fondazione Marconi, January 30–March 15, 2008). Milano, Skira.

Pellegrini, E. (2017). *Voglia d'Italia. Il collezionismo internazionale nella Roma del Vittoriano*. (exhibition catalogue – Rome, Palazzo Venezia e Gallerie Sacconi al Vittoriano) Napoli: Arte'm.

Restany, P. (1959). *Arman* (exhibition catalogue—Milan, Galleria Apollinaire, December 1959). Milan, Galleria Apollinaire.

Restany, P. (1973). *Nuovo realismo*. Milano: Prearo.

Salvi, S. et al. (1987). *Pop Art America Europa: dalla collezione Ludwig* (exhibition catalogue—Firenze, Forte di Belvedere, July 4–October 4, 1987). Milan, Electa.

Sanguineti, E. (1957). *Enrico Baj: dipinti e ceramiche* (brochure of the exhibit, Turin, Galleria Il Prisma, October 10–23, 1957). Turin, Galleria Il Prisma.

Sanna, A. (2018) *Enrico Baj. Automitobiografia*. Milano: Johan&Levi.

Sauvage, T. (1952). *Baj et Dangelo Peintures Nucléaires* (exhibition catalogue—Bruxelles, Galerie Apollo, March 4–17, 1952). Bruxelles, Galerie Apollo.

Schroeder, J. E. (1997). Andy Warhol: consumer research. *Advances Consumers Research*, 24, 476–82.

Schroeder, J. E. (2005). The artist and the brand. *European Journal of Marketing*, 39, (11–12), 1291–305.

Sperone, G. E. et al. (1965). *Pop: Dine, Lichtenstein, Oldenburg, Pistoletto, Rauschenberg, Rosenquist, Warhol, Wesselmann* (exhibition catalogue—Turin, Gian Enzo Sperone Arte Moderna, June–July 1965). Turin, Galleria Gian Enzo Sperone.

Sundell, M. (2002). *From Pop to now: selections from the Sonnabend Collection* (exhibition catalogue—Saratoga Springs, Wachenheim Gallery, Malloy Gallery, State Farm Mezzanine Gallery, Winter Gallery, June 22–September 29, 2002). Saratoga Springs, The Frances Young Tang Teaching Museum.

Swenson, G. R. (1962). The new American 'sign painters'. *Arts News*, 61 (5), 45–7.

Swenson, G. R. (1964a). What is Pop Art? (Interviews). *Arts News*, 62 (7), 24–7, 60–64.

Swenson, G. R. (1964b). What is Pop Art? (Interviews). Part II. *Arts News*, 6 (10), 40–44, 62–7.

The Andy Warhol Foundation for the Visual Arts (n.d.a). *Foundation Past and Present. Creative Impact.* http://warholfoundation.org/foundation/index.html.

The Andy Warhol Foundation for the Visual Arts (n.d.b). *The Andy Warhol Foundation for the Visual Arts 20 years report 1987–2007.* http://warholfoundation.org/pdf/volume1.pdf.

The Andy Warhol Museum (n.d.a). https://github.com/thewarholmuseum/digitalstrategy/blob/master/01_Introduction.md.

The Andy Warhol Museum (n.d.b). The Warhol: give. https://secure2.convio.net/cmp/site/Donation2?16520.donation=form1&df_id=16520.

Toschi, Paolo (1960). *Arte popolare italiana.* Roma: Carlo Bestetti-Edizioni d'arte.

Vivaldi, C. (1961). *Festa* (brochure of the exhibit, Galleria La Salita, May 1961). Rome, Galleria La Salita.

Warhol, A. (1975). *The Philosophy of Andy Warhol (From A to B and Back Again).* New York: Harcourt Brace Jovanovich.

Zingarelli, N. (1941). *Vocabolario della lingua italiana.* Bologna: Nicola Zanichelli Editore.

Afterword by Maurizio Dallocchio

I teach Corporate Finance, Mergers and Acquisitions and also Corporate Restructuring. Why should I be interested in a publication focused on artisanal and craft products and markets? And why did the authors invite me to write an Afterword?

Let me first of all say that I am sincerely excited about this task, in particular after reading all the parts and chapters of the book and understanding its potential at the cultural, social and economic level. My interest for this world goes back in time and is deeply rooted in the research I carried out to demonstrate the importance of craftsmanship, qualified artisans and masters of arts for economic growth, workforce development and capability of attraction of touristic flows. This brought me to accept roles in the governance of institutions like "Altagamma" or "Fondazione Cologni per i Mestieri dell'Arte"; both Italian foundations with a strong international vocation, whose objectives are the development and growing consideration of high-end products and craft productions mastered by Masters of Arts.

I am profoundly convinced that several European countries (geographically speaking) must design their industrial strategy, relying on two main pillars: (a) artisanal and high-end SMEs and (b) large corporations that operate in sectors where quality and performance (and not quantity or price competition) are key factors.

It is pretty clear that nations with a history of culture, respect, artistic and aesthetic values, and strong regulation at all levels, will find it difficult to compete in a court where mass production and standardization are imperatives; where cost-cutting is vital to compete and massification is the password to success. In a context with limited access to natural resources and with an unfriendly demography, key success factors and preconditions for long-term sustainability are quality, innovation, personalization.

These key success factors are typical features of artisanal and craft products and markets. And another feature I would definitely add to this world is flexibility. The Covid-19 pandemic showed the entire world that craft or artisanal products are extraordinarily resilient to crises, because of the fast response entrepreneurs offer to dramatically negative changes and because of their incredible capability to modify their business model, once threatened by an external aggression. While mass productions, indistinct goods and standardized models are typically rigid and difficult to remodel (also due to the high cost of reshaping a Ford-T-like product) craft products are an example of elasticity and openness to change, even in a dangerously worsening environment. The reader can easily find here examples of artisanal producers that grow and generate value in sectors where larger operators suffer from a strong malaise.

This is one of the outcomes of different chapters of this book, where a solid empirical approach is matched with a rigorous academic DNA. What I also understood while reading this book is that it has an uncommon potential for disseminating the "artisanal brand", attracting the interest of largely different readers: young generations hopefully in pole position. They can in fact find food for their thoughts (and future jobs ...), fed by authenticity, beauty, creativity, artistic contents. All values that young people respect, research and admire.

While browsing the pages of this book, I also discovered something unexpected; something that can disruptively impact on widely shared preconceptions. Let me mention the case of innovation. The latter is normally considered the typical output of large corporations that invest robust resources in R&D. On the other side, artisans are normally considered as custodian of heritage, as defendants of traditions. In this book I discovered (or found confirmation ...) that they can also be disruptive innovators, leveraging – it is just an example – on digital manufacturing. 3D printing technologies are a potential revolution ready to be introduced in the business models of craft-based companies. And digital transformation is another opportunity ready to integrate traditional operating methods.

If you are reading these notes, I probably do not need to convince you about the qualities of this publication. Having said that, its focus on sustainable consumption and reduction of waste, customer engagement as a push to educate towards a "slow production and use" and its powerful push towards a better world, will surely make you happier.

Maurizio Dallocchio
Bocconi University Professor of Corporate Finance
SDA Bocconi Professor of Corporate Finance
Past Dean of SDA Bocconi School of Management

Afterword by Franco Cologni

To explore the universe of artistic crafts is a process that should always encompass a double level of commitment. First of all, it is fundamental to shine the spotlight on the great master craftspeople who dedicate their lives and talent to the creation of lasting beauty. And then, it is pivotal to work in order to help young artisans identify the values they should pursue to achieve a level of craftsmanship worthy of a "living treasure", as the greatest holders of an intangible culture are named in Japan.

For this reason, the Cologni Foundation has created a matrix to evaluate artisanal excellence, based on the analysis of 11 values that always distinguish the real masters: savoir-faire, creativity, talent, interpretation, education, territoriality, originality, authenticity, competence, innovation and tradition. The goal of this approach, obtained after two years of research and now available as an assessment tool on the website of the Michelangelo Foundation for Creativity and Craftsmanship, was not simply to define an impersonal matrix, the product of abstract calculations, which might be appropriate for the cold realm of finance but for the passionate universe of crafts.

We aimed to be inclusive, directing a loving and admiring gaze on artisanal excellence. In the process, which in our opinion every researcher should keep in mind, we identified and analysed those criteria that we believe come closest to tracing an ideal path that transcends national boundaries – a universal matrix that highlights and celebrates the rich diversity of the artistic crafts in all the countries where workshops, ateliers and small enterprises flourish, and where the "intelligent" hand of the master craftsperson gives substance to the creative vision of the designer.

Words are the building blocks by which we give substance to our thoughts: this is why we feel that, at the heart of every process of analysis and assessment, it is important to create a language that could be shared with confidence and ease by all those who strive to safeguard and promote fine craftsmanship.

A brave undertaking, no doubt, for any researcher: and not without its pitfalls. It is nonetheless a necessary undertaking if we have to advance the networking activities of a young generation of scholars and researchers, which will help develop (as it is already doing) a fruitful and constructive awareness. The master artisans represent not only a particular territory, but also an approach: this is why every analysis must always start from their own words, ideas, perspectives. Their point of view, therefore, is in itself paradigmatic of a perspective that is not confined by national boundaries and speaks to all those who appreciate and seek hand-made perfection.

The testimony of the artisans, who devote their skill wholeheartedly to the creation of beautiful and well-made objects, will always provide any skilled researcher an invaluable affirmation of the real assessment criteria to define and promote excellence, which have to be applicable even in contexts that are geographically distant but culturally close. Once again, by the union of similarities and differences, we can generate an important vision: a specialized, evocative and authentic common language by which to discover and observe Europe's intangible cultural property, a heritage that gives us a fundamental competitive advantage and nourishes our identity and value every day.

Fully aware of the long path that lies ahead of us, we would like to recommend to every young and promising researcher to draw particular attention to the real and direct relationship with the master artisans: their intellectual integrity, typical of those who recognize the beauty, worth and truthfulness of genuine craftsmanship, provides us with an important insight into the future of the artistic crafts, namely that it is beauty itself that feeds the joy of making, of being, of living. In a world pervaded by tautology it is the joy we feel when a simple object speaks directly to our hearts that can make the difference. Today, more than ever.

Franco Cologni
Founder and President of Cologni Foundation for the Métiers d'Art

Index

3DiTALY 103, 107, 109, 110, 111, 112, 114
3D
    printer 110, 112
    printing 67, 72, 73, 103, 105, 106, 107, 109, 110, 113, 114, 140

Abate Zanetti Glass School 85
Abdulhameed, Osama 105
Adamson 14, 15, 18, 24
Adamson, Glen 14, 15, 18, 24, 66, 67, 69, 70, 71, 137, 138
additive manufacturing 105
add value 17
Adriano Berengo 82, 88, 89, 95
advertising 210, 214, 215
aesthetic regimes 197
aesthetics 57, 200
affective labour 8, 133
Afuah, Allan 96
Agrawal, Jagdish 159
Ahmed, Zafar 161
Ai, Weiwei 88, 93
Akkaya, Bulent 137, 138, 139
à la façon de Venise, 88
Alario, Leonardo 209, 221
Alkassim, Rukayya, S 194
Amazon 33
American Pop Art 210, 211, 213
American Studio Glass Movement 89, 91
analytics and supplier support 147
Andéhn, Mikael 162
Anderson, David, M 165
Anderson, Glen 140
Andy Warhol Foundation, The 216, 217, 225
animal butchers 181, 184
Antica Dolceria Bonajuto 112
anti
    -capitalism 177
    -consumerism 178, 190
    -consumption 10, 177, 178, 183, 189
    -corporate branding 177
    -globalization 177
    -materialism 178
Antoldi, Fabio 14, 24, 138
apprenticeships 36
Arendt, Hannah 14, 18, 24
Argy-Rousseau 83
Arnould, Eric 3
art 2, 16, 69
    fairs 219
    galleries 211
Art Aurea 88
Art Deco 83
artefacts-as-means 69
Artemest 137
Artemest, 145
arte
    paesana 209
    popolare 209, 210, 211, 212, 213, 214, 225
artisan 1, 15, 17, 18
    brand 1, 2
    community 165
    economy 2, 17
    entrepreneurs 158, 165, 168, 171
    maker 82, 99
    market system 214, 219
    products 15
    thinker 82, 99
    worlds 123
artisanal 3, 14, 15, 16, 17, 18, 20, 21, 23, 24
    brands 170
    economies 42
    entrepreneurs 171
    entrepreneurship community 171
    glass 65
    goods 42
    knowledge 57

labour 53
markets 43, 48, 53, 57
practice 66, 67
production 49, 193, 220
products 64, 193, 210
tradition 140
artisans 15, 17, 21, 24, 195
artisanship 14, 15, 16, 17, 18, 20, 21, 23, 24, 42, 140, 157
artist 209, 212, 213, 214, 215, 217, 218, 219, 224
as brand 215
artistic glass 81, 82, 84, 85
artists 210, 211, 212, 213, 214, 215, 216, 217, 218, 219, 220, 221
arts 4, 21, 23, 24
Arts and Crafts Movement 83
artwork 210, 213, 219
artworks 210, 214, 215, 217, 218, 219, 221
Arvidsson, Adam 193
Asian Art News 88
Atkinson, Tracy 210, 222
atmosphere 194, 199, 203
Atti, Giovani 139
attitude-behaviour gap 162
aura 1
authenticity 1, 2, 3, 4, 5, 16, 18, 21, 23, 24, 31, 32, 37, 38, 42, 48, 50, 66, 67, 71, 75, 76, 77, 78, 122, 125, 130, 131, 133, 136, 139, 140, 177, 178, 194, 199, 200, 201, 202, 203, 204
'authentic' places 203

B2B (business-to-business) 136, 142, 144
B2C (business-to-consumer) 136, 150
Bain Altagamma Luxury Study 150, 151
Baines, Sue 123, 128
Bakhshi, Hasan 37
Bakos, Yannis 199
Balabanis, George 161
Balocco, Raffaello 104
Bandini, Mirella 218, 222
Banga, Sunil 198
Bank of Italy 102
Banks, Mark 15, 24, 32
Barbero, Luca, M 214, 222
Barney, Jay 86

Baron, Robert, A 104
Barovier & Toso 81, 89
Barros, Ana B 25
Batra, Rajeev 157, 160
Battilana, Julie 170
Battisti, Eugenio 213, 218, 222
Bauhaus 83
Baumann, Shyon 177, 193
Beaman, Jean 180
Bean, Jonathan 14, 24
beauty 4, 21, 23, 24
Becker, Frawley 2
Becker, Howard 14, 16, 24, 123, 128, 129, 132, 134
Beckert, Jens 43, 44, 45, 46, 47, 51, 52, 53, 56
Beckman, Christine 105
behavior 21
Belk, Russell, W 160
Bell, Emma 193
Benjamin, Walter 1, 2, 202
Benson-Rea, Maureen 157, 162, 163, 170
Berengo Studio 82, 83, 87, 88, 89, 91, 92, 93, 95, 96, 99
Berman, Saul, J 104
bespoke 150
prototyping 73
Beverland, Michael, B 200, 202
Bhaskaran, Suku 162
Bhattarai, Abha 198
Biennale museums 84
Bike Shed 51
Bille, Mikkel 203
Binkley, Sam 177
Bjerregaard, Peter 203
Bloemer, Josee 159
Bloom, Marta 37
Blown Away 34
Blundel, Richard 158
Boersma, Kees 103
Boltanski
Eve 199
Luc 198, 199
Bonfanti, Angelo 102, 104, 139, 141
Bonito Oliva, Achille 218, 222, 223
book repairers 181
Borer, Michael A 180
Boss 54
Bossaglia, Rossana 214, 222

Bourdieu, Pierre 52, 180
boutique 54, 55
  guitar pedals 43, 54, 57, 58
brand 32, 34, 87, 158, 215, 216, 217,
    218, 224
  association 31
  communities 3
  community 2
  identity 160, 161
  image 170
  origin 159, 160
  value 170
branding 3, 27, 130, 162, 203, 204
  strategies 200
branded world 216
brands 162, 215, 216
Branzi, Andrea 138
Braque 83
Brat Style 50
Braverman, Harry 197
Brem, Alexander 105
Brexit 29, 38
Brezzo, Irma 209, 222
brick-and-mortar stores 200, 204, 205
British Empire 157
Britton, Alison 66, 67, 70
Brodie, Roderick, J 157, 162, 163, 170
Bromley, Rosemary, D F 198
Brown
    Julie 157, 158
    Stephen 1
Bull, Glen 114
Burrows, Matthew 34
Burt, Steve 199
business 210, 216, 217, 219
    model 55, 104, 150
        innovation 104
    models 102, 103, 104, 142, 144,
        145
butchery 182, 187, 189
buyer profiles 35
Byrd, Cathy 220, 222

CAD (Computer Aided Design) 72, 105
150
    modeling 109
Camerani, Roberto 37
Cameron
    Dan 217, 222
    Douglas 203

Campbell, Colin 32
Cannarella, Camelo 82
Cannatelli, Benedetto, L 158
Capelli, Chiara 24
capital
    cultural 48
    intellectual 48
    reputational 48
    social 48
Carosso, Marinella 221, 222
Casadei, Partizia 37
Castelli, Leo 214, 215, 223, 224
Cauldwell-French, Evy 30
Cavalli, Alberto 15, 24, 138
Cavallo, Angelo 104
Celant, Germano 213, 222
Centroni, Alessandra 209, 222
ceramic artists, 66
Chagall, Marc 83
Chapman, Jonathan 76
Charmaz, Kathy 164, 165
Chatterjee, Sumsita 15, 24
Chayka, Kyle 178
Chen, Danfang 105
Cherrier, Helene 178
Chesbrough, Henry, W 104
Chiapello, Eve 198, 199
Chiara Squarcina 86
chocolate 3
Choi, Chang, W 160
Choo, Jimmy 74
Cicalini, Giorgia 218, 222
Cisventi, Carlo 213, 222
Clarke, Ian 198
Claval, Paul 23, 24
climate crisis 70
Clinton, Michael 123
Coad, Alex 81
Cobel-Tokarska, Marta 177
cocktail bartending 181, 184
co-creation 3
    of value 151, 152
    practices 137
COD (country of design) 160
Cog Effects 43, 55
cognitive embeddedness 45
Cohen, David 214, 222
Cohen-Solal, Annie 214, 222
Colgate, Mark 48
collaboration 143, 145

Collier, Anne F 134
Colombo, Paulo 81, 84
colonialism 165
COM (country of manufacturing) 160
Communities of Craft 128
community 37, 56, 129, 157, 158, 165,
    168
    of likeminded people 2
competition 142
    advantage 141
conceptual framework 17
conditions of uncertainty 46
Conejo, Francesco 162
Confartigianato 81, 84, 85, 86, 90
    Vicenza and Veneto 144, 160
confidence 53
connoisseur consumer 55, 58
connoisseurship 58, 141
Consorzio Promovetro Murano 84
consumer 15, 18, 210
    behavior 23, 24, 159
    capitalism 178, 190
    choice 185
    confidence 48
    culture 67, 70
    demand 75
    education 67, 189
    experience 23
    loyalty 144
    markets 198
    perceptions 17, 18
    taste 198, 199, 203
    understandings 68
consumers v, 4, 14, 15, 16, 17, 18, 20,
    21, 23, 24, 25, 215, 216
consumption 10, 16, 21, 69, 177
    ethical 70
    habits 144
    patterns 140, 142
    trends 193
contemporary design 26
Content and Digital production 147
COO (country-of-origin) 159, 160, 161,
    162, 170, 171
    brand 163
    branding 170
    effect 157, 158, 162, 163, 165, 167,
        170
Cooksey, Ray, W 157
cooperation 123

cooperative working 123
co-opetition 142
coordination problems 46
co-production 111
Corbinc, Juliet 108
Corbusier 83
Corning Museum of Glass, The 94
Costa, Janeen A 44, 45, 46, 51, 56
Costantini, Egidio 83, 89
Costin, Cathy, L 14, 24
cost of energy 85
country brand identity 159
Cova
    Bernard 3
    Veronique 3
Covid-19 5, 28, 29, 32, 34, 38, 120, 122,
    123, 128, 133, 134, 137, 139,
    144, 151
craft 14, 15, 16, 17, 20, 21, 22, 23, 24,
    25, 209, 210, 211, 214, 215, 219,
    221
    beer 180, 202, 203
    brewers 178, 180, 197
    businesses 5, 38, 124
    cocktails 184
    consumption 32, 35, 178, 193
    definition 28
    design 74
    distillers 181, 183
    economy 16, 124, 140, 195, 197
    enterprise 122
    fairs 34
    firms 3, 99
    galleries 34
    intermediaries 34
    marketing 4
    objects 76
    production 3, 15, 139, 195, 199
    products 15, 20, 21, 86, 136, 138,
        203
    retailing 194
    sector 28, 32, 114, 115, 143
    skills 30, 141
    tradition 210
    washing 1
    work 177, 188
Crafts Council, The 35
craftsmanship 3, 55, 121, 136, 137, 144,
    146, 164, 169, 180, 209, 210, 211
crafts 15, 16, 18, 24, 209, 210, 213, 214,

219
Crafts Council, The 36, 42, 43, 139, 140
craftsmen 15, 16, 18, 23, 24, 77
craftsperson 65
Crang, Mike 4, 23, 24
Crawford, Matthew 121, 125, 128, 177,
    178
creative
    clusters 37
    economy 26
    education 37
    enterprise 121, 124, 125
    freelancers 30
    industries 32, 37, 122
    production 48
    sector 83
Creative Industries Federation 28
Creative Industries Policy and Evidence
    Centre 36
creativity 4, 8, 21, 23, 24, 66, 103, 110,
    113, 114, 121, 124, 127, 128,
    130, 132, 133, 134
Credendino, Marco 146, 151
Credit collection 148
Cressy, Robert 87
Crossick, Geoffrey 195, 196
Cui, Connie 104
cultural 23
    arbiters 58
    capital 56
    economy 23
    embeddedness 45
    field 43, 44, 47, 50, 51, 53, 55, 57,
        59
    goals 87
    heritage 99
    industry 82
    intermediaries 51, 54
    knowledge 187
    marketing 209, 215, 218, 219
    omnivorousness 177, 193
    tradition 84
culture 4, 23
curation: 146
Cusatelli, Giorgio 212, 222
customer
    care 148
    -oriented perspective 142
    satisfaction 142
    taste 204

customization 15, 110, 136
customized products 141
Cuthbertson, Richard 199

Dahler-Larsen, Peter 47, 50, 52, 56
Dallocchio, Maurizio 15, 24, 136, 137,
        138, 139, 140
DAMA (Digital Arts & Manufacturing
        Academy) 113
D'Andrea, Guillermo 198
Danilowicz, Casimir 222
Daum, Honoré 83
Dauter
    Luke 45
    Paul 51
Davidson, Elizabeth 102
Dawkins, Nicole 8, 120, 121, 123, 125,
        130, 133, 134
DDM (direct digital manufacturing) 105
Dellaert, Benedict, G. C 106, 111, 113
De Marchis, Giorgio 214, 222
De Martiis, Plinio 220, 223
democratization of the production 114
Department for Digital, Culture, Media
        and Sport 35
Dequech, David 45, 52
descriptive statistics 18
design 63, 69, 74
    capability 36
Designer Lounge' 148
Design Miami 91
de-skilling 197
developing economies 157
Devoto, Giacomo 212, 223
Dewettinck, Koen 25
Dezecot, Jonathan 1, 2, 144
Dichter, Ernest 159
Dickie, Virginia A 17, 25
Dickson, Peter, R 200
digital 221
    activities 221
    artisan 110
    design 67, 106
    distribution 105
    ecosystems 105
    entrepreneurs 105
    entrepreneurship 104
    fabrication 67, 106, 107, 113, 114,
        140
    innovation 73

digital makers 16
digital manufacture 65
digital manufacturing 71, 72, 102,
    103, 107, 114
    manufacturing 109
    marketing 105
        strategies 144
    platform 148
    platforms 104, 136, 141, 143, 194
    revolution 139
    sales 105, 140
        platforms 26
    selling 33
    strategies 221
    technologies 65, 67, 76, 102, 103,
        110, 113, 152
    technology 137
    transformation 102, 103, 104, 109,
        139, 140
    trends 199
Digital Age 140
Digital Arts & Manufacturing
    Academy 112
digitalization 3, 145
    of production 141
    of retail 198
Digital Platform Ecosystems 141
DiMaggio, Paul 44
Dinnie, Keith 159
Disembedding 56
distinction 52
distinctiveness 194, 200, 202
diversification 196, 202
DIY 53, 54, 58
    philosophy 110, 114
Douglas, Evan, J 159
Dubois, Anna 107
Dutta, Soumitra 87

Earle, Timothy 63, 75
Easton, Eliza 30
e-commerce 5, 136, 143, 144, 148, 194,
    199
    vendors 151
economic
    actors 43
    growth 15
    sustainability 16
eco-systemic approach' 151
education

audience 75
    consumer 70
effects pedals 55
Ekinsmyth, Carol 120, 121
Electro-Harmonix 54, 55
Elliott, Richard 54
Elwyn, Glyn 111
email marketing 148
embeddedness 43, 44, 45, 46, 51, 53, 55,
    56, 57, 58, 158
Embodied practice 124
emotion 124
emotional durability 73, 76
empirical study 17
endogenous preferences 47
Enlightenment 137
enterprise 127
entertainment television 34
entrepreneurialism 8, 37, 121, 133
entrepreneurial
    mindset 37
    skills 87
entrepreneurship 34, 102, 104, 122
environmental impact 65, 70
environmentalism 74
environmentally conscious 69
Erdogan, Irmak 136, 144
Espalin, David 106
ethical consumerism 33
Etikan, Ilker 194
Etsy 33, 120, 193
European Parliament 93
Evrad, Philippe 87
excellence 16, 146
exhibitions 216, 217, 219
experience economy 30

Fab Labs 140
face-to-face retailing 193
Fagiolo dell'Arco, Maurizio 214, 223
family units 15
Fariello, Anna 221, 223
Farrelly, Francis, J 200, 202
fashion 165
Ferreira, Joao, J M 105, 159
fetishization of commodities 49
fetishized consumption 190
fields 47
Fillis, Ian 86, 121, 122, 124, 126, 128,
    129, 130, 131, 132, 133

financial crisis 102
Findlay, Ian 88
Fine, Gary A 31, 181
Fingar, Courtney 157
Fleck-Dousteyssier, Nathalie 1, 2
Fleck, Nathalie 144
flexibility in work 127
Fligstein, Neil 45, 51
floating signifier 3
Flohr, Miko 1
Florianus, Domenico 82
folkloristic 210, 211
Folksy 33, 120
Fondazione Berengo 95, 98
    Art Space 95
Fondazione Cologni dei Mestieri
    d'Arte 140
Fondazione Musei Civici di Venezia 86
Fontana 83
food truck 203
    operators 194, 200
Fordism 137, 193, 194, 196, 198, 200,
    204, 205
Fordist retailing 198
foreign brands 160
Foss, Nicolai, J 102, 104
foundations 209, 214, 219
Francesconi, Elisa 214, 223
Frank, Gelya 17, 25
Frayling, Christopher 121
functional value 48

Gadde, Lars-Erik 107
Galdaston, Giorgia 218, 223
Galle, Émile' 83
gallerists 214, 215, 220
Gallo, Francesco 214, 218, 223
Gandini
    Alessandro 204
    Manuela 215, 223
Gandolfo, Enza 120, 124, 126, 130, 133
Garavaglia, Christian 1, 15, 25, 137
Gasparetto 82
Gauntlett, David 121, 125, 128
GB (Great Britain) 165
Gellynck, Xavier 25
Gerosa, Alessandro 197
Gershenfeld, Niel 140
Ghezzi
    Antonio 104

Simone 221, 222
Gibbs, Graham R 195
Gibson
    Chris 178
    Ian 105, 106
gig economy 122
Gilmour, James H 31
Ginter, James, L 200
Gioia, Dennis, A 164
Giones, Ferren 105
Giudici, Alessandro 158
glass 82
    artifacts 82
    blowing 65, 72, 75, 77, 83
    making 63, 65, 70, 77
Glass Masters of Murano 85
Glass Practice 70
Glasstress 87, 92, 94, 95
    Gotika 95
global economy 17
globalization 3
Glynn, Mary A 158
Goodnough, Abby 217, 223
Goods Dominant logic 143
Goodstain, Richard 199
Goolsbee, Austin 198
Go Takamine 49
Goulding, Christina 108
Grace, Marty 120, 124, 126, 130, 133
Granovetter, Mark 44, 51, 55
Grant, Robert, M 86
Gray, Ann 82
Grayson, Kent 200, 202
Great British Sewing Bee, The 34
Great Pottery Throw Down, The 34
green consumerism' 65
Greenhalgh, Paul 64
green
    marketing 68
    movement 74
greenwashing 65, 67
Grewal, Dhruv 199
Groves, Angela, M 17, 18, 25
Groves, James 114
Guadagnini, Walter 214, 218, 223
Guastalla
    L, Laura 223
    M, Marco 223
Guba, Egon, G 164
guitar effects pedals 54

Guggenheim, Peggy 83, 89
Gupta, Sangita, D 24
Guven, Huseyin 136, 138, 144
Guzmàn, Francisco 215, 223

habitus 47
Hackney, Fiona 123
Hair, Neil 104
Halldorsson, Vidar 25, 180
Hamazaoui, Leila 160
Hamilton, Argentina 198
hand-crafted motorcycles 49, 54
handcrafting 75
handicraft goods 197
handicrafts 143
Handleman, Jay M 177
hand-made 16, 219
Hardill, Irene 23, 25
Haupt, Heinz-Gerhard 195, 196
Hein, Andreas 141, 142
Helm, Sabrina 194
Henderson, Willie 178
heritage 31, 36, 64, 66, 67, 74, 76, 79,
        85, 146, 157, 161, 170, 209, 218,
        219
    skills 26
Heritage Craft Association 36
Herzfeld, Michael 14, 25, 137
Heslop, Louise, A 159, 160, 161, 162
Hess, Martin 44
hic et nunc 1
High Net-Worth Individuals 149
high-quality 15
Hilton, Matthew 193, 196, 197
hipster bar owners 194
'hipster bars' 194
Hirsch, Dafna 197
historical 23
historic culture 65
hobbyists 114
Hoffman, Abbie 178
Hollenbeck, Candice R 177-8
Holmström, Jan 102, 105
Holt, Douglas, B 177, 178, 203
home-working 121, 134
homologated objects 111
homologous relationships 52, 56
Horsley, Carter 217, 220, 223
Huang, Peng 105
Hubbard, Phil 177

Huberman, A. Michael 164
Hughes
    Cathy 198
    Karen D 122, 123, 127
    Tom 54
Hull, Clyde, E 104, 105
human capital 140
Humphery, Kim 194
Hunter, Sam 215, 223
Huong Nguyen, Thi Thu 65

iconography 218
ICT (Information and Communications
        Technology) 104, 137, 141, 142,
        144
identity 21, 210
    artisanal 75
    neo artisan 78
Igwe, Paul A 158
impostor syndrome 132
indigenous values 165-7
indirect prototyping 106
individualisation 16, 136, 141
industrial
        classifications 35
        design 219
        production 196
        products 15, 198
industrialisation 70
Industrial Revolution 82
industrious economy 193
industry associations 163
innovation 16, 64, 75, 87, 103, 104, 139,
        140, 141, 142, 144
    theory 142
Innovation Through Crafts:
        Opportunities for Growth 140
Instagram 34
Institut National des Metiers d'Art 140
intermediaries 193, 197
international sales 29
Internet 147
    of Things 140
    technologies 104
intuition 132
investment 37
Italian
        consumers 17, 24
        Pop artists 218
        Printing Store 109

tradition 210, 213
Italy 16, 18, 23, 25, 209, 211, 212, 214,
    219, 220, 221, 224

Jackson, Cath 198
Jakob, Doreen 15, 25, 32, 33, 78, 177
Janis, Sidney 214, 223
Javier Pérez 94
Jerolmack, Colin 179
jewellery 29, 35
Johannsen, Gunnar 102
Johnson, Lester, W 65
Johnston, Josee 177, 193
jua kali 159
Jun, Jong W 160

K1 Flea market 165, 168, 169, 170
Kacker, Madhav, P 198
Kaleidoscope Career Model 121, 122,
    123, 127, 129, 130, 132, 133, 134
Kamakura, Wagner 159
Kapp, Paul H 177
Kenya 157, 158, 163
Kern, Roger M 177, 199
Kerr, John, M 18, 25
Khanh Cao, Tuan 65
Khan, Shamus 177, 179
Kim, Soo H 194
Kingma, Sytze 103
Klein
    Amelia 75
    Naomi 178
know-how 16, 58
Kogelnik, Kiki 92
Kondo, Marie 178
Korn, Peter 43
Kotler, Philip 203
Kozinets, Robert V 177
Kozloff, Max 213
Klynveld Peat Marwick Goerdeler
    (KPMG) 141
Krippner, Greta R 44, 51
Krugh, Michelle 178
Kühne, Bianka 25

Lagoon of Venice 90
Lahne, Jacob 17, 25
Lalique, René 83
Lareau, Annette 180
large-scale retailing 198
Laroche, Michel 159

laser cutting 67, 73
Lavack, Anne Marie 160
Lawson, Cynthia 14, 25
learning by doing 97
Lee, Michael S. W 177
Leissle, Kristy 1, 3, 15, 17, 25, 138
Lemon, Ketherine, N 142
Leslie, Esther 14, 25
L'espoir Decosta, Jean-Noel, P 162
Levine, Edward 16, 25
Le Zotte, Jennifer 50
Lieberman, Leonard 221, 224
Lieberman, L, Leslie 224
lifestyler 131
Li, Liang 103, 109
Lim, Kenny 161
Lincoln, Yvonna, S 164
lineage 64
Littleton
    Karen 120, 121, 123, 126, 130
local
    brands 160, 162
    products 158
localism 69, 183, 210, 211
locality 37
logistics 147
Lopez-Aleman, Belen 198
Lounsbury, Michael 158
Lublin, Mary 214, 224
Luckman, Susan 8, 120, 121, 122, 123,
    124, 125, 126, 128, 129, 130,
    131, 132, 133
Lusch, Robert, F 106, 110, 141, 142, 143
Ludwig, Reinhold 88
luxury 21, 24
    products 146
    status 65
Lyon, Thomas, P 67

Macconi, Ilaria 24
Made-in-Italy 84, 146, 151, 152
    brand 210
Made in Kenya 158, 164, 170, 171
made-to-measure 21, 24
Madichie, Nnamdi, O 158
Maffei, Stefano 142, 144
Maffesoli, Michel 3
Magnusson, Peter 160, 162
Maheswaran, Durairaj 157, 159, 161,
    162

Mainiero, Lisa A 122, 123, 126, 127, 128, 133
maker businesses 35
Makhitha, Khatutshelo 37
Mallé, Luigi 218, 224
Manrai, Lalita, A 161
manual
    labor 15
    skills 15, 16
manufacturing 15, 16
Marconi, Giorgio 218, 222, 224
Margetts, Martina 66, 67, 70
Margozzi, Mariastella 218, 224
Marino, Vittoria 221, 224
market
    as meaning 57
    exchange 46
    for craft 5, 26, 35, 38
    research 131
    segmentation 198, 200
marketing 3, 5, 15, 17, 20, 23, 27, 31, 33, 37, 38, 43, 53, 58, 65, 67, 69, 70, 74, 78, 90, 120, 130, 139, 190, 200, 202, 219
online 78
social media 73
marketing 75
    4.0 136
    channels 219
    organisations 163
    strategies 210
marketisation 32, 50
Market for Craft, The 4, 27
markets 219
    from meaning 47, 53
    of uncertainty 43
Marques, Carla S 15, 25
Marshall, Alfred 158
Martinec, Radan 200, 202
masculinity 182
Mason, Jennifer 126
Massa, Lorenzo 104
Massari, Silvia 209, 224
mass
    consumption 198
    customization 105, 143
    manufacturing 70
    -produced 18
    production 15, 68, 216, 219
    standardisation 198

'master of craft' 197
Masucci, Monica 37
Mateos-Garcia, Juan 37
materialization of digital information' 106
materials 15
Mazzella, Elio 218, 224
McAdam, Rodney 199
McAlexander, James, H 3
McAuley, Andrew 83
McCray, Patrick 84
McGuinnan, Jim 82
McKitterick, L 199
McRobbie, Angela 8, 121, 122, 124, 126, 133
Mecacci, Andrea 214, 224
mechanisation 67
Megicks, Phil 198
merchandise 217
merchandising 34
Merunka, Dwight 160
Metcalf, Bruce 83
Metropolitan Museum of Art in New York 87
MHM (Morris Hargreaves McIntyre) 27, 28. 29, 30, 32, 33, 34, 38
Micelli, Stefano 138, 139
Migliorini, Bruno 212, 224
Miles, Matthew, B 164
Miller, Danny 87
Millesgården Museum in Stockholm 94
Mirizzi, Ferdinando 209, 221
Mischler, Elliot 126, 134
mixology 182, 197, 203
modernisation 67
Mokyr, Joel 196
Molteni, M 158
Montebello, Philippe de 87
Montgomery, A Wren 67
Moradi, Hadi 160
Morris, Michael 96
Mulholland, Jon 45
Muniz, Albert, M 2, 3
Muranese glass masters 83
Murano
    glass 148
    glassmaking , 83, 84, 85
    Island 81, 97
murrine 93
Musa, Sulaiman, A 194

museum 209, 210, 211, 214, 215, 217, 218, 219, 220, 221
Museum Moderner Kunst Kärnten 94
Mussini, Mauro 1, 15, 25, 137
MXR 54

Nairobi 157
Nambisan
    Satish 102, 104, 142, 143
    Stefano 143
Napolitano, Maria, R 221, 224
narration 76
narratives 70, 74, 76, 78
national culture 161
natural cosmetics 165, 168
Naudin, Arnette 193
Ndemo, Bitange 163
neighbourhood 205
neo
    -artisan 63, 65, 68, 69, 71, 74, 75, 77, 78
    -artisanal
        practice 65, 70
        production 78
    -artisans 64, 69, 74
    -classical economics 44, 49
    -craft
        entrepreneur 205
        food retailing 200
        industries 193
        retailer 199, 200, 202, 203
        retailing 194, 197, 199, 200, 202, 203, 204
networking 103, 143
network
    model 142
networks 111, 128, 129, 134, 159, 162
Newbery, R 158
New Economic Sociology 44
new
    economy 63, 68, 69, 70, 74, 75, 78, 79
    technologies 16, 64, 70, 74
    wave custom motorcycles 43
'New Wave Custom' motorcycles 49
Ngoasong, Michael, Z 104
Nguyen, Ninh 65
Nordfalt, Jens 199
nostalgia 50, 64, 65, 67, 75, 76, 78, 79, 198

Nostalgia 75
Nuo Capital 151

objects 209, 210, 211, 212, 213, 214
O'Cass, Aaron 161
Ocejo, Richard 8, 42, 68, 76, 121, 123, 124, 127, 129, 133, 177, 179, 181, 193, 197, 199
O'Guinn, Thomas, C 2, 3
Old Empire Motorcycles 43, 50
Oli, Gian C 223
Olma Luxury Holdings 151
omnichannel
    retailing 199
    strategy 142
online
    commerce 147
    forums 57
    marketing 67, 120, 124, 130, 132
    markets 120
    retailing 199
    shopping 33
    shops 21
    products 182
originality 15
Ostrom, Vincent 138
Ouweneel, Else 109
Owen, Paula 221, 223
Ozcan, Kerimcan 106
Ozerkov, Dimitri 95
Ozretic-Dozen, Durdana 160

paintings 213, 214, 221
Palmer, Robert, R 212, 224
Pan, Shan, L 104
Papadopoulos, Nicolas 159, 160, 161, 162
Pappu, Ravi 157, 159
Parini, Liceo 85
Paswan, Audhesh, K 215, 223
Patel, Karen 193
Paz, O 224
pedal manufacturers 55
perceptions 17
Pereira, Arun 159
Perry, Grayson 64, 78, 79
personal identity 23
personalisation 3, 16, 110, 113, 114, 138, 139, 140, 142
personality 15

Peterson, Richard, A 31, 75, 177, 199, 200
Pharr, Julie, M. 159
Picasso, Pablo 83, 89
Piccioni, Valeria 82
Pine, B Joseph 31
Piotrowicz, Wojciech 199
place 158
    atmosphere 203
Podolny
    Greta R 44
    Joel M 44
Polanyi, Karl 44
Pop Art 209, 210, 211, 212, 213, 214, 215, 219, 220, 221, 222, 223, 224, 225
popular art 210
Porter, Michael E 48, 81
portfolio
    careers 30, 123
    portfolio careers 123
    workers 37
    working 123, 128
post-Fordism 194
pottery 188
Potts, Ruth 74
Power WASP model 112
precarity 29
pre-Fordism 197
premium brand 157
price 160
Price
    Linda, L 3, 170
    Robert 199
problem
    of competition 46, 51, 56
    of cooperation 46
    of valuation 46
process 209, 211, 213, 214, 215
    -implicit knowledge 68
    knowledge 68
producer 17
product
    differentiation 46, 198, 200
    diversification 199
    innovation 104
production 15, 16, 17, 18, 67, 211
    process 213
    systems 152
    lifecycle 68

qualities 74
products 15
professionalization 138
progressive commodification. 32
prosumers 111
prototyping 77, 106
Puccinelli, Nancy M 199
purchase 15
purchasing behavior 20
Pushkin State Museum of Fine Arts 93

quality 1, 42, 43, 46, 47, 49, 51, 52, 53, 54, 55, 56, 58, 69, 75, 157, 160, 170, 183, 197, 199, 202
    -driven 15
    markers 46
Quester, Pascale, G 157
questionnaire 18
questionnaires 18
Quinn, Barry 199

race 181
Radke, Andreas, M 110, 113
Raghubir, Priya 199
Ramaswamy, Venkat 106
rapid
    prototyping 109
    tooling 106
Ratten, Vanessa 15, 25, 159
Ratto, Matt 106
Ravisi, Davide 43, 48, 52, 56, 57
Ree, Robert 106
Renaissance, The 2, 137
reputation 53, 197, 219
reputational position 58
research 215, 216, 219, 221
resilience 5, 38
resistance to consumption 177
resource management 104
Resources-Based View 86
Restany, Pierre 220, 224
'retail apocalypse' 194, 198, 199
Rhindova, Violina 43
Ricci, Alessandra 14, 24, 137, 138
Richmond, Susan 220, 222
Rickenbacker 54
righteous
    consumers 182
    consumption 10, 178, 183
    production 178, 187, 189, 190

Rindfleisch, Aric 106
Rindova, Violina 48, 52, 56, 57
risk-taking 87
Ritzer, George 111
Roggeveen, Anne, L 199
Rojas-Méndez, Jose 161
romance 71
Roman Empire 82
Romeo, Jean, B 159, 161
Rosner, Daniela 24
Rostagno, Ippolita 145, 146, 148
Roth, Martin, S 159, 161
routes to market 26, 27, 34
Royal Warrant Holders Association,
    The 36
Ryan
    Jason 161
    Louise 45

Saebi, Tina 102, 104
Saldana, Johnny 126
Salvi, Sergio 214, 224
Samiee, Saeed 161
Sams, Doreen, E 2
Sanders, Charles 202
Sanguineti, Edoardo 213, 224
Sanna, Angela 213, 224
Santos, Gina 25
satisfaction 23
Sauvage, Tristan 213, 224
savoir-faire 16
scalable business' 37
Schilling, Melissa 142
Scholder, Amy 217, 222
School of Drawing for Glassmakers 85
Schor, Juliet B 177
Schouten, John, W 3
Schroeder, Jonathan, E 215, 216, 224
Schwartz, Mary 123
Scott, Allen, J 68
Scrase, Timothy, J. 42
Second World War 209
seed capital 199
Seipel, Josh 37
self
    -actualisation 125
    -employed workers 28
    -employment 123, 127
    -manufacturing 106
Sennett, Richard 8, 15, 25, 42, 51, 77,

82, 120, 121, 123, 127, 128, 133,
    138, 177, 180, 189, 195
Serra, Rosanna 218, 222
Service Design 142
    Thinking 151
service
    dominant logic 142, 143
    economy 142
    ecosystems 143
    teaching 68, 76, 77, 78
Shepherd, Dean, A 159
Shiner, Larry, E 14, 25, 137, 138
shopkeepers 197, 198
shopping centres 198
SIC (Standard Industrial Classification)
    codes 35
Siffusdottir, Inga D 25, 180
Simkus, Albert 177
Simms, Andrew 74
Simpson, Barbara 87
skill 32
skilled 16
slow
    fashion 69
    making 68
    production 66, 70, 183
Slywotzky, Adrian J 48
small
    and independent retailers 198
    and micro-firms 87
    batch production 72, 74
    craft businesses 37
    retailers 198
    -scale production 15
    shops 199
SMEs (small and medium enterpris-
    es) 114, 164
Smith
    Adam 137
    J. Brock 48
Smith Maguire, Jennifer 199
Smith, Wendel, R 200
sociable expertise 51, 123
social
    distinction 160
    embeddedness 50
    media 33, 53, 58-9, 65, 67, 73, 76,
        77, 78, 132, 136, 148
    networks 44, 58
    prestige 196

values 8, 124, 133
Sofa Chicago 91
Sofa New York 91
sole traders 37
Sombart. Werner 195
Sonnabend, I, Ileana 223
Sonnabend, M, Michael 223
sound 55, 56
    quality 57, 58
Sparks, Leigh 199
specialist knowledge 35
specialization 142
specialized 15
Sperone, Gian E 215, 224
standardisation 67
standardised goods 198
State Hermitage Museum of St.
    Petersburg 95
status identity 31
Steel, William, F 158
Steenkamp, Jen-Benedict, E M 157, 159,
    160, 161, 162
Štefko, Robert 136
Stengel, Alejandro 198
Stern, Barbara 162
Stevens, Dennis 32
Steward, David, W 199
Storey, David, J 87
storytelling 15, 146
strategic
    development 16
    marketing 209
    model 219
Strauss, Anselm 108
Sukumaran, Nishal 162
Sullivan, Sherry 122, 123, 126, 127,
    128, 133
Sundell, Margaret 215, 225
supermarkets 198, 200
supply chains 35, 148
survey 14, 18, 23
sustainability 3, 5, 16, 26, 33, 37, 50, 64,
    65, 67, 68, 70, 74, 76, 78, 121,
    140, 184, 187
sustainable
    consumption 42
    economies 74
    production 65, 67
    products 70
Swenson, Gene 213, 225

Sydow, Alisa 158, 165, 170
symbolic
    capital 56
    products 16
    value 48, 56, 57
    values 58

Tabak, Akif 137, 138, 139
tailored 21
tailor made 140
taste 68, 157, 180, 182, 197
    community 181
Tatarkiewicz, Wladyslaw 137
Taylorist 137
Taylor, Stephanie 120, 121, 123, 126,
    130
technical skill 36
techniques 15
technological entrepreneurship 105
Telford, Nicholas 121
Tene, Ofra 197
testimonials 57
Thakor, Mrugank, V 160
Thomas
    Colin, T 198
    David, R 164
Thorlindsson, Thorolfur 14, 25, 180
Thrift, Nigel 178
throw-away society 50
Thurnell-Read, Thomas 178, 193, 199
Tiffany 83
Tignor, Robert L 157
Tonkinwise, Cameron 69
Toschi, Paolo 209, 225
tourism 31, 166
trading zones 47, 56, 58
tradition 16, 70, 76, 157, 201, 210, 211,
    213, 214, 216, 222
traditional 16, 18
    craft 74
        practices 64, 71
    -innovation paradox 144
traditions 167, 170, 209, 210, 211, 214
traditiovation 82
Tregear, Angela 158
Trilling, Lionel 200
trust 45, 46
Tseng
    Mitchell, M 110, 113
    Ting-Hsiang 161

Tucci, Christopher, L 104

UK (United Kingdom) craft market 26
Ulaga, Wolfgang 48
umbrella brands 163, 170
uniqueness 2, 15, 16, 18, 138, 139, 199, 202, 203
unity 21
Upadhyay, Parijat 24
Upbin, Bruce 68
USA (United States of America) 211, 212, 213, 214, 220, 221

user
    -design driven approach 143
    experience 142
Usunier, Jean-Claude 159, 162
Uzzi, Brian 51

Vaast, Emmanuelle 102
Vachhani, Sheena 193
value 47, 48, 51, 52, 58, 65, 69, 137, 141, 163, 209, 215
    co-creation 142, 144, 145
        practices 143
    emotional 75
values 124
  consumer 75
Van Bockstaele, Filip 25
Vanderstuckken, Koen 83
Van de Walle, Davy 25
Van Riper, Silvia 194
Vargo, Stephen, L 106, 110, 141
Varman, Rohit 44, 45, 46, 51, 56
Velez Ospina, Jorge 37
Veller, Christian 144
Venetian glass 82
Venice Biennale of Art 92, 93
Venier, Francesco 140
Venini 89
Verhoef, Peter, C 139, 142
Verlegh, Peeter, W J 157, 159, 160, 161, 162
vertical marketplaces, 144
Villette, Solange M 23, 25
Visual Arts 216, 217, 225
Vitorino, Joao 105
Vivaldi 214, 225
Vizzaccaro, Matteo 24
von Hippel, Eric 106

Waldman, Kurt 18, 25
Wallace Collection of London, The 94
Warburton, Annie 139
Warhol, Andy 209, 211, 212, 215, 216, 217, 218, 219, 221, 223, 224, 225
Warhol Museum, The 218
Warnaby, Gary 198
water jet cutting 67, 73
Wattanasuwan, Kritsadarat 54
web-based technology 78
website development 27
Weiss, Tim 163
wellbeing 33
West, Candace 187
Westerman, George 103
Western
    brands 167
    products 167
Wheelock, Jane 123, 128
Wherry, Frederick, F 17, 25
White
    C. A, Cynthia 25
    Harrison, C 16, 25
whiteness 181
Wiecek, Annika 106, 111, 113
willing to pay 15
Wilson, Andrew 1
Winstanley, Michael, J 196
Womack, James, P 105, 110
women makers 28
women's careers 122
Wonderful World of Crafting, The 34
Wooliscroft, Ben 162
Woolley, Martin 120, 121, 124, 125, 128, 133
working from home 120, 130
Wright, Kristina, D 157, 159

Yair, Karen 33, 123
Yang, Zhi 65
Yasin, Norjaya, M 159
Yin, Robert, K 107
YouTube 53

Zalewska, Joanna 177
Zarantonello, Lia 160
Zarei, Azim 160
Zatti, Susanna 214, 222
Zavetoski, Stephen 178
Zhou, Nan 160

Zhuang, Guijun 157
Zimmerman, Don H 187
Zingarelli, Nicola 212, 225

Zinkhan, George M 178
Zukin, Sharon 44, 199, 200